Welcome to Ethos Logos
Classical Educational Products

Published by Ethos Logos.
Ethoslogos.org
Tucson, AZ. 85718

Most Ethos Logos books are available at special discounts for bulk purchases for classroom use, homeschool use, promotions, premiums, fundraising, and other educational needs. For details, contact; sales@ethoslogos.org.

ISBN: 979-8-88743-038-6

While the author has made every effort to provide accurate information at the time of publication, neither the publisher nor the author assumes any responsibility for errors or for changes that occur after publication. The publisher worked closely with teachers, educators, and designers to curate this work. All images, paintings, product names, and other trademarks mentioned or pictured in this book are used for educational purposes only. No association with or endorsement by the owners of the trademarks is intended. Each trademark remains the property of its respective owner. We strive for excellence, not perfection. Should you find an error in this edition, please email us at orders@ethoslogos.org.

Printed in the United States of America

Table of Contents

MCMCXIX5.211

ETHOS LOGOS
Classical Curriculum

Classical High School English

Logic to Rhetoric Stage of Learning

In the late Logic and beginning of the Rhetoric stages of Classical Education, scholars are transitioning from *"how do the facts of the world work together?"* to *"how do I explain what I know and express myself?"*. This transition f is part of your scholar's more profound exploration of their world.

For the high school years, the focus on English and History moves to writing, explaining, and expressing. By this stage, much of our work in literature analysis, grammar skills, and vocabulary expansion is building upon prior knowledge.

Scholars read the great works from ancient, Middle Ages, and modern classical times. The sequence we teach starts with American Literature in 9th grade, moves to British Literature in 10th grade, World Literature in 11th grade, and Classical Literature in 12th grade. In addition to English courses, our model combines a comprehensive historical analysis. Scholars will dig into the ideas, lives, arts, and literature from the Greek world (namely Plato/Aristotle); the major world religions; plays (both comedy and tragedy); key religious texts; Rhetorical skills (logos, pathos, ethos.); speechmaking & satire; and so on.

An essential aspect of the Classical Education model is that knowledge does not exist in a vacuum. We are intentional about the literature choice and the traverse through history, culture, art works, and how all these subjects tie back to the literature being covered.

Welcome to Classical Literature

The Ethos Logos system uses history as the foundation of our entire grade/year of instruction. We break history into four parts. These four time periods are repeated three times. Each time your scholar explores a time period, the depth of learning builds upon their prior exposure to the time period. In the early grades (Grammar Stage), your child is exposed to the basic facts, dates, and important events of a time period. By the second exposure (Logic Stage) and the third exposure (Rhetoric Stage), we build upon prior foundations for a deeper, more nuanced understanding of each historical period. The four time periods we study include:

Ancient History – (1st, 5th, 9th Grades)
(Mesopotamia to the Fall of Rome – 10,000 BC to 432 AD)

Medieval Times – (2nd, 6th, 10th Grades)
(The Fall of Rome to The Enlightenment – 432 AD to 1700)

America's Founding – (3rd, 7th, 11th Grades)
(Pre-Columbian America to Pre-Civil War – 1500 to 1850)

Modern History (4th, 8th, 12th Grades)
(The Civil War to 9/11 – 1865-2001)

These four periods repeat such that a scholar in our system will see a particular time period three times in their 1st to 12th-grade schooling experience. Within each time period, we break down the school year into 10 units. Each unit is designed to be covered in one month.

Within each unit, there are countless ways in which you can tailor a lesson for your scholar. The lesson cards include bullet points, general categories, and question prompts, which you can explore and have fun with.

Each lesson card features one or more of the Ethos Logos 100. We specifically call these 100 events/people or things out so that you will make sure that these items are explored deeply at each grade level. The rest of the content is your choice based on your scholar's interests or your family's decisions.

Classical Education is about making deep connections and exploring the great works of science, literature, poetry, artists, musicians, religions, and people from history. We paired suggested lesson cards in these and other categories to the particular history card so that you can continue to move deeper and deeper into a time period. Gather the cards for the month across various curriculum content areas and use these lesson cards as the foundation of your teaching and learning.

To complement our lesson card, we offer a workbook full of questions. These questions are grade leveled and aligned to each month-long history unit. The power of the right question is the essence of learning. These question banks help you to further plan and deliver interesting lessons on the topics you decide to explore.

We also offer a digital platform that, again, lines up to the lesson cards and walks your scholar through a day-by-day, week-by-week, pre-programmed lesson sequence from model lessons built by our classroom teachers. These pre-built lessons can be customized using our large selection of lesson resources should you wish to further build upon our platform.

The back side of each history overview card lists lesson topics in each subject that align to the time in history for that month.

Each card subject is color coded so you are able to find the corresponding cards with ease. As you pull the cards for the month, double check that the month number at the bottom of the front of the card matches the current month you are studying and the month of the overview card. Below is an example of what cards to pull if you bought the complete grade lesson card set.

Example of a Monthly Curriculum Overview Card

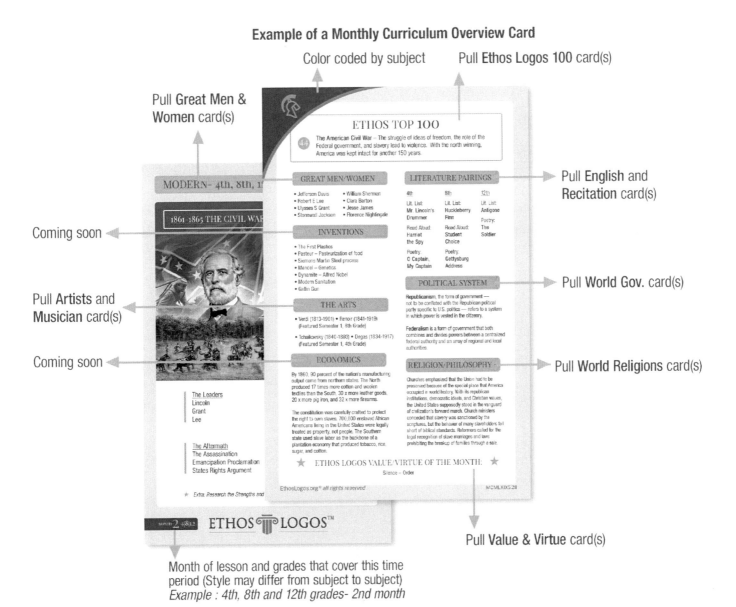

Color coded by subject

Pull **Ethos Logos 100** card(s)

Pull **Great Men & Women** card(s)

Pull **English** and **Recitation** card(s)

Coming soon

Pull **Artists** and **Musician** card(s)

Pull **World Gov.** card(s)

Coming soon

Pull **World Religions** card(s)

Pull **Value & Virtue** card(s)

Month of lesson and grades that cover this time period (Style may differ from subject to subject)
Example : 4th, 8th and 12th grades- 2nd month

ETHOS TOP 100
The American Civil War – The struggle of ideas of freedom, the role of the Federal government, and slavery lead to violence. With the north winning, America was kept intact for another 150 years.

MODERN– 4th, 8th, 1...

1861-1865 THE CIVIL WAR

GREAT MEN/WOMEN
- Jefferson Davis
- Robert E Lee
- Ulysses S Grant
- Stonewall Jackson
- William Sherman
- Clara Barton
- Jesse James
- Florence Nightingale

INVENTIONS
- The First Plastics
- Pasteur – Pasteurization of food
- Siemens Martin Steel process
- Mendel – Genetics
- Dynamite – Alfred Nobel
- Modern Sanitation
- Gatlin Gun

THE ARTS
- Verdi (1813-1901) • Renoir (1841-1919) (Featured Semester 1, 8th Grade)
- Tchaikowsky (1840-1893) • Degas (1834-1917) (Featured Semester 1, 4th Grade)

ECONOMICS
By 1860, 90 percent of the nation's manufacturing output came from northern states. The North produced 17 times more cotton and woolen textiles than the South, 30 x more leather goods, 20 x more pig iron, and 32 x more firearms.

The constitution was carefully crafted to protect the right to own slaves. 700,000 enslaved African Americans living in the United States were legally treated as property, not people. The Southern state used slave labor as the backbone of a plantation economy that produced tobacco, rice, sugar, and cotton.

LITERATURE PAIRINGS
4th:	8th:	12th:
Lit. List: Mr. Lincoln's Drummer	Lit. List: Huckleberry Finn	Lit. List: Antigone
Read Aloud: Harriet the Spy	Read Aloud: Student Choice	Poetry: The Soldier
Poetry: O Captain, My Captain	Poetry: Gettysburg Address	

POLITICAL SYSTEM
Republicanism, the form of government — not to be conflated with the Republican political party specific to U.S. politics — refers to a system in which power is vested in the citizenry.

Federalism is a form of government that both combines and divides powers between a centralized federal authority and an array of regional and local authorities.

RELIGION/PHILOSOPHY
Churches emphasized that the Union had to be preserved because of the special place that America occupied in world history. With its republican institutions, democratic ideals, and Christian values, the United States supposedly stood in the vanguard of civilization's forward march. Church ministers conceded that slavery was sanctioned by the scriptures, but the behavior of many slaveholders fell short of biblical standards. Reformers called for the legal recognition of slave marriages and laws prohibiting the breakup of families through a sale.

★ ETHOS LOGOS VALUE/VIRTUE OF THE MONTH: ★
Silence – Order

The Leaders
Lincoln
Grant
Lee

The Aftermath
The Assassination
Emancipation Proclamation
States Rights Argument

★ Extra: Research the Strengths and...

MCMLXIX5.2II

MONTH 2 4|8|12 **ETHOS LOGOS™**

Lesson Card Subject Color Code:

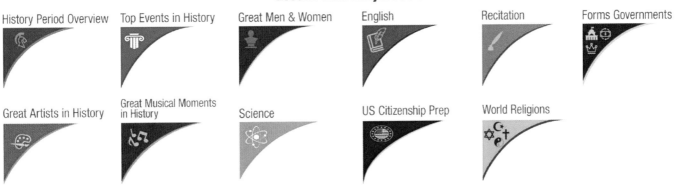

History Period Overview	Top Events in History	Great Men & Women	English	Recitation	Forms Governments

| Great Artists in History | Great Musical Moments in History | Science | US Citizenship Prep | World Religions | |

How To Use This Workbook

This workbook is broken into an overview of the connecting subjects to our HISTORY lesson cards. Each month-long unit starts with a point in history and includes the English, values/virtues, Great Men and Women, artists, musicians, and Ethos 100 history tie-ins. The entire course of instruction starts with HISTORY lesson cards....

LESSON CARD:

This month's snapshot covers the time period, lesson card, grade band, literature suggestions, artists and musicians, values and virtues, and great men and women from history, governance, and religion for particular months worth of instruction.

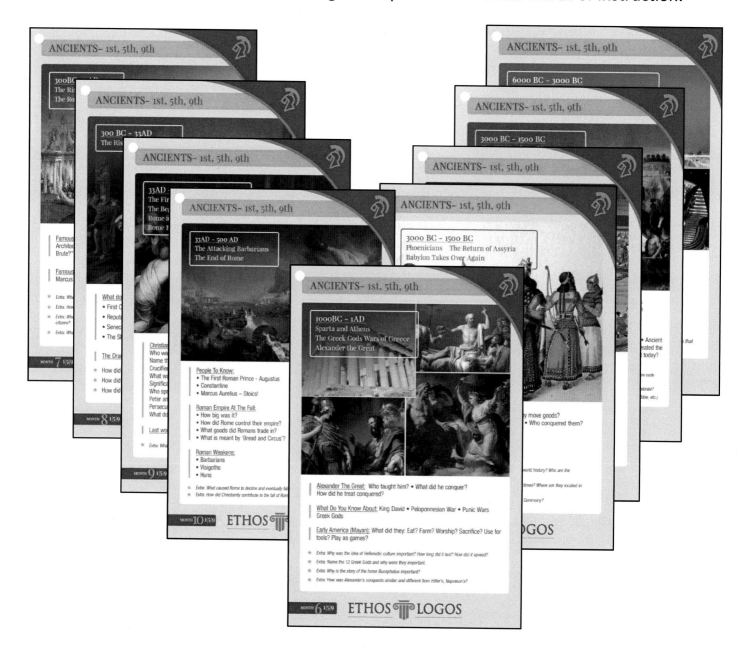

How To Use This Workbook

TERMS and VOCABULARY

The terms are a starting point for you and your scholar to become familiar with the concepts that may be new. The terms/vocabulary can become part of your opening exercise. Your scholar researches some or all of the terms and builds word webs or Frayer vocabulary model exercises to become familiar with the new terms.

QUESTION BANK

We have broken down a series of questions based on their complexity and provided them for you as a guide towards building your unit/month-long instruction. The questions help familiarize your scholar with the basic facts. In the early grades (Grammar), we explore the basic questions of **WHO, WHEN, WHERE**, and **HOW** of a time period. The middle stage questions are a bit more complex and designed to help you scholars think deeper about the historic areas we are covering. During the Logic stage, we are looking to move our scholars beyond facts and into the **WHY** events occurred and the deeper patterns or trends within history. The final, Rhetoric stage of questions is designed to synthesize and connect the topics to personal beliefs, other subjects, and even current events.

The grade-level questions are only suggestions. Feel free to view all the questions, regardless of grade level bands, in building your lessons.

SAMPLE Projects

At the end of the history units, you will find sample assignments that can be adapted to almost any unit or time frame in history. These sample assignments range in complexity and estimated time to completion. These are actual assignments that our classroom teachers use to build their lessons.

CAPSTONE Projects

Capstone projects are typically month, semester, or year-long projects that tie together a number of the learning concepts and targets we cover through the year. These suggested Capstone assignments can be tailored to your particular scholar or family's interests. The Capstones should be your scholar's best work and be worked on over a long period of time. The goal is to connect personal experiences and ideas with what we are learning in our history units.

Our Lesson Cards and Lesson Guides are designed for you and your scholar to explore topics that are interesting and engaging to you. We provide you with the tools, but you have the freedom to customize everything we outline. Be creative and have fun!

The One Million and One Question Project

Accompanying the graphical lesson cards are dozens of lesson guides and workbooks full of grade- appropriate questions to explore.

Our classroom teachers build each of their daily lessons around an ESSENTIAL QUESTION or a guiding inquiry that they ask their scholars to explore. The **One Million and One Project** is a ban of thousands and thousands of questions aligned to our curriculum cards and organized in our workbooks for the homeschool and classroom teachers to use.

The Power Of The Great Questions

Socrates was famous for wandering the streets of ancient Athens and asking question after question. He proclaimed to know nothing! Socrates was so famous for the idea of asking the perfect question that today, we practice the Socratic Method of instruction in our schools. We believe this idea of the perfect question has survived for 2500 years because asking the right question and having the scholars search, compile and synthesize the answer themselves is where deep learning takes place.

Information Overload

We live in an age where information is as available as the smartphone in your pocket. Our entire print offering, from the graphical and bullet pointed curriculum cards to the accompanying **One Million and One Question** workbooks, are designed to allow you and your scholar to tailor lessons to concepts and ideas your family is interested. Gone are the days when a textbook manufacturer shares what they want you to know. With our curriculum cards and question bank, you pose the question, and your instructional work is to find, research, and present the answer creatively.

We offer three ways for you to maximize your experience with our Classical Education platform. Without Lesson Cards and Lesson Guides, you can fully plan and implement a Classical Education in your home setting. Add in our digital subscription platform, and we take the Lesson cards and build you a day-by-day platform of what to teach. These pre-built lessons take much of the work out of your daily instruction. You and your student have access to content on every subject and every topic. Finally, with our teacher-supported platforms, you can have our experienced classroom teachers delivered right to your home with either their artistically built lessons within our digital platform or life, one-on-one, or group instruction.

Ethos Logos
3 Delivery Options

We built our program for **flexibility, customization, and ease.**

1. Lesson Cards & Guides (Great)

- Graphical Lesson Cards Detail Each Subject
- <u>800+ Cards</u>: History, English, Science, Arts
- Powerful Question To Guide Learning

2. Pre-Built Digital Lessons (Better)

- Each Subject With Step-By-Step Content
- Use Our Template or Customize or BOTH
- Make Your Own Course With From Our Library

3. Our Master Teachers (Best)

- Chose From Top Teachers in the USA
- Drop-In To A Live Zoom or Group Class
- Schedule A One On One Master Teacher

using the
Ethos Logos Digital Delivery Platform

Built For:
Homeschool Families
Classical Charters
Public Schools

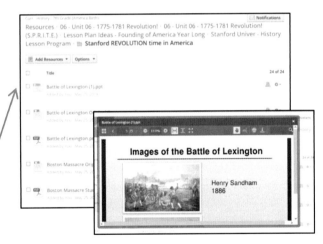

Visit EthosLogos.org to view pricing and enrollment options.

Ethos Logos
English - Language Arts

From Grammar & Spelling to Values & Virtues

English courses in our model are extremely important and have a number of aspects which we'll break down below. The Medici Classical English scope, sequence, and selection took years of classroom teachers back and forth to develop. We looked at top Classical schools around the country and interviewed teachers to find out which novels worked, and which didn't. We added and subtracted and continue to do so. As you explore our selections, realize that you have complete flexibility in what to teach in English. If you follow our unit (monthly) sequence, the benefits of thematic units and cross-connections that make Classical education so impactful will be seamless.

We are firmly anchored in the classics, but we've incorporated abridged versions of classic novels for some of our lower grades and full versions for upper grades. The abridged versions introduce students to famous English, American, European, and World literature. Our curriculum supports are built around novels, plays, poetry, short stories, speeches, and quotations from the great works of literary history.

Since many of these books have been in print for decades, many can be found online for no charge, used, or easily available from online booksellers.

- Novel Historical Setting
- Author Intent and Voice
- Themes and Characters
- Spelling/Vocabulary

From the Novel
Latin Root Words
Scripps Spelling

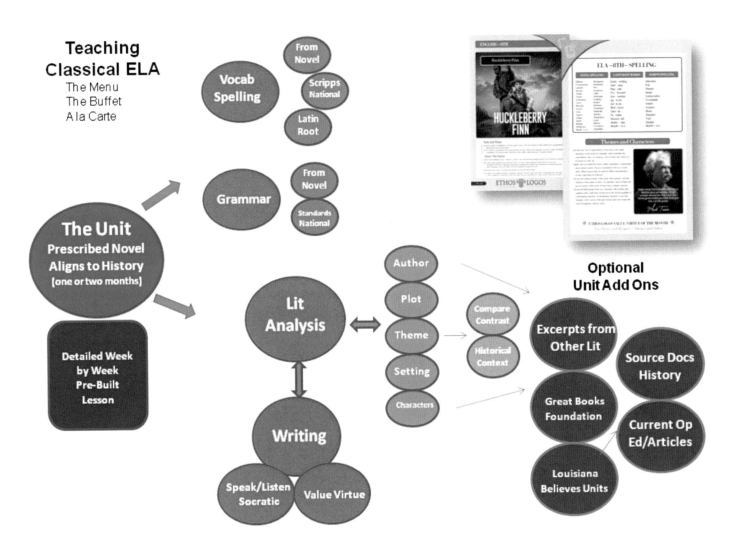

Age Appropriate - We use the **Lexile** score benchmark to align age-appropriate books to a particular grade. As our scholars get older, they are able to handle more adult topics. Some of the books on our reading lists have been banned over time for being too far to the left or the right politically. We believe that you have total agency as to which books to teach your child and would encourage you to research and read the novels you are teaching. When we come upon a difficult subject, we see those as a learning opportunity to think critically and compare and contrast life in the past to life today.

Literature Review - As your child continues through their education, the ability to dissect, identify and compare literature becomes an important tool. In our digital platform, we help you with pre-built lesson plans and then help you and your student identify the plot, theme, author's intent, and much more. In many cases, we suggest snippets of other great works (movies, book exerts, articles, source documents) and spell out ways that you can craft assignments that compare and contrast various literary devices.

Spelling - Novel Words - Latin - Scripps Spelling - Each unit features a novel. We identify spelling words from the novel and suggest a few ways to have your student learn and master those spelling words. We also include Latin root words and Scripps Spelling words for each month.

Grammar - In our digital support system, we spell out the grammar targets that your student should have mastered by specific grade levels. Exercises, worksheets, and practices are available to help you both cover the nuances of the English language.

Historic Alignment - History is the backbone of each of our units. In our system, scholars see a time in history a total of three times. The more we can immerse our students into what it was like to live, work, worship, or experience a particular time, the more aware they become of the past and the more context they have to understand current or future events. The powerful combination of history instruction (source documents, facts/dates, Great Men and Women, inventions, scientific advancement, etc.), with arts instruction with deep and rich stories in English, is what Classical education is designed around.

Value and Virtues - The novels we chose have characters, many the same age as your child, experiencing trials and joys as they move through the story. We have built into our curriculum prompts, suggestions, and training on how your child has experienced those struggles and persevered. At home, you can feature values like Courage or Responsibility, Forgiveness or Humility through the eyes of a particular character in a novel. We give you a number of ways to make these connections, all aimed at anchoring a sense of right from wrong.

Poetry - Age Appropriate and Memorized - Beginning in Kindergarten, each month, our students memorize and recite an age-appropriate poem. These poems have been curated and outlined with each English unit. The great poets from history, including Walt Whitman, Robert Frost, Rudyard Kipling, Langston Hughes, Wordsworth, Shakespeare, Longfellow, Shelly, and Robert Lewis Stevenson, are all included.

Plays and Theater In Older Grades - Units in high school include Our Town by Oscar Wilder, Death of A Salesman by Arthur Miller, and more.

Writing Prompts - Being able to formulate ideas and then communicate those ideas in clear and concise writing is the mark of a well-rounded education. We include in our digital offerings step-by-step training and writing assignments that are tied to our novels and our history prompts. We transverse between, Expository, Opinion/Persuasive, and Informative in our English and History subjects and scientific writing in our science units.

Presentation Skills - Classical Education culminates in the forgotten art of Rhetoric. After years of practice, we strive to ensure that all of our students can present their ideas and persuade their audiences. This is done via writing as well as in group presentations. Our platform includes Capstone projects that are programmed into 5th, 8th/9th, 10th, 11th, and 12th grades. These projects allow our students to tie everything together and deeply think about what is important to them.

Balanced Informational Text and Fiction - As we built our model, public schools have a real focus on informational text, which we think is important, but our curriculum has a balanced approach with story-driven fiction novels. The power of story is the power of Classical Education, and we made sure this balanced approach is included in each unit. We cross teach in science, history, and the arts for informational text, so your child receives an ample amount of informational text. English, in our model, has a heavier concentration of fiction.

Socratic Prompts - The power of a great is what Classical Education platforms strive for. Facts, dates, and memorization have their place in K12 education, but a deeper understanding and critical thinking take training and time. We have built-in Socratic discussion starters into English and history units. These questions can be used as writing prompts or discussion starters to check your child for a deeper understanding of topics. In science, we've put together prompts around the ethics of science and advancements from time. A good teacher and a good Classical Education will always be looking for ways to synthesize content and go deeper into the good, true and beautiful.

K3 Scholars Early Reading:

Early Reading Step By Step Plan - Below, you will find the specifics of our emergent readers program. We work within the Bookworms platform, which has strong research behind it, and it has many of the characteristics we look for in a Charlotte Mason - Classical school.

Charlotte Mason Read Aloud - 18th-century educator Charlotte Mason advocated for reading to her students using classical stories that may be a bit harder to comprehend than their grade level. She believed that listening, hearing new vocabulary, and gathering inference from context was important part of learning to read. Our early reading program, Bookworms, believes the same. We recommend continuing read alongs up into 5th or 6th grades.

Whole Word and Phonetic Awareness - The debate has raged between whole word and phonetic instruction. We integrate both into our curriculum. Bookworms

Struggling Readers Diagnostics and Tools - Because our curriculum is used in public schools, we've built a check and balance system based on the latest in literary research to help you identify reading gaps in your homeschool student. Contact our team for more info on diagnostics and intervention strategies to ensure your child gets the help they need in learning to read.

Handwriting - Cursive - We strive for mastery of cursive writing by 5th grade. Within our curriculum map, we include learning targets and practice materials to ensure that your child is progressing with their cursive skills at each grade level.

Dyslexia Accommodations - When available, we include a link to the audio version of most of our assigned novels
.

Benchmark Standards - Should You Wish To Follow - Since our curriculum is built for public and private schools as well as the home school community, we have a number of the state standards called out in the resource folders of each novel unit. You can easily see which skills your child should master by which grade.

Recitations

Starting in Kindergarten and continuing into high school, we recommend and instruct on our campuses a monthly recitation. These recitations are from notable poets, powerful speeches, or historical documents like the Preamble to the US Constitution.

The act of memorizing and presenting in from their peers gives our scholars confidence and a deeper understanding of the English language's Good, True and Beautiful aspects.

"If children know eight nursery rhymes by heart by the time they're four years old, they're usually among the best readers. "Why do children love poems?

Fox, Mem. (2001). Reading Magic, Why Reading Aloud to Our Children Will Change Their Lives Forever. San Diego, CA: Harcourt.

Wordsworth
Shakespeare
Robert Lewis Stevenson
William Blake
Robert Burns
AA Milne
Henry Wadsworth Longfellow
Langston Hughes
Walt Whitman
Robert Frost
Martin Luther King Jr.
Edward Guest
Rudyard Kipling
Emily Dickenson
Francis Scott Key
ETHOS LOGOS
Elie Wiesel

**Rhymes are important for language development and cognitive development.
Social/emotional development and physical development.**

1) Language Development:

Rhymes make it easier for kids to learn new words. Learning new words appears effortless because the rhythmical structure of the stanzas creates a familiar context for unfamiliar words. Moreover, reading rhymes aloud or repeating rhymes helps their practice pitch, voice inflection, and volume. It may seem trivial to a grown-up, but the level of coordination required to master all the variables of voice is extremely complex.

> *"Poetry provides a relaxed and pleasant way for students to practice language skills"*
> Source: Nancy L. Hadaway, Sylvia M. Vardell and Terrell A. Young. The Reading Teacher Vol. 54, No. 8, Embracing Pluralism Worldwide, Part 2: Classrooms in the U.S. (May, 2001), pp. 796-806

2) Physical Development

This brings us to the impact of rhymes on physical development. Breath coordination and tongue and mouth movements are made easier by the musical structure of the rhyme. Rhymes create a perfect environment for children because it looks like the right things happen easily. Rhymes help you understand when you need to breathe and for how long, with no need of theory of explanation. The physical awareness developed through rhymes can be naturally applied to prose as the kids grow older.

> *"Phonemic Awareness is the ability to hear, identify, and use the individual sounds or phonemes in spoken words.*
> *Helping children understand rhyming is one key skill of phonemic awareness"* (Block & Israel, 2005)

3) Cognitive Development

Through rhymes and poems, children understand that there are words which are similar in sound but with different meanings. They learn what a pattern is and become capable of recognizing patterns. They understand, through patterns, what a sequence is. They have fun memorizing rhymes, thus practicing their memory, both linked to audio and visual events. (Listening to someone reading rhymes or reading themselves). Memory, patterns, and sequences are also extremely helpful for approaching math and new languages.

> *"Working with teachers in sharing poetry across the curriculum has shown us that students need to practice developing their oral fluency and that they find poetry a particularly unintimidating and fun way to do it "*
> (Hadaway, Vardell & Young, 2001)

4) Social/Emotional Development

This is a dimension that we particularly care about. We want them to be able to establish healthy relationships with kids and grown-ups around them. Rhymes encourage kids' sense of humor, and sharing rhymes with their family creates space for inside jokes and for an emotional attachment to the stories kids read together with their parents. When children feel lonely or need comfort, they can easily recall the rhymes they shared with their parents and feel cherished, also if they're not with their family at that exact moment. http://timbuktu.me/

As an example, during the Black Ships Before Troy, a two-month unit, the teacher has options for ready built and provided for them, or the teacher can build their own lessons with a buffet of items to help make the novel come alive.

•**Writing Prompts** which focus on Narrative/Explanative, Argumentative/Opinion, Expository, or Research writing prompts a tied to prompts in the novel as well as source documents found in the Great Books Foundation text.

•**Grammar Skills** are pulled from the novels being studied and aligned to State standards. If the teacher sees that the students need additional work on a grammar concept from 5th grade or from a prior year, there is a resource bank with hundreds of grammar worksheets that can be brought in as supplementation. All these tools are at the teacher's disposal for every grammar skill from K to 12.

•**Literary Analysis** is loaded into the Ethos Logos curriculum in a chapter-by-chapter format, all aligned to State standards. The Exit Tickets define what the students should master at the 5th-grade level, and the teacher can once again use the pre-built lesson outlines or use any of the resources (powerpoints, compare contrast prompts) at their disposal.

•**Vocabulary** is a mix of Scripps high frequency, grade-aligned words, a Latin root word group to focus on (aligned with science), and vocabulary directly from the books being studied.

•**Historical Background on the Author**, the period the book is set, or the impact the novel made in history are all built into the 72 novels that are covered in the Classical model from K to 12. For example, during the 8th-grade novel Huckleberry Finn, there are interviews from 60 Minutes on the controversy of the novel in the modern-day, as well as long-form radio interviews with Harper Lee. These historical add-ins allow a teacher to put a novel into the context of its historical significance.

English Curriculum Cards Middle School

The WHY of reading the great works.

Socratic Question Prompts help the teacher start deep discussions, which are a hallmark of Classical Education. Socratic lesson prompts are sprinkled throughout the Ethos Logos curriculum. In ELA, Science, History, and in some cases Art, the teacher will find prompts or big questions to use as lead-ins to Socratic discussions. These discussions will happen from Kindergarten all the way to graduation. In addition to the prompts, our PD department spends the time showing teachers the Art of a good discussion. Their portfolio of work and additional compensation are tied to a teacher's ability to master the skill of Socratic learning.

Value and Virtue Prompts help a homeschool teacher to embed the alignment with the monthly focus, which is being covered school-wide. These prompts may be in the form of writing assignments, Socratic discussions, or small group analyses. Ask most teachers why they chose the profession of teaching, and undoubtedly, you will hear their desire to impact individual students and their communities.

Digital Instructional Options

Example: 6ᵗʰ Grade – ELA Unit

The Hero's Journey (4 months)

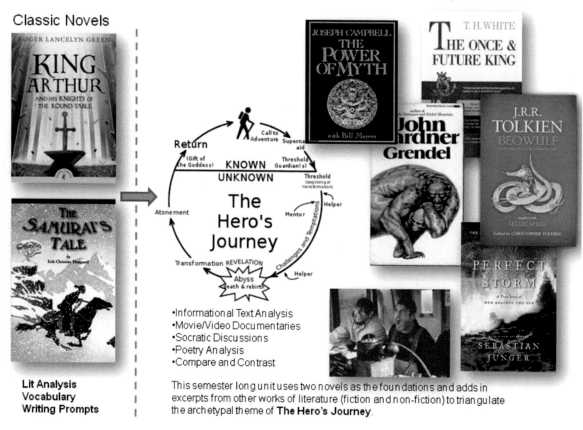

Classic Novels

Lit Analysis
Vocabulary
Writing Prompts

- Informational Text Analysis
- Movie/Video Documentaries
- Socratic Discussions
- Poetry Analysis
- Compare and Contrast

This semester long unit uses two novels as the foundations and adds in excerpts from other works of literature (fiction and non-fiction) to triangulate the archetypal theme of **The Hero's Journey**.

Example: 6ᵗʰ Grade – ELA Unit

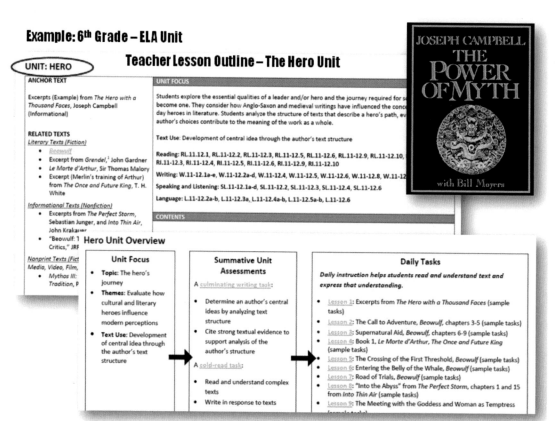

Charlotte Mason Philosophy

The Charlotte Mason influence focuses on the students as adults becoming, and two key ideas that our schools embed into the Classical model are "Education is an atmosphere, a discipline, a life" and "Education is the science of relations." Her motto for students was "I am, I can, I ought, I will."

Mason coined the phrase *"living books that spark the imagination of the child through the subject matter."* I know that this concept can be nuanced to you as a parent, but the best way I can surmise the blend of our model between Classical and Charlotte Mason is that the Classical element is the black and white photo of an Ansell Adams. The Charlotte Mason is the vibrant pallet of a Monet. Both are masterpieces. The combination of the two complements each with other and has overlapping mastery but very different styles.

Writing Across Grades and Subject
Alignment with History

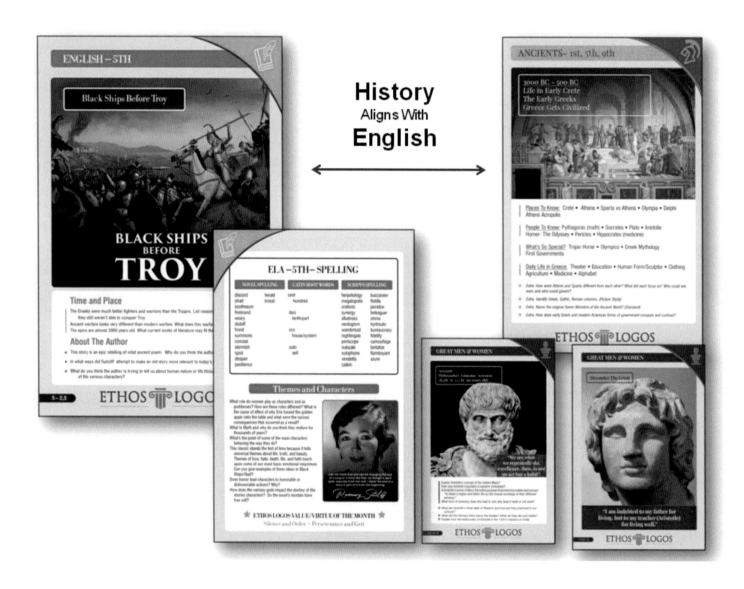

In our high school English sequence, we have aligned our novel selection to a year of American Literature (9th grade), British Literature (10th grade), World Literature (11th grade), and Classical Literature (12th grade). If your family would like to maintain literature and historic alignment, we have added into each unit of this workbook the corresponding ACTUAL historical period in which the novel is set.

	Literature	Read Aloud	Recitation
Aug	The Iliad - Homer	Student Choice	A Psalm of Life – HW Longfellow
Sept	Antigone - Sophocles	Student Choice	The Soldier – Rupert Brooke
Oct	The Odyssey – Homer	Biography	Ulysses, Lord Tennyson
Nov	The Odyssey - Homer	Biography	The New Colossus – Lazarus
Dec	Hamlet - Shakespeare	Gap Month	The Second Coming – WB Yates
Jan	Hamlet - Shakespeare	Classical Teacher Choice	Sonnet 29 - Shakespeare
Feb	Gulliver's Travels - Swift	Classical Teacher Choice	What Has Meaning – DF Wallace
March	Gulliver's Travels - Swift	Historical Fiction Teacher Choice	Still I Rise – Maya Angelou
April	Don Quixote - Cervantes	Historical Fiction Teacher Choice	The Negro Speaks of Rivers – L Hughes
May	Don Quixote - Cervantes	Gap Month	The Builders – HW Longfellow

Language Progressive Skills, by Grade

The following skills, marked with an asterisk (*) in Language standards 1-3, are particularly likely to require continued attention in higher grades as they are applied to increasingly sophisticated writing and speaking.

Standard	Grade(s)							
	3	4	5	6	7	8	9-10	11-12
L.3.1f. Ensure subject-verb and pronoun-antecedent agreement.	■	■	■	■	■	■	■	■
L.3.3a. Choose words and phrases for effect.	■	■	■	■	■	■	■	■
L.4.1f. Produce complete sentences, recognizing and correcting inappropriate fragments and run-ons.		■	■	■	■	■	■	■
L.4.1g. Correctly use frequently confused words (e.g., to/too/two; there/their).		■	■	■	■	■	■	■
L.4.3a. Choose words and phrases to convey ideas precisely.*		■	■					
L.4.3b. Choose punctuation for effect.		■	■	■	■	■	■	■
L.5.1d. Recognize and correct inappropriate shifts in verb tense.			■	■	■	■	■	■
L.5.2a. Use punctuation to separate items in a series.*			■	■	■	■	■	■
L.6.1c. Recognize and correct inappropriate shifts in pronoun number and person.				■	■	■	■	■
L.6.1d. Recognize and correct vague pronouns (i.e., ones with unclear or ambiguous antecedents).				■	■	■	■	■
L.6.1e. Recognize variations from standard English in their own and others' writing and speaking, and identify and use strategies to improve expression in conventional language.				■	■	■	■	■
L.6.2a. Use punctuation (commas, parentheses, dashes) to set off nonrestrictive/parenthetical elements.				■	■	■	■	■
L.6.3a. Vary sentence patterns for meaning, reader/listener interest, and style.†				■	■	■	■	■
L.6.3b. Maintain consistency in style and tone.				■	■	■	■	■
L.7.1c. Place phrases and clauses within a sentence, recognizing and correcting misplaced and dangling modifiers.					■	■	■	■
L.7.3a. Choose language that expresses ideas precisely and concisely, recognizing and eliminating wordiness and redundancy.					■	■	■	■
L.8.1d. Recognize and correct inappropriate shifts in verb voice and mood.						■	■	■
L.9-10.1a. Use parallel structure.							■	■

Welcome to 12 th grade English. Following are the areas of English we will be exploring this year. These learning targets are here to help you better understand where you current are and where we are going to end up by the end of the year.

11th and 12th Grade Grading and Time Focus:

25% Literature
35% Writing
15% Info Text
20% Speaking and Listening
5% Language

Literary Skills By Grade

Skill	K	1	2	3	4	5	6	7	8	9	10	11	12
Describe how word choice and imagery contribute to the meaning of a text.													
Compare and contrast various forms and genres of fictional text.													
Identify conventional elements and characteristics of a variety of genres.													
Identify the source, viewpoint, and purpose of texts.													
Explain the use of symbols and figurative language.													
Compare and contrast author's styles.													
Identify and ask questions that clarify various viewpoints.													
Analyze details for relevance and accuracy.													
Use literary terms in describing and analyzing selections.													
Identify literary and classical allusions and figurative language in text.													
Explain the relationship between and among elements of literature: characters, plot, setting, tone, point of view, and theme.													
Analyze the cultural or social function of a literary text.													
Explain the influence of historical context on the form, style, and point of view of a written work.													
Identify characteristics of expository, technical, and persuasive texts.													
Identify a position/argument to be confirmed, disproved, or modified.													
Compare and contrast the use of rhyme, rhythm, sound, imagery, and other literary devices to convey a message and elicit the reader's emotion.													
Identify universal themes prevalent in the literature of different cultures.*													
Compare and contrast literature from different cultures and eras.*													
Distinguish between a critique and a summary.													
Compare and contrast character development in a play to characterization in other literary forms.													
Analyze the use of literary elements and dramatic conventions including verbal, situational, and dramatic irony.													
Generate and respond logically to literal, inferential, evaluative, synthesizing, and critical thinking questions before, during, and after reading texts.													
Analyze two or more texts addressing the same topic to identify authors' purpose and determine how authors reach similar of different conclusions.													
Identify false premises in persuasive writing.													
Recognize and analyze the use of ambiguity, contradiction, paradox, irony, overstatement, and understatement in text.													
Recognize the characteristics of major chronological eras.*													
Compare and contrast traditional and contemporary poems from many cultures.*													
Compare and contrast dramatic elements of plays from American, British, and other cultures.*													

KEY	
	The skill is introduced and appears in the grade-level reading standards.
	The skill is not formally introduced in the grade level reading standard. Students should be knowledgeable about the skill from previous instruction. Teachers should review skills taught in previous grades.

Grammar (New Skills)

Use verbals and verbal phrases to achieve sentence conciseness and variety.

•**Demonstrate** command of the conventions of standard English grammar and usage when writing or speaking. a. Apply the understanding that usage is a matter of convention, can change over time, and is sometimes contested. b. Resolve issues of complex or contested usage, consulting references (e.g., Merriam-Webster's Dictionary of English Usage, Garner's Modern American Usage) as needed.

•**Demonstrate** command of the conventions of standard English capitalization, punctuation, and spelling when writing. a. Observe hyphenation conventions. b. Spell correctly.
Apply knowledge of language to understand how language functions in different contexts, to make effective choices for meaning or style, and to comprehend more fully when reading or listening. a. Vary syntax for effect, consulting references (e.g., Tufte's Artful Sentences) for guidance as needed. b. Apply an understanding of syntax to the study of complex texts when reading.

•**Determine** or clarify the meaning of unknown and multiple-meaning words and phrases based on grades 11-12 reading and content , choosing flexibly from a range of strategies. a. !Use context (e.g., the overall meaning of a sentence, paragraph, or text; a word's position or function in a sentence) as a clue to the meaning of a word or phrase. b. Identify and correctly use patterns of word changes that indicate different Grades 11-12 meanings or parts of speech (e.g., conceive, conception, conceivable). c. !Consult general and specialized reference materials (e.g., dictionaries, glossaries, thesauruses), both print and digital, to find the pronunciation of a word or determine or clarify its precise meaning, part of speech, etymology, or standard usage. d. Verify the preliminary determination of the meaning of a word or phrase (e.g., by checking the inferred meaning in context or in a dictionary).

•**Demonstrate** understanding of figurative language, word relationships, and nuances in word meanings. a. Interpret figures of speech (e.g., hyperbole, paradox) in context and analyze their role in the text. b. Analyze nuances in the meaning of words with similar denotations.

---

11. M.1 Trace and analyze the influence of mythic, traditional, or classical literature on later American literature and film.

12.M.1 Trace and analyze the influence of mythic, traditional, or classical literature on later British or other world literature and film.

Literature: (25% of this year's focus)

Key Ideas and Details

RL.11-12.1 Cite strong and thorough textual evidence to support analysis of what the text says explicitly as well as inferences drawn from the text, including determining where the text leaves matters uncertain.

RL.11-12.2 Determine two or more themes or central ideas of a text and analyze their development, including how they interact and build on one another to produce a complex account; provide an objective summary of the text.

RL.11-12.3 Analyze the impact of the author's choices regarding how to develop and relate elements of a story or drama.

Craft and Structure

RL.11-12.4 Determine the meaning of words and phrases as they are used in the text, including figurative and connotative meanings; analyze the impact of specific word choices on meaning and tone, including words with multiple meanings or language that is particularly

 fresh, engaging, or beautiful.

RL.11-12.5 Analyze how an author's choices concerning how to structure specific parts of a text contribute to its overall structure and meaning as well as its aesthetic impact.

RL.11-12.6 Analyze a case in which grasping a point of view requires distinguishing what is directly stated in a text from what is really meant.

Integration of Knowledge and Ideas

RL.11-12.7 Analyze multiple interpretations of a story, drama, or poem, evaluating how each version interprets the source text.

RL.11-12.9 Demonstrate knowledge of foundational works of American and world literature, including how two or more texts from the same period treat similar themes or topics. Language in Reading: Literature RL.11-12.10 Apply knowledge of language to understand how language functions in different contexts, to make effective choices for meaning or style, and to comprehend more fully when reading. RL.11-12.11 Determine or clarify the meaning of unknown and multiple-meaning words and phrases based on grades 11–12 reading and content, choosing flexibly from a range of strategies.

Key Ideas and Details

1. Cite strong and thorough textual evidence to support analysis of what the text says explicitly as well as inferences drawn from the text, including determining where the text leaves matters uncertain.

2. Determine two or more themes or central ideas of a text and analyze their development over the course of the text, including how they interact and build on one another to produce a complex account; provide an objective summary of the text.

3. Analyze the impact of the author's choices regarding how to develop and relate elements of a story or drama (e.g., where a story is set, how the action is ordered, how the characters are introduced and developed).

Craft and Structure

4. Determine the meaning of words and phrases as they are used in the text, including figurative and connotative meanings; analyze the impact of specific word choices on meaning and tone, including words with multiple meanings or language that is particularly fresh, engaging, or beautiful. (Include Shakespeare as well as other authors.)

5. Analyze how an author's choices concerning how to structure specific parts of a text (e.g., the choice of where to begin or end a story, the choice to provide a comedic or tragic resolution) contribute to its overall structure and meaning as well as its aesthetic impact.

6. Analyze a case in which grasping point of view requires distinguishing what is directly stated in a text from what is really meant (e.g., satire, sarcasm, irony, or understatement).

Integration of Knowledge and Ideas

7. Analyze multiple interpretations of a story, drama, or poem (e.g., recorded or live production of a play or recorded novel or poetry), evaluating how each version interprets the source text. (Include at least one play by Shakespeare and one play by an American dramatist.)

8. Analyze a work of fiction, poetry, or drama using a variety of critical lenses (e.g., formal, psychological, historical, sociological, or feminist).*

9. Demonstrate knowledge of eighteenth-, nineteenth- and early-twentieth-century foundational works of American literature, including how two or more texts from the same period treat similar themes or topics.

Info Text: (10% - Focus on historic and informational text)

Key Ideas and Details

RI.11-12.1 Cite strong and thorough textual evidence to support analysis of what the text says explicitly as well as inferences drawn from the text, including determining where the text leaves matters uncertain.

RI.11-12.2 Determine two or more central ideas of a text and analyze their development over the course of the text, including how they interact and build on one another to provide a complex analysis; provide an objective summary of the text.

RI.11-12.3 Analyze a complex set of ideas or sequence of events and explain how specific individuals, ideas, or events interact and develop over the course of the text.

Craft and Structure

RI.11-12.4 Determine the meaning of words and phrases as they are used in a text, including figurative, connotative, and technical meanings; analyze how an author uses and refines the meaning of a key term or terms.

RI.11-12.5 Analyze and evaluate the effectiveness of the structure an author uses in his or her exposition or argument, including whether the structure makes points clear, convincing, and engaging.

RI.11-12.6 Determine an author's point of view or purpose in a text in which the rhetoric is particularly effective, analyzing how style and content contribute to the power, persuasiveness or beauty of the text.

Integration of Knowledge and Ideas

RI.11-12.7 Integrate and evaluate multiple sources of information presented in media or formats as well as in words in order to address a question or solve a problem.

RI.11-12.8 Delineate and evaluate the reasoning in seminal U.S. and world texts, including the application of constitutional principles and use of legal reasoning and the premises, purposes, and arguments in works of public advocacy.

RI.11-12.9 Analyze foundational documents of historical and literary significance for their themes, purposes, and rhetorical features.

Language in Reading: Informational

RI.11-12.10 Apply knowledge of language to understand how language functions in different contexts, to make effective choices for meaning or style, and to comprehend more fully when reading. RI.11-12.11 Determine or clarify the meaning of unknown and multiple-meaning words and phrases based

Informational Text

Key Ideas and Details

1. Cite strong and thorough textual evidence to support analysis of what the text says explicitly as well as inferences drawn from the text, including determining where the text leaves matters uncertain.

2. Determine two or more central ideas of a text and analyze their development over the course of the text, including how they interact and build on one another to provide a complex analysis; provide an objective summary of the text.

3. Analyze a complex set of ideas or sequence of events and explain how specific individuals, ideas, or events interact and develop over the course of the text.

Craft and Structure

4. Determine the meaning of words and phrases as they are used in a text, including figurative, connotative, and technical meanings; analyze how an author uses and refines the meaning of a key term or terms over the course of a text (e.g., how Madison defines faction in Federalist No. 10).

5. Analyze and evaluate the effectiveness of the structure an author uses in his or her exposition or argument, including whether the structure makes points clear, convincing, and engaging.

6. Determine an author's point of view or purpose in a text in which the rhetoric is particularly effective, analyzing how style and content contribute to the power, persuasiveness, or beauty of the text.

Integration of Knowledge and Ideas

7. Integrate and evaluate multiple sources of information presented in different media or formats (e.g., visually, quantitatively) as well as in words in order to address a question or solve a problem.

8. Delineate and evaluate the reasoning in seminal U.S. texts, including the application of constitutional principles and use of legal reasoning (e.g., in U.S. Supreme Court majority opinions and dissents) and the premises, purposes, and arguments in works of public advocacy (e.g., The Federalist, presidential addresses).

Range of Reading and Level of Text Complexity

10. By the end of grade 11, read and comprehend literary nonfiction in the grades 11–CCR text complexity band proficiently, with scaffolding as needed at the high end of the range.

By the end of grade 12, read and comprehend literary nonfiction at the high end of the grades 11–CCR text complexity band independently and proficiently.

Writing: (40% of this year's focus should be on writing)

Text Types and Purposes

W.11-12.1 Write arguments to support claims in an analysis of substantive topics or texts, using valid reasoning and relevant and sufficient evidence.

W.11-12.2 Write informative/explanatory texts to examine and convey complex ideas, concepts, and information clearly and accurately through the effective selection, organization, and analysis of content.

W.11-12.3 Write narratives to develop real or imagined experiences or events using effective technique, well-chosen details, and well-structured event sequences.

Research to Build and Present Knowledge

W.11-12.7 Conduct short as well as more sustained research projects to answer a question (including self-generated question) or solve a problem; narrow or broaden the inquiry when appropriate; synthesize multiple sources on the subject, demonstrating understanding of the subject under investigation.

W.11-12.8 Gather relevant information from multiple authoritative print and digital sources, using advanced searches effectively; assess the strengths and limitations of each source in terms of the task, purpose, and audience; integrate information into the text selectively to maintain the flow of ideas, avoiding plagiarism and overreliance on any one source and following a standard format for citation.

W.11-12.9 Draw evidence from grades 11-12 literary or informational texts, to support analysis, reflection, and research.

Language in Writing

W.11-12.10 Demonstrate command of the conventions of standard English grammar and usage when writing.

W.11-12.11 Demonstrate command of the conventions of standard English capitalization, punctuation, and spelling when writing. a. Observe hyphenation conventions. b. Spell correctly.

Range of Writing

W.11-12.12 Write routinely over extended time frames (time for research, reflection, and revision) and shorter time frames (a single sitting or a day or two) for a range of tasks, purposes.

Text Types and Purposes

1. Write arguments to support claims in an analysis of substantive topics or texts, using valid reasoning and relevant and sufficient evidence.

a. Introduce precise, knowledgeable claim(s), establish the significance of the claim(s), distinguish the claim(s) from alternate or opposing claims, and create an organization that logically sequences claim(s), counterclaims, reasons, and evidence.

b. Develop claim(s) and counterclaims fairly and thoroughly, supplying the most relevant evidence for each while pointing out the strengths and limitations of both in a manner that anticipates the audience's knowledge level, concerns, values, and possible biases.

c. Use words, phrases, and clauses as well as varied syntax to link the major sections of the text, create cohesion, and clarify the relationships between claim(s) and reasons, between reasons and evidence, and between claim(s) and counterclaims.

d. Establish and maintain a formal style and objective tone while attending to the norms and conventions of the discipline in which they are writing.

e. Provide a concluding statement or section that follows from and supports the argument presented.

Text Types and Purposes (Cont)

2. Write informative/explanatory texts to examine and convey complex ideas, concepts, and information clearly and accurately through the effective selection, organization, and analysis of content.

    a. Introduce a topic; organize complex ideas, concepts, and information so that each new element builds on that which precedes it to create a unified whole; include formatting (e.g., headings), graphics (e.g., figures, tables), and multimedia when useful to aiding comprehension.

    b. Develop the topic thoroughly by selecting the most significant and relevant facts, extended definitions, concrete details, quotations, or other information and examples appropriate to the audience's knowledge of the topic.

    c. Use appropriate and varied transitions and syntax to link the major sections of the text, create cohesion, and clarify the relationships among complex ideas and concepts.

    d. Use precise language, domain-specific vocabulary, and techniques such as metaphor, simile, and analogy to manage the complexity of the topic.

    e. Establish and maintain a formal style and objective tone while attending to the norms and conventions of the discipline in which they are writing.

    f. Provide a concluding statement or section that follows from and supports the information or explanation presented (e.g., articulating implications or the significance of the topic).

3. Write narratives to develop real or imagined experiences or events using effective technique, well-chosen details, and well-structured event sequences.

    a. Engage and orient the reader by setting out a problem, situation, or observation and its significance, establishing one or multiple point(s) of view, and introducing a narrator and/or characters; create a smooth progression of experiences or events.

    b. Use narrative techniques, such as dialogue, pacing, description, reflection, and multiple plot lines, to develop experiences, events, and/or characters.

    c. Use a variety of techniques to sequence events so that they build on one another to create a coherent whole and build toward a particular tone and outcome (e.g., a sense of mystery, suspense, growth, or resolution).

    d. Use precise words and phrases, telling details, and sensory language to convey a vivid picture of the experiences, events, setting, and/or characters.

    e. Provide a conclusion that follows from and reflects on what is experienced, observed, or resolved over the course of the narrative.

3a. Demonstrate understanding of the concept of theme by writing short narratives, poems, essays, speeches or reflections that respond to universal themes (e.g., challenges, the individual and society, moral dilemmas, the dynamics of tradition and change).

Writing: (40% of this year's focus should be on writing)

Production and Distribution of Writing

W.11-12.4 Produce clear and coherent writing in which the development, organization, and style are appropriate to task, purpose, and audience.

W.11-12.5 Develop and strengthen writing as needed by planning, revising, editing, rewriting, or trying a new approach, focusing on addressing what is most significant for a specific purpose and audience.

W.11-12.6 Use technology, including the Internet, to produce, publish, and update individual or shared writing products in response to ongoing feedback, including new arguments or information.

Production and Distribution of Writing

4. Produce clear and coherent writing in which the development, organization, and style are appropriate to task, purpose, and audience. (Grade-specific expectations for writing types are defined in standards 1–3 above.)

5. Develop and strengthen writing as needed by planning, revising, editing, rewriting, or trying a new approach, focusing on addressing what is most significant for a specific purpose and audience. (Editing for conventions should demonstrate command of Language standards 1–3 up to and including grades 11–12 on page 60.)

6. Use technology, including the Internet, to produce, publish, and update individual or shared writing products in response to ongoing feedback, including new arguments or information.

Writing: (40% of this year's focus should be on writing)

Production and Distribution of Writing

W.11-12.4 Produce clear and coherent writing in which the development, organization, and style are appropriate to task, purpose, and audience.

W.11-12.5 Develop and strengthen writing as needed by planning, revising, editing, rewriting, or trying a new approach, focusing on addressing what is most significant for a specific purpose and audience.

W.11-12.6 Use technology, including the Internet, to produce, publish, and update individual or shared writing products in response to ongoing feedback, including new arguments or information.

Production and Distribution of Writing

4. Produce clear and coherent writing in which the development, organization, and style are appropriate to task, purpose, and audience. (Grade-specific expectations for writing types are defined in standards 1–3 above.)

5. Develop and strengthen writing as needed by planning, revising, editing, rewriting, or trying a new approach, focusing on addressing what is most significant for a specific purpose and audience. (Editing for conventions should demonstrate command of Language standards 1–3 up to and including grades 11–12 on page 60.)

6. Use technology, including the Internet, to produce, publish, and update individual or shared writing products in response to ongoing feedback, including new arguments or information.

Writing: (40% of this years focus should be on writing)

Research to Build and Present Knowledge

W.11-12.7 Conduct short as well as more sustained research projects to answer a question (including self-generated question) or solve a problem; narrow or broaden the inquiry when appropriate; synthesize multiple sources on the subject, demonstrating understanding of the subject under investigation.

W.11-12.8 Gather relevant information from multiple authoritative print and digital sources, using advanced searches effectively; assess the strengths and limitations of each source in terms of the task, purpose, and audience; integrate information into the text selectively to maintain the flow of ideas, avoiding plagiarism and overreliance on any one source and following a standard format for citation.

W.11-12.9 Draw evidence from grades 11-12 literary or informational texts, to support analysis, reflection, and research.

Research to Build and Present Knowledge

7. Conduct short as well as more sustained research projects to answer a question (including a self-generated question) or solve a problem; narrow or broaden the inquiry when appropriate; synthesize multiple sources on the subject, demonstrating understanding of the subject under investigation.

8. Gather relevant information from multiple authoritative print and digital sources, using advanced searches effectively; assess the strengths and limitations of each source in terms of the task, purpose, and audience; integrate information into the text selectively to maintain

9. Draw evidence from literary or informational texts to support analysis, reflection, and research.

   a. Apply grades 11–12 Reading standards to literature (e.g., "Demonstrate knowledge of eighteenth-, nineteenth- and early-twentieth-century foundational works of American literature, including how two or more texts from the same period treat similar themes or topics").

   b. Apply grades 11–12 Reading standards to literary nonfiction (e.g., "Delineate and evaluate the reasoning in seminal U.S. texts, including the application of constitutional principles and use of legal reasoning [e.g., in U.S. Supreme Court Case majority opinions and dissents] and the premises, purposes, and arguments in works of public advocacy [e.g., The Federalist, presidential addresses]").

Range of Writing

10. Write routinely over extended time frames (time for research, reflection, and revision) and shorter time frames (a single sitting or a day or two) for a range of tasks, purposes, and audiences.

Writing

Routine writing (summaries, writing to learn tasks, response to a short text or open-ended questions
Advanced/Mastery of 5 Paragraph Essay Format
Informative/Explorative (18 weeks)
    8-12 informative pieces – examine a topic – analysis essay
Argument (18 weeks)
    16-24 argumentative pieces – analysis essay
10-12 short research connections – pick a theme connecting units – suggest tie in with History, Science to ELA novel/story
10-12 narratives detailing a real or imagined experience
Logic Advanced/Mastery (2nd Sem 6th Grade Forward)– Incorporate into writing

Standard	Grade(s)												
	K	1	2	3	4	5	6	7	8	9	10	11	12
Differentiate pictures from writing.													
Use available technology for reading and writing.													
Generate ideas.													
Focus on one topic.													
Revise writing.													
Use complete sentences in final copies.													
Begin each sentence with a capital letter and use ending punctuation in final copies.													
Use correct spelling for commonly used sight words and phonetically regular words in final copies.													
Organize writing to include a beginning, middle and end for narrative and expository writing.													
Expand writing to include descriptive detail.													
Identify intended audience.													
Use a variety of prewriting strategies.													
Write a clear topic sentence focusing on the main idea.													
Write a paragraph on the same topic.													
Use strategies for organization of information and elaboration according to the type of writing.													
Include details that elaborate the main idea.													
Recognize different modes of writing have different patterns of organization.													
Write two or more related paragraphs on the same topic.													
Use transition words for sentence variety.													
Utilize elements of style, including word choice and sentence variation.													
Write multiparagraph compositions.													
Compose a topic sentence or thesis statement if appropriate.													
Select vocabulary and information to enhance the central idea, tone, and voice.													
Expand and embed ideas by using modifiers, standard coordination, and subordination in complete sentences.													
Use clauses and phrases for sentence variety.													
Distinguish between a thesis statement and a topic sentence.													
Communicate clearly the purpose of the writing using a thesis statement where appropriate.													
Arrange paragraphs into a logical order.													

1

Speaking/Listening: 15%

Comprehension and Collaboration

SL.11-12.1 Initiate and participate effectively in a range of collaborative discussion (one-on-one, in groups, and teacher-led) with diverse partners on grades 11-12 topics, texts, and issues, building on others' ideas and expressing their own clearly and persuasively.

SL.11-12.2 Integrate multiple sources of information presented in diverse formats and media in order to make informed decisions and solve problems, evaluating the credibility and accuracy of each source and noting any discrepancies among the data.

SL.11-12.3 Evaluate a speaker's point of view, reasoning, and use of evidence and rhetoric, assessing the stance, premises, links among ideas, word choice, points of emphasis, and tone used.

Presentation of Knowledge and Ideas

SL.11-12.4 Present information addressing opposing viewpoints and using supporting evidence, clearly, concisely, and logically for a specific purpose, audience, and task.

SL.11-12.5 Make strategic use of digital media in presentations to enhance understanding of findings, reasoning, and evidence and to add interest.

SL.11-12.6 Adapt speech to a variety of contexts and tasks, demonstrating a command of formal English when indicated or appropriate.

Language in Speaking and Listening

SL.11-12.7 Demonstrate command of the conventions of standard English grammar and usage when writing or speaking.

SL.11-12.7.a Vary syntax for effect, consulting references for guidance as needed.

SL.11-12.7.b Apply the understanding that usage is a matter of convention, can change over time, and is sometimes contested. SL.11-12.8 Acquire and use accurately general academic and domain-specific words and phrases, sufficient for the college and career readiness level; demonstrate independence in gathering vocabulary knowledge when considering a word or phrase important to comprehension or expression.

Speaking and Listening

1. Initiate and participate effectively in a range of collaborative discussions (one-on-one, in groups, and teacher-led) with diverse partners on grades 11–12 topics, texts, and issues, building on others' ideas and expressing their own clearly and persuasively.

> a. Come to discussions prepared, having read and researched material under study; explicitly draw on that preparation by referring to evidence from texts and other research on the topic or issue to stimulate a thoughtful, well-reasoned exchange of ideas.
>
> b. Work with peers to promote civil, democratic discussions and decision-making, set clear goals and deadlines, and establish individual roles as needed.
>
> c. Propel conversations by posing and responding to questions that probe reasoning and evidence; ensure a hearing for a full range of positions on a topic or issue; clarify, verify, or challenge ideas and conclusions; and promote divergent and creative perspectives.
>
> d. Respond thoughtfully to diverse perspectives; synthesize comments, claims, and evidence made on all sides of an issue; resolve contradictions when possible; and determine what additional information or research is required to deepen the investigation or complete the task.

2. Integrate multiple sources of information presented in diverse formats and media (e.g., visually, quantitatively, orally) in order to make informed decisions and solve problems, evaluating the credibility and accuracy of each source and noting any discrepancies among the data.

3. Evaluate a speaker's point of view, reasoning, and use of evidence and rhetoric, assessing the stance, premises, links among ideas, word choice, points of emphasis, and tone used.

Presentation and Knowledge of Ideas (Rhetoric – Ethos, Logos, Pathos)

4. Present information, findings, and supporting evidence, conveying a clear and distinct perspective, such that listeners can follow the line of reasoning, alternative or opposing perspectives are addressed, and the organization, development, substance, and style are appropriate to purpose, audience, and a range of formal and informal tasks.

5. Make strategic use of digital media (e.g., textual, graphical, audio, visual, and interactive elements) in presentations to enhance understanding of findings, reasoning, and evidence and to add interest.

6. Adapt speech to a variety of contexts and tasks, demonstrating a command of formal English when indicated or appropriate. (See grades 11–12 Language standards 1 and 3 on page 60 for specific expectations.)

Writing Standard

Write arguments to support claims with clear reasons and relevant evidence. a. Establish a thesis statement to present an argument. b. Introduce claim(s), acknowledge alternate or opposing claims, and organize the reasons and evidence logically. c. Support claim(s) with logical reasoning and relevant evidence, using accurate, credible sources and demonstrating an understanding of the topic or text. d. Use words, phrases, and clauses to create cohesion and clarify the relationships among claim(s), reasons, and evidence. e. Establish and maintain a formal style. f. Provide a concluding statement or section that follows from and supports the argument presented.

Write informative/explanatory texts to examine a topic and convey ideas, concepts, and information through the selection, organization, and analysis of relevant content. a. Establish a thesis statement to present information. b. Introduce a topic clearly, previewing what is to follow; organize ideas, concepts, and information, using strategies such as definition, classification, comparison/contrast, and cause/effect; include formatting (e.g., headings), graphics (e.g., charts, tables), and multimedia to aid comprehension, if needed. c. !Develop the topic with relevant facts, definitions, concrete details, quotations, or other information and examples. d. Use appropriate transitions to create cohesion and clarify the relationships among ideas and concepts. e. !Use precise language and domain-specific vocabulary to inform about or explain the topic. f. Establish and maintain a formal style. g. Provide a concluding statement or section that follows from and supports the information or explanation presented.

Produce clear and coherent writing in which the development, organization, and style are appropriate to task, purpose, and audience. (Grade-specific expectations for writing types are defined in standards 1-3 above.)

Conduct short research projects to answer a question, drawing on several sources and generating additional related, focused questions for further research and investigation.

Write narratives to develop real or imagined experiences or events using effective technique, relevant descriptive details, and well-structured event sequences. a. Engage and orient the reader by establishing a context and point of view and introducing a narrator and/or characters; organize an event sequence that unfolds naturally and logically. b. Use narrative techniques, such as dialogue, pacing, and description, to develop experiences, events, and/or characters. c. Use a variety of transition words, phrases, and clauses to convey sequence and signal shifts from one time frame or setting to another. d. Use precise words and phrases, relevant descriptive details, and sensory language to capture the action and convey experiences and events. e. Provide a conclusion that follows from and reflects on the narrated experiences or events.

With some guidance and support from peers and adults, develop and strengthen **writing as needed by planning, revising, editing**, rewriting, or trying a new approach, focusing on how well purpose and audience have been addressed. (Editing for conventions should demonstrate command of Language standards 1-3 up to and including grade 7.)

Language: 5% - Should be mastered grade

RL.11-12.4 Determine the meaning of words and phrases as they are used in the text, including figurative and connotative meanings; analyze the impact of specific word choices on meaning and tone, including words with multiple meanings or language that is particularly fresh, engaging, or beautiful.

RL.11-12.5 Analyze how an author's choices concerning how to structure specific parts of a text contribute to its overall structure and meaning as well as its aesthetic impact.

Conventions of Standard English

1. Demonstrate command of the conventions of standard English grammar and usage when writing or speaking.
a. Apply the understanding that usage is a matter of convention, can change over time, and is sometimes contested.
b. Resolve issues of complex or contested usage, consulting references (e.g., Merriam-Webster's Dictionary of English Usage, Garner's Modern American Usage) as needed.
2. Demonstrate command of the conventions of standard English capitalization, punctuation, and spelling when writing.
a. Observe hyphenation conventions.
b. Spell correctly.

Knowledge of Language

3. Apply knowledge of language to understand how language functions in different contexts, to make effective choices for meaning or style, and to comprehend more fully when reading or listening.
a.   Vary syntax for effect, consulting references (e.g., Tufte's Artful Sentences) for guidance as needed; apply an understanding of syntax to the study of complex texts when reading.

Vocabulary Acquisition and Use

4. Determine or clarify the meaning of unknown and multiple-meaning words and phrases based on grades 11–12 reading and content, choosing flexibly from a range of strategies.
    a. Use context (e.g., the overall meaning of a sentence, paragraph, or text; a word's position or function in a sentence) as a clue to the meaning of a word or phrase.
    b. Identify and correctly use patterns of word changes that indicate different meanings or parts of speech (e.g., conceive, conception, conceivable).
    c. Consult general and specialized reference materials (e.g., dictionaries, glossaries, thesauruses), both print and digital, to find the pronunciation of a word or determine or clarify its precise meaning, its part of speech, its etymology, or its standard usage.
    d. Verify the preliminary determination of the meaning of a word or phrase (e.g., by checking the inferred meaning in context or in a dictionary).
5. Demonstrate understanding of figurative language, word relationships, and nuances in word meanings.
    a. Interpret figures of speech (e.g., hyperbole, paradox) in context and analyze their role in the text.
    b. Analyze nuances in the meaning of words with similar denotations.
6. Acquire and use accurately general academic and domain-specific words and phrases, sufficient for reading, writing, speaking, and listening at the college and career readiness level; demonstrate independence in gathering vocabulary knowledge when considering a word or phrase important to comprehension or expression.

Why We Study Literature – Discussion Questions

1. Why even study literature?
2. How does literature reflect a society's culture?
3. How does the idea of a hero change, develop, or stay the same throughout cultures and history?
4. What religious ideas drive characters, and what personal motives drive them?
5. How do our own cultural biases affect the way we view literary characters or even the world itself?
6. What are the canons of classical writing, and how do we use them to organize our work?
7. How do we use rhetorical appeals to strengthen our writing and arguments?

8. How do I analyze, transcribe, and explicate poetry?
9. How can we analyze poetry?
10. What is satire, and what are the two types thereof?
11. How can an effective satirical piece change a societal or political problem?
12. How did the English language come into existence?
13. How did the English language originally look?

14. How do social expectations shape the development of our identity/identities?

15. How did ancient humanity attempt to explain or rationalize the world about them?
16. Why do we see so many similarities between creation myths, despite their separation by vast expanses of time and/or distance?
17. What were the first literary works of humanity?
18. Who is the first credited author of humanity?
19. What are some of the first surviving literary works of the English language?

How can literature help us reach a deeper understanding of ourselves and our growth as moral and ethical people? How can it help shape the way we think and act?

How can we cultivate in each other and ourselves the values, experiences, and skills we need to build a stronger democracy?

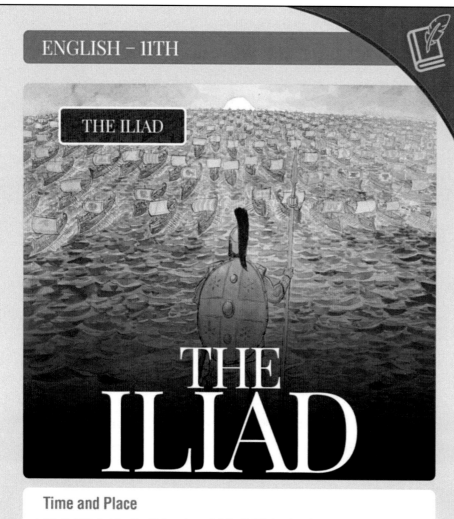

ENGLISH – 11TH

THE ILIAD

THE ILIAD

Time and Place

What is Achilles' relationship with the various gods in The Iliad? Explore the gods and mortals' relationship in the story. What role do fate play and the role of the gods in the story outcome? What larger points does Homer seem to be making by depicting the gods as he does?.

Elements of The Iliad are accurate depictions of relationships of Ancient Greek society. Do the relationships resemble modern–day relationships? Give examples and perhaps use popular culture references to illustrate the similarities.

Authors Intent

★ Achilles is acknowledged to be the greatest Greek warrior. Yet Homer focuses on Achilles' quarrel with Agamemnon and its effect upon the Greeks rather than on his heroic exploits. Why?

11-1

ETHOS LOGOS

Unit #:   1 (August)

Novel: **The Iliad**

Grade: **12th**

History:
1825-1861
HEADING TOWARDS WAR -
Expansion Underground
Railroad

Artists - Musician:
Verdi
Whistler

Value/Virtue:
Excellence – Respect

Religion:
Pan Theism (Indian)
Puritan (Christian)

Governance:
Monarchy
Colony
Tribe

Cultural Saying Unit 1
- Miss the boat
- Teacher's pet
- Good Samaritan

The Iliad – Pre-Read

What is the Iliad?

The Iliad is an epic poem written by Homer in around 8th century BC. It is a tale about two great armies, the Greek and the Trojans, and their hero's, Achilles and Hector. The poem starts by bringing you into the midst of the war when Achilles decides that his king, Agamemnon, hurt his honor so much that he would not fight any longer. Being the Achaeans best soldier, this made a very interesting turn of the tides on the battlefield. With the Gods playing with both armies as if they were their toys, they constantly change the fate of the war and produce very intense scenes that keep your blood pumping and your heart churning at the grizzly descriptions of battle.

The **Iliad** Ancient Greek: (sometimes referred to as the Song of Ilion or Song of Ilium) is an ancient Greek epic poem in dactylic hexameter, traditionally attributed to Homer. Set during the Trojan War, the ten-year siege of the city of Troy (Ilium) by a coalition of Greek states, it tells of the battles and events during the weeks of a quarrel between King Agamemnon and the warrior Achilles.

Before you begin reading, consider these *Pre-reading Questions*:

1. What do you think would be worth fighting for, dying for?
2. Do you know anyone who follows a code of honor in certain situations?
3. Have you ever known anyone who felt that his / her life had somehow been touched by or guided by divine forces?

The Iliad – Chapter Questions

Book 1. Read all. [Start reading Introduction xvii-xxix (skip xx) and xlii-lviii]

Notes and Questions, Book 1
(1) *Chryses* is the priest of Apollo. His daughter, named *Chryseis*, has been taken as a prize of war by Agamemnon, leader of the Greek forces. The father and daughter are from a city named *Chryse*.
(11) *Achilles, in tears* It was OK for real men to cry in Archaic Greece. (But see p. 305.) *Thetis*, Achilles' mom, comes out of the sea because she's a sea-nymph (minor goddess).

1. According to the first 8 lines, what will this poem be about?
2. What do you think the quarrel between Agamemnon and Achilles is about? Compare / contrast to the "quarrel" that started the war. Do gods or men or both cause the quarrel?
3. What do you think of Apollo's murderous response (2-3) to Chryses' prayer? What do you think of Zeus's response (16-17) to Thetis' request?
4. What accusations do Achilles and Agamemnon level at each other? Do you think these charges are just?
5. Who do you think is in the right in this quarrel? Who do the Achaeans think is in the right? Why? Why do you think Achilles and Agamemnon fail to take Nestor's advice?
6. What kind of people do you think Agamemnon and Achilles are?
7. How do you think Achilles "decides" to refrain from killing Agamemnon (7-8)? Why does Achilles give up Briseis (8-10)? What do you think of Achilles' refusal to fight?
8. In what senses is Agamemnon more powerful than Achilles?
9. How do men get gods to do what men want?
10. Name some similarities between Zeus and Achilles (and Zeus and Agamemnon).
11. How do you react to the way women (mortal and immortal) portrayed in Book 1?
12. What do you think the heroes in the *Iliad* are fighting for? Do the heroes seem to *like* fighting? (See pp. 6, 22, 31, 72, 110, 145, and question # 8 under "Book 9.") What do the gods seem to care about? How are their concerns like / unlike the heroes' concern for honor and glory? (71-72).
13. How do you know who has the most honor? Why do you think Zeus honors Thetis' request (16-17)? What do you think of Zeus' response to her (lines 549-559)?
14. In what ways do you think the men's and gods' quarrels are like / unlike? Why do you think these quarrels have different outcomes?

The Iliad – Chapter Questions

Book 2.

Read pp. 20-34. Optional: pp. 35-49, the Catalogue of Ships and Men. The troops are outlined here, first those of the Danaans (i.e. Greeks). There are 29 "platoons." Homer tells their regional affiliations and, variably, something of the geography, culture, history, the number of ships, their style of weapons or dress, and the names of the captain or captains (leading warriors). Note that Agamemnon has the largest platoon; Telamonian Ajax has the smallest. The Trojan platoons and their allies are described last--only 13 of these and much briefer descriptions.

Books 3-4. Read all.

Books 2-4

(27) *Thersites* = "bold one." *the ugliest* = *aischistos* = "most ugly, most shameful."

(29) *It seems like just yesterday . . . at Aulis*: actually, it was nine years before.

(33) *aegis* = a sort of shawl that Athena (and other gods) wear and use like a shield—for protection and to strike terror into the hearts of their enemies. It is mentioned again on page 105.

(78) *Ares . . . sister Eris* = "Strife."

1. What do you think Homer intends to show the reader (about Agamemnon's character, about the morale of the Achaeans, about Odysseus) in the scenes detailing Agamemnon's plan to "test" (22-26) his troops and its result?

2. Why do you think Homer included the episode of Thesites' abuse of Agamemnon and his chastisement by Odysseus (27-28)? Why is it OK for Achilles to abuse Agamemnon but not OK for Thersites to disrespect him? Why do you think the troops laugh?

3. What do you think the scepter / staff could symbolize? (See pp. 8, 23, 26-28.)

4. What do you think of Paris' answer to Hector (52)? Why do you suppose the people of Troy haven't just gotten rid of Paris and / or Helen? (See also pp. 54-55; 138-139.)

5. Why do you think Menelaus agrees to the truce and single combat?

6. What do you think is Helen's view of her situation? Who does she blame for her predicament? Who would you blame? (See pp. 54-55, 62-63; 122.)

7. Now a strange question: where do you think Helen's emotions come from?

8. What do you think would happen to Helen if Aphrodite "let go" of her (63)?

9. Why does Aphrodite rescue Paris? Why do you think Helen gives in to Paris (63-64)? Vase Painting: Helen meets Paris for the first time (Perseus).

10. Why do you suppose Homer organized Book 3 in the following way?

     a) Battlefield: Hector chides Paris; Paris suggests duel and oaths; Achaeans accept, suggest sacrifice (50-53).

     b) Troy: Old men converse; Helen and Priam look at soldiers (54-57).

     a) Battlefield: Priam goes out; sacrifices, oaths; the duel; Aphrodite intervenes (breaks chinstrap; hides Paris in cloud 58-62).

     b) Troy: Helen and Aphrodite; Helen and Paris (62-64).

     a) Battlefield: Menelaus looks for Paris (64).11. Give some reasons for why the gods love some men, women, and cities and try to destroy others (65-67). Why does Hera want peace?

11. Why do you think breaking the truce brings "glory" to Pandarus (68, 71)?

Books 5 - 7. Read all. [Keep reading Introduction xvii-xxix (skip xx) and xlii-lviii.]

Book 8. Entire book optional, pp. 143-159. Zeus assembles the gods and orders them not to interfere in the war again. Athena asks whether she and Hera can at least be war counselors, and Zeus, after giving an indefinite answer, sits on a crest of Olympus to watch the battle, confident that the Trojans will have a winning day. He throws thunderbolts to scare off the Achaeans and help Hector. Athena and Hera try to sneak out of Olympus in battle gear and chariots to help the Achaeans, but Zeus spots them and sends Iris to warn them. (He threatens to smash up their chariots.) They obey but are angry. Zeus tells them of his will--as promised to Thetis--that Hector will be victorious only until Patroclus is killed and Achilles re-enters the battle (lines 482-490). That night Hector orders the Trojans to camp on the plains with lighted fires so that the Greeks cannot escape, and the Trojans will be ready for battle at dawn. Note the wonderful description of the armies encamped at night [p. 159; lines 563-577]).

The Iliad – Chapter Questions

Books 5-8(103) *his father . . . for now* = Zeus.

(105) The *Gorgon* is a female monster with snaky hair, bulging eyes, and menacing tusks. A Gorgon's head was a common design on Greek shields—note the description of Agamemnon's shield at 11.32-36.
(116) *generations are like leaves* —some of the most famous lines in the *Iliad* introduce a rather long-winded digression on the hero Bellerophon.
Andromache = "fighting with the men."

1. What do you think of the gods' behavior in Book 5? Can the gods be heroic? Why or why not? (For more on the gods, read Murnaghan's Introduction xxv-xxix.) Why do you think Book 5 concentrates so much on Diomedes' heroic feats?
2. Why do you think Diomedes and Glaucus exchange armor on pp. 118-119? Does their friendship pact make any sense to you?
3. Compare / contrast the three scenes in book 6: a) Agamemnon's attitude (113-14), b) Glaucus and Diomedes (115-119), and c) Hector in Troy (119-127).
4. Why is it important that Menelaus not be killed? (See pp. 69-70, 100, 129-30.)
5. Why won't they let Menelaus fight Hector in book 7? Do you think Pandarus wins glory by wounding Menelaus, as Agamemnon says he does (71)?
6. Does Paris tell his brother the whole truth at the top of p. 122? What do you think of Helen's speech on the same page?
7. Have any of the events in Book 6 altered your view of what the heroes are fighting for? If yes, which events and why?
8. What are the Trojans fighting for? What do you think Hector is fighting for?
9. If Hector knows that "holy Ilion will perish" (6.471), then why do you think he keeps on fighting and wants his son to be just like him? In what ways do you think Hector is like / unlike Achilles? (selfish?)
10. Compare / contrast Andromache's attitude towards the war with Helen's. What do you think of Andromache's advice to Hector?
11. Why do you think Homer put in the scene with the child becoming afraid? Do you think that Homer would like to perpetuate the honor / glory system as Hector does?
12. Why do you think Hector decides to challenge the best of the Achaeans? (What might this challenge accomplish militarily?) What do you think of duel's outcome (137)? Vase Painting: Ajax vs. Hector (Notice Athena on the left, Apollo on the right).
13. Once again, one of the Trojans, Antenor, suggests they just give Helen back (138-139). But they don't. How are their reasons for their actions similar and different from the scene on pp. 54-55?

The Iliad – Chapter Questions

Book 9. Read all. [Read Introduction xxix-xxxvii, "Achilles" and "Hector."]
(163) *I was mad* = "I was in the grip of blindness or folly sent by the gods." The word translated as "mad" here is the Greek *Atê* (see <u>Atê</u> note 377).
(169) *the same reward* —The word *reward* translates the Greek word for "honor"—*timé*.
(175) *his wife, Cleopatra* —not the famous one, but the name is apparently a deliberate inversion of *Patroclus*. For clarification of Phoenix' example, see introduction, p. xxxii.

1. After studying carefully Achilles' long answer to the ambassadors (168-171), list some reasons why Achilles spurns Agamemnon's generous truce offer. (Who is "the man who says one thing and thinks another" [line 318]?) Do you think his reasons are good ones? Why or why not? What emotions and thoughts strike you as most important in this speech and why?
2. Do you think Achilles is questioning or redefining honor and glory at 9.320-343 and 9.415-422? Why or why not? What do you think he means when he says, "my honor comes from Zeus" (176)? (See Murnaghan's introduction, pp. xxx-xxxiii.)
3. If Achilles won't take all the stuff Agamemnon offers, then what *would* it take to pay him "in full" for "all [his] grief" (*Iliad* 9.400)? Compare / contrast Agamemnon's gifts with the exchanges of gifts between Glaucus and Diomedes (115-119) and Hector and Ajax (137).
4. Why do you think that none of the arguments of Odysseus, Phoenix, and Ajax can persuade Achilles to swallow his rage and re-enter the war?
5. Which arguments do you find most convincing and why?
6. Do you think that Achilles owes his comrades any loyalty? (See pp. 167 and 177.) (Why do you suppose he won't help his comrades?) Why do you think he stays angry?
7. What qualities make Achilles godlike? Do you like him? Why or why not?
8. Can you tell from his descriptions and similes of battle, killing, and wounds what Homer thinks of war and heroic glory? (See pp. 70-71, 79-88, 100-01, 113-114, 201-202, 278-280, 317, 405-406.) What different kinds of images and similes does Homer employ to describe the deaths of warriors? What do you think is Homer's attitude towards the dead? Does he think the glory is worth all this death? Why do you think Homer spends so much time describing wounds, boasts, and families of the heroes?

A note on the position of the ships and the wall.
In book 9, Achilles says:

> *I won't lift a finger in this bloody war*
> *Until Priam's illustrious son Hector*
> *Comes to the Myrmidons' ships and huts*
> *Killing Greeks as he goes and torching the fleet.*
> *But when he comes to my hut and my black ship*
> *I think Hector will stop, for all his battle lust. (9.673-678)*

The Iliad – Chapter Questions

Book 10.
Entire book optional, pp. 180-197. Agamemnon, having a sleepless night, calls on Nestor, who recommends an assembly of captains. Nestor asks for volunteers to spy on the Trojans for information on their strategy for morning. Diomedes and Odysseus go: they capture Dolon, who tells them enough details to enable them to kill many Trojan allies and steal their horses.

Book 11. Read pp. 198-202 and 221-223. [Pages 203-220 optional.] Agamemnon fights heroically until he is wounded. Hector fights heroically. Paris wounds Diomedes in the foot with an arrow (209), and wounds Machaon and Eurypylos. Odysseus is wounded. Ajax is forced to retreat. Achilles watches the battle from the stern of his ship and surmises that soon the Achaeans will come begging to him for help (lines 646-649). He sends Patroclus to Nestor's tent to find out who is wounded. Patroclus declines to sit down, wanting to return quickly so as not to anger Achilles (lines 690-697), but Nestor detains him with a long story of one of his own youthful heroic adventures and finally reminds him of the instructions that Patroclus' father had given Patroclus--to give Achilles reasonable counsel. Nestor asks Patroclus to fight in Achilles' place.

Book 12. Read pp. 224-226. [Pages 227-238 optional.] The two Ajaxes and Teucer, the archer, defend the sea walls against the Trojan attack. Sarpedon tells Glaucus why heroes are honored with choice meats and good land—because they must risk their lives for others (lines 320-342)—thereby encouraging him to fight harder. Hector breaks through the gates and the Greeks run for their ships. (Note the description of Hector p. 237-238.)

Book 13. Entire book optional, pp. 239-264. While Zeus takes his eyes off Troy to watch something else, Poseidon comes in disguise to help the Greeks, who push back the Trojans and kill many of them. Polydamas, the seer, warns Hector to draw back and consolidate the Trojans' position (p. 261, lines 768-789). Hector agrees with him, but then, upon seeing Paris, gets caught up in the battle again.

Book 14. Read all.

Book 15. Read pp. 281-283—Zeus' plan. The rest (pp. 284-304) is optional. Zeus wakes up very angry and threatens Hera, again telling her that his plans will not be changed. He sends Iris to order Poseidon to withdraw from the battle. Poseidon grudgingly assents. Zeus sends Apollo to help Hector recover from his injury and to storm the ships. Together they knock down part of the sea wall. Patroclus leaves the wounded Eurypylus to try to persuade Achilles to fight again (p. 293). Hector continues to confront Ajax and urges the Trojans to fire the ships. Ajax manages to wound any Trojan who comes close and knocks their torches away.

The Iliad – Chapter Questions

Book 16. Read all.
Books 10-16
1. Do you think Zeus is a heartless, pitiless god? (See 8.481-489; 11.78-83; 20.21-33.)
2. Why will the gods break down the seawall after the war? (See pp. 141-142, 224-225.)
3. What do you think of Hera's behavior in Book 14? How do you think the Greek audience reacted to Zeus' seduction lines (14.318-33)?
4. Can you account for the fresh grass at 14.353?
5. Do you think Zeus is in charge of fate? (See 15.49-78 [Zeus' plan for the war] and 16.469-496 [Sarpedon's fate].)
6. Book 16 is often called the "little *Iliad*"--what themes of the larger book are developed on a smaller scale here?
7. Why do think Achilles compares Patroclus to a "little girl" (305)? What do you think Achilles is feeling here? What point(s) could Homer be making here?
8. Why do you think Achilles lets Patroclus go and fight for him? (See pp. 306-08, 310-12.) Describe Achilles' state of mind in this scene, concentrating on his use of the word "honor" (lines 84-101). What do you think of Achilles' wish at the top of p. 308?
9. Do you think Achilles to blame for Patroclus' death? Is Patroclus partially responsible?
10. Why do you think Patroclus' death is so different from other deaths? Name his killers (357). (See 18.490, 19.442-3.) Why do you think there are so many? Why do you think Homer calls Patroclus "you" after p. 325?
11. Is it OK to boast and trash talk or not? (See pp. 323, 327, 330.)
12. What do you think Achilles' (old) armor could symbolize? Notice what happens to whoever tries to wear this armor.

Book 17.
Entire book optional, pp. 332-354. Menelaus guards Patroclus' body. Apollo calls Hector to fight Menelaus. Hector strips the body of its (Achilles') armor. Menelaus calls to Ajax for help. Hector puts on the armor, and Zeus pities him because he will die soon. Achilles wonders why Patroclus isn't returning, while both sides fight for hours for the body and Achilles' divine horses weep for Patroclus (pp. 344-345, lines 438-454). (Note Zeus' response to this weeping in lines 455-461). Aeneas and Hector try to take Achilles' horses but fail. Zeus sends lightning and thunder, which help to start a panicked flight of the Greeks. Ajax prays to Zeus at least to let him die in sunlight and Zeus disperses the clouds (page 351; lines 660-665). Menelaus sends Antilochus to inform Achilles of Patroclus' death and to ask him to help save the body.

Books 18 and 19. Read all.

Book 20. Entire book optional, pp. 387-402. Zeus calls the gods together and tells them they can now take whatever part in the war they wish, perhaps because Achilles is so fearsome that he threatens to "exceed his fate" and destroy the walls of Troy (lines 30-33—see also pp. 328 and 418). Apollo inspires Aeneas to face Achilles, but before danger can come to either of them, Poseidon saves Aeneas so the Dardanian line will not utterly perish: Aeneas' fate, because he is "guiltless" and always gives gifts pleasing to the gods (lines 298-314), is to establish a new line of Trojans. (Keep this in mind for the end of the semester when we read the *Aeneid*.) Hector prepares to face Achilles, but Apollo warns him away. However, when his youngest brother Polydorus is killed, Hector turns again to Achilles. Neither is injured because Athena is defending Achilles and Apollo is helping Hector. Achilles then kills many other Trojans.

Books 21 and 22. Read all.

Book 23. Read pp. 440-448. [Pages 448-466, the Funeral Games for Patroclus, are optional.] Achilles sets the prizes and acts as the judge. The games include a chariot race, a boxing match, a wrestling match, a foot race, a sword fight, an iron-lump throw, an archery contest, and a javelin throw. Interesting in this section are the parallels to the "war game": participants pray to and receive help from the gods; worry about their honor (winning); and are extremely competitive for the prizes, which are mostly war booty—armor, functional metal such as cookware (tripods), and female slaves. Also, all of the athletic events are those which serve a warrior well. (Remember this when we read about games in the *Odyssey*.) Throughout the games, Achilles is a gracious host. (Notice how he awards Agamemnon with "an unfired cauldron, worth an ox, embossed / With flowers" without bothering to make him compete for it [lines 910-920].)
Book 24. Read all. [Read Introduction xxxvii-xlii, "The Enduring Heart."]

The Iliad – Chapter Questions

Books 17-24

(372) *the Linos song* = an ancient dirge or lament, parallel to laments for dying and rising fertility gods like Adonis.

(377) *Atê* = "divine temptation or infatuation" (Dodds 2). Also translated as "folly" (9.519) and "passion" (24.511), *atê* is a kind of "partial and temporary insanity; and like all insanity [among the Greeks], it is ascribed, not to physiological or psychological causes, but to an external, 'daemonic' agency" (Dodds 5). Dodds contends that Agamemnon is not offering a cheap alibi here, but genuinely explaining what happened (see 1.429-431, 9.388, and 19.288-93). What do you think?

1. Why do you think it is important for each side to have possession of Patroclus' body? Why do you think bodies are so important? (Cf. Hector, pp. 430, 434-5, 467-69, 482-92.)
2. Notice how Achilles reacts to Patroclus' death, especially what happens to his anger and to his notions of honor and glory (356-58, 365, 378, 429, 435) Do you think he revises his ideas of honor and glory? How would you describe their relationship?
3. Do you think Achilles ever finally lets go of his anger? (See pp. 442-46 and 484-85.) What do you think is Homer's view of this anger? (justified, heroic, tragic?)
4. Why do you think Homer spends so much time describing Achilles' new armor, especially, his shield (369-373)? Compare / contrast how Achilles and the men react to the new armor when it is delivered (374-375).
5. What do you think the scenes on the shield could symbolize? Why would a weapon of war have so many peaceful scenes on it? Compare and contrast these scenes with events in the *Iliad*.
6. What do you think of Agamemnon's apology (376-78)? Didn't Achilles blame Zeus also (382)? Why do you think Achilles refuses to eat (380, 383)?
7. Compare and contrast Achilles' treatment of Lycaon and his speech on death (405-406) with his speech in the underworld in the *Odyssey*, Book 11 (265-266).
8. Why do you think Homer included the episode of Achilles fighting the river? Compare / contrast with the idea of "exceeding" one's fate (16.819; 20.30-33; 21.529-31).
9. What do you think makes Hector decide finally to face and fight Achilles?
10. Is Achilles' treatment of Hector's body justified (in Greek terms)?
11. How are Hector and Patroclus similar? Do you see any similarities in the behavior of Achilles and Priam? (Describe Achilles' states of mind in the scene with Priam.)
12. What do you think is the message of Achilles' fable of Zeus' jars (483-484)? Why do you think Homer put sensible advice about grief (484-86) in the mouth of Achilles? 13. In what ways can you relate Achilles' altered notions of honor and glory to the changes we see in his anger and grief in Book 24? (Read carefully pp. 483-486.) Notice when Achilles' and Priam's griefs coincide, and when they are at odds.
13. Why do you think Homer ends the poem in the way he does? What is his point in ending that way? Why didn't Homer end the poem with Achilles' death or the capture of Troy? (In other words, why do you think Homer wants to stress the reconciliation and the end of Achilles' anger in book 24?)
14. Why do you think this poem is not called the *Achillead*?
15. Which hero do you like best, Achilles, Hector, or some other? Why? What (if anything) makes Achilles a hero?
16. What are some of the meanings of fate in the epic? (See question 7 above.)
17. Do you think women are depicted sympathetically in the epic? (Andromache, books 6 and 24, Helen, books 3 and 6, Briseis, pp. 382-383.) Given the emotions in the final scenes of the epic, what do you think is Homer's opinion of the war on Troy?
18. Do you think Achilles is a tragic hero? Look for examples of *hubris* on his part (12 boys 365, 404, 441, 445; Lycaon 405-06; fighting the river; treatment of Hector 433, 468-9). Name some aspects of Achilles' story and character that might be seen as "tragic." If you do not think that Achilles is tragic, give reasons for your views. Are any other persons or events "tragic" in the *Iliad*?

Personal Reflection

ELA –11th– English

What Does The Story Mean To You?

Research three Greek gods from the Iliad. What did he or she rule? What animals or symbols are associated with your god or goddess and why? What are the specialties of your god or goddess? What is the relationship between your god and the others? To what extent is your god involved in the lives of humans? In what stories or myths does your god take part? Is there any other interesting knowledge you acquired in your search?

How can a person become a hero or are they born that way? What traits must a person posses to become a hero?

In The Iliad, why is a person's reputation worth more than wealth and power? Where is this shown in the story?

What is the influence of the Iliad in today's world? What was it's influence in the ancient world? Does Homer glorify war?

Why do you think the ancient Greeks believed in so many gods and goddesses?

Why did the ancient Greeks dedicate so many rituals, festivals, statues, and buildings to their gods?

In what ways are the religious beliefs of the ancient Greeks like some religious beliefs practiced today?

What is the moral message of the Iliad?
Would you rather take a risk and fail or never have taken the risk in the first place? Are there any personal examples in your life where failure taught you something important?

1. What makes a hero?
2. What makes a good leader?
3. Girls, would you allow a war to be started over you? A fight?
4. Boys, would you start a war over a girl?
5. Would you fight for a family member even if you knew they were wrong?
6. Is war ever a good idea?
7. When a politician today does not win, who or what does he blame it on?
8. In society how do we gain glory?
9. How do you control your rage?
10. What is hubris? Who is someone who is hubris?

The Iliad – Essay and Socratic Questions

Ideas of beginning Socratic Seminar discussion questions:

1. What makes a hero?
2. What makes a good leader?
3. Would you fight for a family member even if you knew they were wrong?
4. Is war ever a good idea?
5. In society, how do we gain glory?
6. How do you control your rage?
7. What are the devastating effects of bitterness?
8. Is Helen guilty or innocent?

Bromance: as old as recorded history.
In both the Epic of Gilgamesh and the Iliad, the convention of the importance male-male friendships is preeminent.
- Achilles and Patroclus
- Gilgamesh and Enkidu

Identify one or more modern examples from literature/film/etc. that also contain this convention and explain the similarities and differences therein.
Appraise the necessity of this convention: Why does this convention appear in the literature of Sumerian, Greek, and modern culture?

The Roman concept of Pietas implies four levels of responsibility: to the gods, to the state, to the family, and to fellow human beings.
Evaluate Pietas. Is this motivating force for Aeneas superior to the individualistic motivations of Greeks like Achilles? Why or why not? Do people still value something like pietas today? How so? Explain giving specific examples.

The Greeks lived in what is sometimes called a "shame culture," an other-directed culture in which one's worth is based on how one's peers value him.
1. A warrior's worth is based on the prizes awarded him by the army.
2. When Agamemnon strips Achilles of one of his prizes—the slave girl—Achilles loses face.
3. Agamemnon would lose face by backing down to Achilles before the whole army, which he commands, and so they reach an impasse.

Regarding this quarrel between Agamemnon and Achilles, with which of them do you find yourself sympathizing? Who is in the right? Who the wrong? On what basis can we decide in this kind of conflict?

Greek vs. Roman Heroes Where the Greek heroes have epithets like "swift-footed" (Achilles) or "many-faceted" (Odysseus), the Roman Aeneas is pius, which means "responsible" or "dutiful."
- Greek hero = individualistic, shame cultured / reputation oriented, impulsive, fulfills nature
- Roman hero = individual needs subordinate to the group, personal sacrifice, fulfills duty

Consider a modern hero in a modern novel or movie and try to decide what motivates him or her.
Is he or she serving personal and individualistic interests in becoming a hero, or is he or she subordinating personal interests to larger issues and causes?

The Iliad – Essay or Socratic Questions

1. The Iliad focuses on the behavior of warriors in time of crisis and examines what each person owes to him- or herself and to the community. What does each of the following characters owe to himself and to others? a) Agamemnon b) Achilles c) Patroclus d) Hector e) Paris
2. Achilles is acknowledged to be the greatest Greek warrior. Yet Homer focuses on Achilles quarrel with Agamemnon and its effect upon the Greeks rather than on his heroic exploits. Why?
3. Achilles is the first tragic hero of literature. What does it mean to be a tragic hero? How does The Iliad develop Achilles into a tragic hero? What is the difference between a tragic hero and a hero?
4. What kind of person is Hector? What tests of character confront him? To what extent does he pass them? What temptations does he resist, and which does he find irresistible? Why? How does his behavior affect his heroic image?
5. Compare and contrast the characterization of ONE character from The Iliad and Troy and the effect differences have on the audience.
6. In The Iliad, why is a person's reputation worth more than wealth and power? Where is this shown in the story? How is this depicted in the film?
7. Elements of The Iliad are accurate depictions of relationships of Ancient Greek society. Do the relationships resemble modern day relationships? How did the film approach this topic?
8. Compare and contrast the choices made by Homer and Petersen & Benioff (director & screenwriters of Troy) to create the key elements of tragedy.
9. Compare and contrast the most effective and least effective aspects of both The Iliad and Troy.
10. What were the most glaring CHANGES the film made? Why did they make them? Were they effective?

Other Possible Discussion Questions:
1. What is the "will of Zeus?"
2. Some have characterized the Iliad as Homer's explication of the origins of human suffering.
3. What are those origins?
4. What sort of character is Apollo?
5. What moves Apollo, Aphrodite Hermes, Hera, Zeus, or another of the gods?
6. What sort of character is Priam
7. Why doe Agamemnon have authority?
8. What sort of relationship does Achilles have with his mother and his father?
9. Who is responsible for Patroclus' death?
10. What is the warrior's code of honor in the Iliad?
11. How does the morality of the people in the Iliad compare to the morality of the gods?
12. Why is the scene between Achilles and Priam so important in so many dimensions?
13. Why is this poem so important to the training of warriors that western military colleges invariably require initiates to read it?
14. Describe the shield of Achilles and explain the symbolism.

Themes and Characters

Achilles is the first tragic hero of literature. What does it mean to be a tragic hero? How does the Iliad develop Achilles into a tragic hero? What is the difference between a tragic hero and a hero? Is there a heroic code that guides the decisions of the characters in The Iliad?

How do Achilles change over the course of the poem?

The Iliad focuses on the behavior of warriors in times of crisis and examines what each person owes to him- or herself and to the community. What does each of the following characters owe to himself and to others?

a) Agamemnon   b) Achilles   c) Patroclus   d) Hector
e) Paris

"Hateful to me as the gates of Hades is that man who hides one thing in his heart and speaks another."
Homer

 ETHOS LOGOS VALUE/VIRTUE OF THE MONTH
Excellence – Respect

Virtues – Examples in Greek Culture

- Beauty—what is it?
- Teamwork (the Greeks fight among themselves)
- Sacrifice (Agamemnon and Iphigenia)
- Honor (Ajax and his humiliation, the oath to Helen)
- War and innocent victims
- The male heir (Telemachus)
- Maternal devotion (Thetis and Achilles)
- Passing the buck (Zeus to Paris)
- Craftiness—survival skill or dishonesty? (Odysseus)
- Symbolism (Achilles' armor)
- Fidelity
- Hospitality
- Migration during wartime (Greek and Trojan refugees)
- Brutality (Achilles' rage)
- Friendship (Patroclus and Achilles)
- Personal weaknesses
- Exploiting weakness (Paris and Achilles)
- Mourning

Themes To Explore

- The glory of war
- Human condition
- The fragility of human life
- Pride
- Competition
- Glory
- The Individual and Society
- Compassion and Forgiveness
- Rivalry
- Anger

The Iliad – Vocabulary

incensed	illustrious
plunder	loitering
sacrosanct	sacrosanct
divine	spurned
brazen	bruit
harrowed	commandeer
bereft	pittance
blazoned	overweening
shambling	vaulting
gallant	exult
distaff	exultant
implore	bulwark
wavered	muster
marshals	ignominious
whetted	citadel
brandished	gargantuan
stinted	harry
lustrous	(harries)
gaunt	decree
	clandestine
	deign
	sumptuous

Grade Level Vocabulary

anachronistic
abbreviate
abdicate
abstinence
adulation
adversity
aesthetic
amicable
anecdote
anonymous
antagonist
arid

assiduous

Latin Root Words

Germ - vital or related
Greg - group
Mar - sea
Prim - first
Pyro - fire
Clam - cry out
Plu - more
Tang - touch
String - bind
Liber - Free
Junct - join
Clud - close
Se - apart

About The Author

The Iliad was written from the Greek poet Homer's point of view. He was known to be personally familiar with the location of Troy as he lived very close to where it was. He was born between the 12th and 8th century BCE but to this day is a mystery to our western culture. He was thought to be blind, and many debated on whether he really existed or not.

Many researchers and experts argue whether in fact Homer was in fact actually alive or even existed and even questions on whether Homer was just one individual or there were multiple people involved. Homer's nationality was in point of fact a Greek, which may have paved way to influences of bias in the recounting of the Trojan war as Homer may have wanted to show the Greeks in a more powerful and victorious light in comparison to them being portrayed as the weaker side. The Iliad is retold predominantly in the perspective of the Achilles who is known to be a great Greek warrior

Homer was a Greek himself his view and perspective on what may have happened during the Trojan War cannot be entirely trustworthy as there may be influences of bias in the retelling.

GREAT MEN & WOMEN

Homer
800 – 701 BC

"Hateful to me as the gates of Hades is that man who hides one thing in his heart and speaks another."

1,5,9 -5,6

ETHOS LOGOS

The Trojan War

This is important in the study of the conflict between the Greeks and the Trojans as it is a recount of the beginnings of the Trojan War, and it gives us an insight into the conflict that occurred between the rivals and the reasons behind why the conflict began . The Iliad also give Homer's interpretation of how much Paris's arrogance and pride played a significant role in starting the war as Helen the Queen of Sparta and Paris fall in love and run away together. Even though this is a story and interpretation of the Trojan War, we can still used to story to learn the outfall from conflict and how the Trojans began to hate the Greek and vise versa.

The values and virtues of the month are **RESPECT** and **EXCELLENCE**.

Weave these traits into your novel studies, other subject areas you are studying, and opportunities to show RESEPCT and EXCELLENCE in your daily life.

TEACHERS

15 WAYS TO INSPIRE YOUR CHILDREN TO EXCELLENCE.

1. Emphasize contribution over achievement
2. Model hard work
3. Give your children descriptive praise
4. Focus on solutions and opportunities, not problems
5. Show your children that you're pursuing excellence, too
6. Don't complain
7. Be enthusiastic about life
8. Lead by example
9. Remind your children that you love and accept them unconditionally
10. Read
11. Stand for something
12. Develop a clear vision for your family
13. Overcome your fears
14. Share your struggles with your children
15. Speak less and listen more

By *Daniel-Wong.com*

FOR PERSONAL EXCELLENCE PRACTICE:

- Discipline
- Commitment
- Emotional control
- Attitude and focus
- Belief and courage
- Calmness and control
- Self evaluation

EXCELLENCE TRAITS TO MASTER:

- Self awareness
- Vision and life purpose
- Positive emotions
- Skill set and abilities
- Adaptability
- Self accountability
- Self transparency
- Growth mindset

READ

- To Kill A Mockingbird – Character Atticus Finch Matilda
- Matilda
- Narrative of the Life of Frederick Douglas
- Team of Rivals – DK Goodwin

WATCH

- Jiro The Art of Sushi (2011)
- Miracle (2004) – 1980 US Olympic Hockey
- The Gardener (2016)
- Ground Hog Day – PG (1993)
- Stand and Deliver (1988)
- Lean on Me (1989)
- Mr. Holland's Opus (1995)
- The Watchmakers Apprentice (2017)

MODELS

- Coach John Wooden (basketball)
- Tony Hawk (skateboarder)
- Laird Hamilton (surfer)
- Serena Williams (tennis)
- Tom Brady (football)

RESPECT QUESTIONS

1. What does the word "respect" mean to you?
2. How do you exemplify respect in your life?
3. How does respect differ from tolerance?
4. How do disrespect, intolerance, prejudice, and discrimination differ from one another?
5. Why is respect important in our world today?
6. Who deserves respect but often does not receive it? How does it feel when someone shows disrespect?
7. What are some good manners you can show at meal time, at the store, or at school?
8. What would happen to bullying if everyone showed respect to one another?

7 EFFECTIVE WAYS TO MAKE OTHERS FEEL IMPORTANT

1. Use their name.
2. Express sincere gratitude.
3. Do more listening than talking.
4. Talk more about them than about you.
5. Be authentically interested.
6. Be sincere in your praise.
7. Show you care.
   – R. Bennett

READ

- The Snowy Day - Ezra Jack Keats
- Going Home – Eva Bunting
- The Way I Act – Steve Metger
- The Recess Queen – Alexis O'Neill
- Don't Call Me Special – Pat Thomas
- Loser – Jerry Spinelli
- Due Unto Otters – Laurie Keller
- Classic of Filial Piety – Confucius
- A Coat of Many Colors, Dolly Parton
- If a Bus Could Talk: The Rosa Park Story, Faith Ringgold

HOW TO SHOW RESPECT TO FRIENDS

1. Be kind and courteous.
2. Listen to others, make eye contact.
3. Be polite and practice manners.
4. Think before you speak.
5. Be humble and considerate.
6. Lend a helping hand or serve others.
7. Be willing to change.
8. Stick to your moral code.
9. Stop gossiping immediately.
10. Learn to appreciate and value diverse views.

WATCH

- Mary Poppins (1964)
- Remember the Titans PG (2000)
- Finding Nemo (2003)
- Wonder (2017)

MODELS

- Bruce Lee (Martial Arts)
- Alfred The Great
- Sir Lancelot
- Marcus Aurelius

The Iliad – Timeline of Ancient Greece

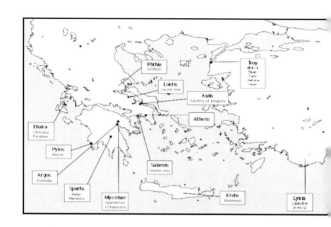

BRONZE AGE (3000-1100)

c. 1800-1250	Troy VI
c. 1500-1120	Mycenaean Civilization
c. 1250	possible date of the historical fall of Troy VI
1183	traditional date of the fall of Troy

DARK AGES (1100-800 BC)

1100-750	Stories of the fall of Troy passed down in oral form
1100	Doric Invasion of Greece
1050-950	Greek colonization of Asia Minor (western coast of Turkey)
900	Beginning of the rise of the polis (city-state)

ARCHAIC PERIOD (800-500 BC)

800-700	Rise of the aristocracies
776	Olympic Games established
750	Greek colonization of Southern Italy and Sicily begins
750	Introduction of a new alphabet; writing introduced
720	Homer, **Iliad**
700	Hesiod, **Theogony** and **Works and Days**
680	Homer, **Odyssey**; Archilochus (lyric poet)
650	Greek colonization around the Black Sea begins
600	Sappho (lyric poet); Thales (philosopher)
594-593	Archonship of Solon in Athens
545-510	Tyranny of the Peisistratids in Athens
540	Singing of Homeric poems begins at Panathenaic festival
533	Thespis wins first tragedy competition at Athens
508	Cleisthenes reforms the Athenian Constitution

CLASSICAL PERIOD (500-323 BC)

490-479	Persian War
458	Aeschylus, **Oresteia**
461-429	Pericles dominant in Athenian politics; the "Periclean Age"
450-420	Herodotus composes his **Histories** about the Persian War.
447	Parthenon begun in Athens
431-404	Peloponnesian War (Athens and allies vs. Sparta and allies)
428	Sophocles, **Oedipus the King**
424-400	Thucydides composes his **History of Peloponnesian War**
404	Athens loses Peloponnesian War to Sparta
399	Trial and death of Socrates

Recitation Pairing

RECITATION – 12TH GRADE

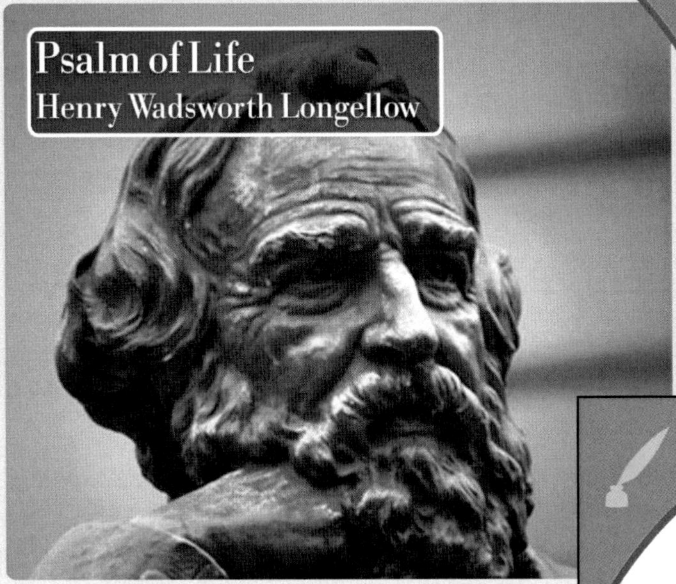

★ **About The Poet**

Henry Wadsworth Longfellow (187-1882) was one of the most widely k
best-loved American poets of the 19th century.

★ **About the Poem**

This 1838 first appeared in New York literary magazine The Knickerboc
poem drafted after a conversations between Longfellow a collogue. The
seeks of seizing the day and that current day life is more preferred than
past. The speaker of the poem is the "Heart of the Young Man," while hi
is a "Psalmist," a writer of biblical psalms.

12-1 ETHOS LOGOS

Psalm of Life

HENRY WADSWORTH LONGFELLOW

Tell me not, in mournful numbers,
Life is but an empty dream!
For the soul is dead that slumbers,
And things are not what they seem.

Life is real! Life is earnest!
And the grave is not its goal;
Dust thou art, to dust returnest,
Was not spoken of the soul.

Not enjoyment, and not sorrow,
Is our destined end or way;
But to act, that each to-morrow
Find us farther than to-day.

Art is long, and Time is fleeting,
And our hearts, though stout and brave,
Still, like muffled drums, are beating
Funeral marches to the grave.

In the world's broad field of battle,
In the bivouac of Life,
Be not like dumb, driven cattle!
Be a hero in the strife

Trust no Future, howe'er pleasant!
Let the dead Past bury its dead!
Act,— act in the living Present!
Heart within, and God o'erhead!

Lives of great men all remind us
We can make our lives sublime,
And, departing, leave behind us
Footprints on the sands of time;

Footprints, that perhaps another,
Sailing o'er life's solemn main,
A forlorn and shipwrecked brother,
Seeing, shall take heart again.

Let us, then, be up and doing,
With a heart for any fate;
Still achieving, still pursuing,
Learn to labor and to wait.

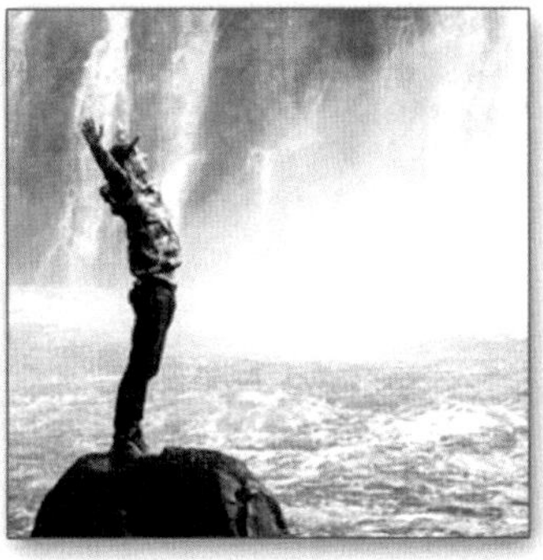

★ ETHOS LOGOS VALUE/VIRTUE OF THE MONTH ★

Excellence - Respect

Historical Pairing

Military Training in Ancient Greece

Athens:
- Goal to produce citizens trained in arts and to prepare for both peace and war.
- Homeschooled until age 6
- 6-14 attend school; read aloud and memorize
- Used tablets and rulers
- Learned Homer & the Lyre
- Other subjects' discretion of teacher (always male)
- High school for 4 years
- Went to military school for 2 years (18-20); then graduated
- Girls didn't attend school but could study at home

Sparta:
- Purpose of education was to produce a disciplined marching army!
- Discipline, self-denial, simplicity
- Required to have "perfect" bodies. Babies that didn't pass the test were killed are sent to be a slave (**helot**).
- Boys sent off to military school at age 6 or 7. Slept in barracks with other boys.
- Taught to read and write, but warfare was most important.
- Training was brutal; they marched without shoes, went without food, etc.
- At age 18-20, boys had to pass a test (fitness, leadership, skill); if they didn't pass, they'd became **perioikas** (middle class with no citizenship).
- If pass, they became a full citizen and Spartan soldier.
- Not allowed to touch money.
- Lived in barracks with their "brotherhood" (even if married).
- Could "retire" at age 60 and go to live with their families.
- Girls were also educated and sent to live with their "sisterhood". If she passed a physical fitness test at 18, she'd be assigned a husband. If not, she'd become perioikas.
- Spartan women had freedom to leave the home.

The Wars
While the varying city-states of Greece were often fighting each other, they'd often form LEAGUES– alliances.

There were many wars, but the 4 main ones were:
> Trojan War,
> Persian,
> Peloponnesian,
> Alexander's Campaigns.

Historical Pairing

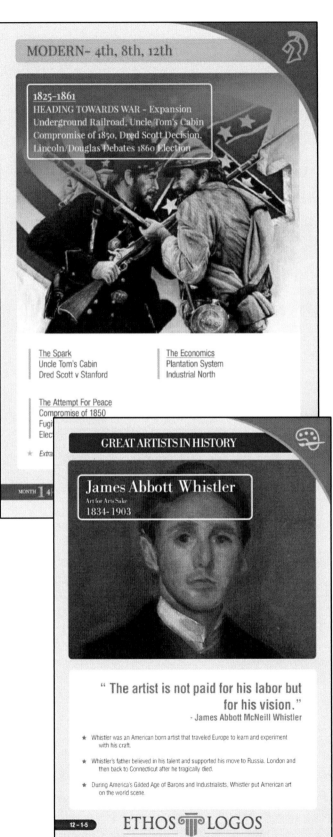

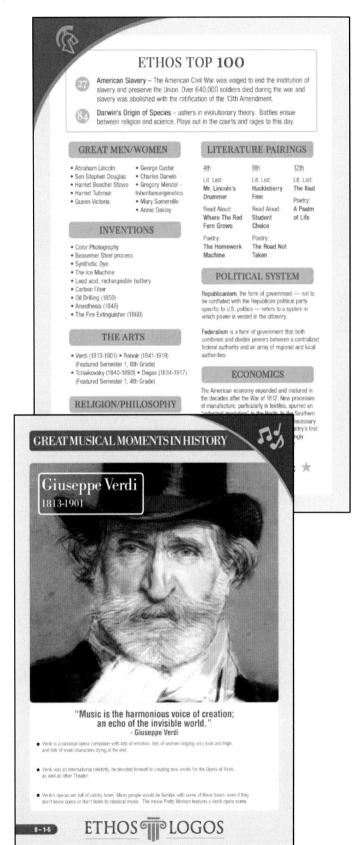

Artists and Musicians Pairing

Historical Pairing
Actual Time Period

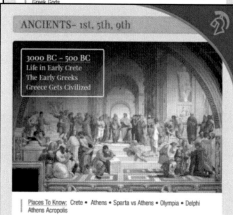

Great Men and Women

ENGLISH – 12TH

ANTIGONE

ANTIGONE

Time and Place

The play Antigone sometimes seems to have two tragic heroes: two characters make decisions that lead to a tragic conclusion. Use Aristotle's Theory of Tragedy to explain which character is the true tragic hero, Creon or Antigone.

Aristotle's rules for drama: catharsis, dramatic unities, hamartia, hubris, recognition and reversal; how do they apply to the play, Antigone?

How does the play "Antigone" relate to Ancient Greece?

Authors Intent

★ Which is more important to Sophocles – family or authority? Look at Antigone, Ismene, Creon, and Haimon, and at what happens to them and their relationships.

★ What is fate to Sophocles?

ETHOS ⬛ LOGOS

Unit #:	**2 (September)**
Novel:	**Antigone**
Grade Levels:	**12th**

History:
1861-1865
THE CIVIL WAR

Artists - Musician:
Verdi
Whistler

Value/Virtue:
Silence - Order

Governance:
Democracy
Republic

Religion:
Christianity

Cultural Saying Unit 2
- Mumbo jumbo
- The world is your oyster
- Gospel Truth

Antigone – Chapter Summary

Antigone Reading Questions, Scene 1 and Ode 1 (700-705)
Answer the questions below. Thorough and thoughtful responses will earn one point.
Scene 1:

1. What is the "Ship of State" that Creon refers to? What are the "recent storms" that threatened it?
2. What kind of ruler is Creon? Explain using a quotation from his monologue.
3. What is the Choragos' response to Creon's edict? Why?
4. What does Creon mean when he says, "And death it is; yet money talks, and the wisest/ Have sometimes been known to count a few coins too many" (64-65)?
5. How does the arrival of the Sentry (page 701) defuse the tension of this scene?
6. What does the Sentry report?
7. Who does Creon think is responsible for burying Polyneices? What literary device is this?
8. True feelings sometimes emerge when one is angry. From Creon's speech in lines 115-141, how do you think he really feels about the elders of Thebes? Include a quotation to support your ideas.
9. What qualities in Creon might Sophocles' audience have found most godlike? What might the audience have considered to be Creon's "human defects"?
10. What does Creon threaten to do to the Sentry if "the man" is not found? What does Creon mean when he says, "Do you understand me? / A fortune won is often misfortune"(140-141)?

11. In Creon's first words to the Chorus, what were the "storms" that threatened to destroy the Ship of State?
12. What reasons does Creon give for not allowing Polyneices to be buried?
13. How does the end of Creon's speech differ from the beginning (lines 45-49)?
14. How does the Choragos feel about Creon's commands (lines 56-59)? How do you know this?
15. Summarize the news that the Sentry must give to Creon?
16. How does the Sentry seem to feel about speaking to Creon? What can we infer about Creon due to the Sentry's reaction?
17. The choragus is bold enough to suggest to Creon that perhaps the gods wanted Eteocles buried. What is Creon's reaction to this suggestion? What assumption does Creon make?
18. What order does Creon give the Sentry before his departure? Quote his exact words from the text that have the order.
19. Define DRAMATIC IRONY using his literary glossary. Explain where the dramatic irony in this scene occurs.
20. Read the verses to the ode and list the three main ideas of it.
21. On the basis of the final verse of Ode 1, why do you think the Chorus supports Creon?

What law does Creon champion in Scene 1, and who supports his view here? What other view has been expressed in the drama so far, and who expresses it?

Antigone – Chapter Summary

RHETORIC: The art of using language to persuade.
Creon's Speech
Scene 1 Rhetorical Analysis
Objective: Use details and evidence from Creon's "Ship of State" Speech to support a rhetorical analysis of his address to the people of Thebes

RHETORICAL STANCE: The speaker's position. What he or she is arguing?
RHETORICAL PURPOSE: What the speaker wants the audience to think or to do. This can often be explained using an infinitive phrase. Example: MLK's purpose in the "I Have a Dream" speech is to create unity among the races.
RHETORICAL STRATEGIES: Any devices of language used by the speaker. Examples include figurative language, connotative language, imagery, diction, syntax (sentence structure/parallelism), irony, tone.
RHETORICAL PROOFS: Logos, ethos, and pathos. The speaker's use of rhetorical strategies will strengthen the rhetorical proofs—and lead to a more persuasive or effective speech.

What are two purposes of Creon's speech? Remember to use infinitive phrases.
      A. **The purpose of Creon's speech is to…**
      B. **The purpose of Creon's speech is to…**

1. At the beginning of the speech, what metaphor does he use to describe the state? Why is this an apt metaphor? (How does it address the concerns of the audience?)
2. Identify the six principles Creon says will help guide him as a ruler.
3. Explain why Creon's principles are admirable. Why would his audience respect him for establishing these as his ethical guidelines?
4. What is his rhetorical stance on the burial of Polyneices? **Creon is arguing that…**
5. What evidence does he use to support his claim? *Cite specific line numbers* that support Creon's claim about Polyneices.
6. How does he address any counterarguments? That is…what specific objections might be raised about his decree regarding the corpse of Polyneices? Why might these objections be raised by the citizens of Thebes? (Hint: Remember ancient Greek burial practices.)
7. What is noble and admirable about this speech? *Cite at least two lines* from the speech and explain why you think they are admirable.
    3. First line(s) you find admirable:
    4. Explanation:
    5. Second Line(s) you find admirable:
    6. Explanation:
8. What aspects of his speech hint at possible conflicts or less than noble aspects of his personality? *Cite at least one specific line* and explain why you think it is less than noble.
9. Tying it all together: Find at least two examples of each of the following:
    3. Words with connotative meanings—be sure to explain effect.
    4. Significant syntactical choices—be sure to explain effect
    5. Diction: Identify the type of diction he uses, and give two examples.
    6. Rhetoric appeals: one example each of logos, ethos and pathos

Antigone – Chapter Summary

Antigone Reading Questions, Scene 2 (707-712)

1. Why is the Sentry so relieved? Why does he return?
2. From Creon's initial reaction, what can you deduce about Creon's relationship with Antigone?
3. Explain the following comparison: "I have seen / A mother bird come back to a stripped nest, heard / Her crying bitterly a broken note or two / For the young ones stolen. Just so, when this girl / Found the bare corpse, and all her love's work wasted, / She wept, and cried on heaven to damn the hands / That had done this thing" (35-41).
4. What reason does Antigone give for violating Creon's decree? What theme of the play does her reasoning express?
5. How does the Choragos describe Antigone?
6. Why does Creon charge Ismene? How do you feel about Creon's accusation of Ismene?
7. In lines 121-127, the Choragos and Creon each apply an image to Ismene. What are the two images? How do these images reveal the different viewpoints of the Choragos and Creon?
8. Considering everything you know about Ismene so far, why do you think she desires death? What is her motivation?
9. How can Antigone's rejection of Ismene be seen as a matter of pride, or hubris?
10. Ismene and Antigone are dramatic foils. In what ways are these two characters different?
11. Explain Creon's final passage in this scene.

12. The sentry returns with someone under arrest? Who is this?
13. What does Creon's reaction in lines 18-21 suggest about his relationship with Antigone? In other words, why would he be surprised that she was the guilty party?
14. Summarize the sentry's report of what he witnessed Antigone doing? What metaphor does he use to describe her actions?
15. Do you feel that the metaphor was effective? Why or why not?
16. Using Antigone's own words, explain why she dared to deny Creon's orders.
17. In lines 106-118, Creon and Antigone are defending their own actions. What reason does each give for doing what they did?
18. Lines 119-127 have contrasting images of Ismene, one from the Choragos and one from Creon. What are they?
19. In this scene, Ismene wants to join Antigone in the death sentence. From what you know of her, what do you think is her motivation?
20. From what you know of Antigone, why do you think she rejects Ismene and excludes her from the death sentence?
21. What new twist to the plot is revealed when Ismene reminds Creon that Antigone is "But your own son's bride!" What is even more shocking about Creon's insistence that Antigone die even after this is revealed?
22. Based on what you know about Creon's personality, do you believe his son will be able to sway his opinion?
23. Use your literary glossary and define FOIL CHARACTER.

"The only power any government has is the power to crack down on criminals. Well, when there aren't enough criminals, one makes them. One declares so many things to be a crime that it becomes impossible for men to live without breaking laws." ~ Ayn Rand
Explain Rand's statement and the way(s) in which it apples to Sophocles' *Antigone*. (Write three to five sentences)

_____

Ismene tells Antigone, "I too have a duty that I must discharge to the dead" (II.138). Write whether you think Antigone is doing the right thing in trying to keep Ismene from fulfilling this duty

_____

What would you say is the greatest force motivating Antigone in Scene Two? Pride, Love or Principle?

Antigone – Chapter Summary

***Antigone* Reading Questions, Scene 3 and Ode 3 (716-721) – Write in complete sentences. Each thorough and thoughtful response will earn one point.**

Scene 3:

1. How is Haimon related to Creon and Antigone?
2. What is your first impression of Haimon's attitude toward his father?
3. What is ironic about Creon giving advice about Antigone?
4. What words are sometimes used to name the kind of leader Creon is describing when he says, "Whoever is chosen to govern should be obeyed— / Must be obeyed, in all things, great and small, / Just and unjust!" (35-37)?
5. What is the point that Haimon is trying to make to Creon in lines 51-91?
6. Haimon uses two analogies, or comparisons, to show Creon that it is wise to be flexible. What are the two analogies?
7. Why do you think the Choragos avoids taking sides in the argument between Haimon and Creon?
8. What character flaws in Creon are revealed when he says, "You consider it right for a man of my years and experience / To go to school to a boy?" (95-96)?
9. Whose view—Creon's or Haimon's—better expresses the Greek ideal of democracy?
10. Although Haimon has not spoken with Antigone since the play began, how does his view echo hers? Include a quotation from this scene to support your ideas.
11. What does Haimon mean when he says, "Then she must die. But her death will cause another" (119)? How does Creon interpret this last sentence?
12. How has Haimon's attitude toward Creon—his father and his king—changed since the beginning of the scene?
13. Whose life is saved in this scene? How do you know?
14. What is Creon's final decision concerning Antigone's punishment? How does Creon's decision "absolve" the State?
15. Based on what you have read so far, would you describe Creon as a good ruler or a poor ruler? Explain.

16. What question does the choragus begin with? What is Creon's response to its question?
17. In his first line, how does Haemon seem to feel towards his father? What motivation might he have for greeting his father in this manner?
18. Why does Creon say that he's actually doing his son a favor by ridding him of Antigone? What does this suggest about his role of women?
19. What reason does Creon give for why he can't pardon her since she's family?
20. What does Creon say that suggests that his manhood feels threatened by Antigone and her actions?
21. What suggestion is Haemon making when he says, "Yet there are other men who can reason, too; and their opinions might be helpful." What reaction from Creon would you expect from this suggestion?
22. What does Haemon reveal about how the people feel about Antigone's punishment?
23. Explain what Haemon is trying to get Creon to understand with his metaphor about the trees bending? (line 80-82)
24. What emotional appeal does Haemon imply when he says "Then she must die. But her death will cause another?"
25. What reversal does Creon make in his punishment of Antigone? Why does he believe that this will be viewed more favorably in the eyes of the people?
26. A syllogism is when a logical conclusion can be inferred based on factual information given. Complete this syllogism that Creon uses in his argument with Haemon:_____

      A. Anarchy can be prevented if all laws are strictly enforced.

"There is nothing I would not do for those who are really my friends. I have no notion of loving people by halves, it is not my nature."
~ Jane Austen, *Northanger Abbey*

Explain the way(s) in which Austen's quote applies to Scene Three of *Antigone*. Write two to four sentences.

Antigone – Chapter Summary

Antigone **Reading Questions, Scene 4 (723-726). Answer the following questions. Write in complete sentences. Each thorough and thoughtful response will earn one point.**

Scene 4:
1. The play is moving toward its climax. What dramatic action is about to occur?
2. Compare and contrast Antigone to the following characters: Niobe – Tantalos
3. What do these characters have in common?
4. What change do you notice in Antigone's manner?
5. What two things does Antigone ask of the elders of Thebes?
6. What does Antigone mean in line 41 when she says that her father's "marriage strikes from the grave to murder" her own marriage? How does the Chorus argue against this view in lines 45-48?
7. Why do you think that Creon publicly reasserts that his hands are clean in this matter? Do you think his hands are clean?
8. Antigone says about Creon, "May his punishment equal my own" (70). If Creon receives a punishment "equal" to Antigone's, what do you think it will be?
9. Include a quotation from this scene that shows that Antigone believes that she has done the right thing.

10. Reread the opening lines of the choragus. What emotion is he feeling regarding Creon's decision to punish Antigone?
11. Antigone compares herself to Niobe. Why might Antigone compare herself to this woman? *Be sure to read the footnote that explains who Niobe was.
12. Who does Antigone cast some of the blame on for her fate? Was she right to assign this individual a portion of the blame? Why or why not?
13. What does the chorus remind Antigone about who controlled her fate?
14. Antigone seems to come to accept her eventual death, but what desire does she express for Creon?
15. Summarize the summaries told in Ode 4. What do these stories seem to have in common with Antigone's?

Write three comments on the drama so far and one question that you would like to see answered by the end of the play. These comments and the questions should focus on key elements, events, or ideas in *Antigone*.

Antigone – Chapter Summary

Antigone Reading Questions, Scene 5 and Paean (728-732)
Answer with complete sentences. One point each
Scene 5:
1.According to Teiresias, what has caused the gods' anger?
2.How do Creon's words to Teiresias demonstrate his pride?
3.Teiresias says, "You are a king because of me" (64). Why is Creon a king because of Teiresias?
4.Who is the child thrust "into living night" (73)? Who is the child "kept from the gods below" (74)? What does Teiresias seem to foreshadow in this speech as a whole?
5.What are Teiresias' "arrows" (84)? How does his word choice connect to earlier words of Creon's in this scene?
6.Creon's confession of pride can be interpreted as the turning point of the play. Immediately after this confession, Creon demonstrates a true change of heart by asking the Choragos for advice and help. Jot down the lines that show that Creon is starting to change.
7.Why do you think Creon decides to save Antigone?

8.What purpose does Tieresias have when visiting Creon?
9.What did Tieresias witness that he believes is a warning sign from the gods?
10.What is Creon's reaction to the advice Tieresias provides?
11.Tieresias tries to caution Creon a second time. Paraphrase the warning he gives in lines 70-87.
12.In the passage listed above, identify one example of a logical appeal Creon uses.
13.In the same passage, identify one example of an emotional appeal Creon uses.
14.At the end of scene 5, Creon finally experiences a change of heart. What evidence did the choragus present before him that makes him realize he was wrong? Does Creon change his decision with an open heart or with reluctance? Support your answer with a specific line reference.
15.Complete the following syllogism that shows the logical reasoning of Creon as he considers what to do to Antigone.

      A. Tieresias is a great prophet that has never been wrong.

      B. Tieresias has predicted that Creon will experience great sorrow if he punishes Antigone.

      C. Therefore, _____.

Paean:
1.Why might Sophocles have interrupted the action at this point to insert a hymn to Dionysos?
2.Describe Dionysos.
3. List the places that are mentioned in this section.
4.List 3 Greek cries.
5.List the people and/or gods and a description for each. *
6.What does the chorus mean by asking Dionysos to come "with clement feet" (13-14)? What is ironic about this plea? *

*Essential Questions to assure knowledge of main idea

Antigone – Chapter Summary

Antigone Reading Questions, Exodos

Answer with complete sentences. One point each

1. The Messenger says, "Fate raises up, / And Fate casts down the happy and unhappy alike: / No man can foretell his Fate" (4-6). To whom does this theme most apply? Why?

2. Who dies? How does each character die?

3. Do you think Creon is justified in placing all the blame upon himself? Explain.

4. How has Creon changed?

5. Why do you think the Choragos addresses the audience directly at the end of the play? Paraphrase the final four lines of the play.

6. In lines 32-76 of the Exodos, the Messenger says that Creon buried Polyneices first and then went to free Antigone. How do you predict events might have turned out if Creon had reversed the order of his tasks? Explain!

7. Describe the major **conflict** in the play.
   1. Is it between absolute good and absolute evil or is the conflict between opposing views of what is good
   2. What position does Sophocles seem to take on this position? Cite evidence from the play to support your response.

8. Find **THREE** lines in the play that you think are especially important. **RECORD THEM:**
   1. Then, state what you think is the main **theme** in the play.
   2. What does this reveal about human life?

9. At the end of this **tragedy**, Eurydice blames Creon for the disastrous turn of events. Creon accepts her curse, saying, "I alone am guilty" (line 121). What do you think of Creon's statement of sole responsibility?

10. Why does the messenger say that Creon is a walking dead man? What has Creon lost?

11. Summarize the news that the messenger gives to Queen Eurydice. What effect does hearing the news have on her?

12. Creon acknowledges that he caused the death of Haemon and Antigone. What other death did he cause indirectly? How does Creon feel about this?

13. Creon wishes for what punishment for his actions? Will the choragus allow Creon to have this punishment? Why or why not?

14. What lesson does Creon finally come to learn from this experience? If he had learned his lesson sooner, what plot events may have been different?

_____

"Where love rules, there is no will to power; and where power predominates, there love is lacking. The one is the shadow of the other." -- Carl Jung

To what extent is this quotation related to King Creon and his regime? Does this statement about power justify Creon's actions? Why or why not?

_____

"Where love rules, there is no will to power; and where power predominates, there love is lacking. The one is the shadow of the other." -- Carl Jung

To what extent is this quotation related to King Creon and his regime? Does this statement about power justify Creon's actions? Why or why not?

<u>Antigone</u> – Wrap Up Questions

1. Explain the type of law Antigone favors/believes versus the type of law Creon favors/believes.
2. What crime has Polyneices committed, according to Creon?
3. Initially, who does Creon believe buries the body of Polyneices?
4. How do the guards manage to capture Antigone?
5. Why is Antigone so angry with Ismene after they've both been brought in to see Creon?
6. What does the blind prophet claim happen that bothers him when he's in augury (2 things)?What does the blind prophet claim MUST be done to repair the evil against the gods (2 things)?
7. What does Creon see when he looks into the tomb at the end of the play (2 things)?
8. Why does Sophocles not have Creon die at the end of the play?
9. Compare and contrast the characters of Antigone and Creon with reference to the precepts of a "tragic hero." Use the entire definition of tragic hero and support your ideas with QUOTED evidence.
10. What does the play suggest about the issue of individual versus the state?
11. What does this play suggest about the nature of leadership?
12. What does this play suggest about the nature of justice and mercy?
13. Is this a feminist play? Before you decide, please review a definition of the word feminist. Then use evidence to support your argument.
14. Discuss the Greek view of catharsis. How does this play achieve catharsis? Explain.
15. Creon argues that it is not right for "a man to go to school to a boy." What is inherently wrong with his logic? Have you ever learned a valuable lesson from someone who is younger than you?
16. Teiresias tells Creon: "The only crime is pride." What does he mean by this? How can pride lead to faulty judgement? How can poor decisions be rectified?
17. Compare and contrast the sister, Antigone and Ismene, and include their philosophies, and their reactions to others in the play.
18. "Antigone" is thousands of years old, and yet you are reading it today. How is the play universal?
19. Explain, in detail, how each of the following characters dies:
    Haimon -
    Antigone -
    Eurydice -

Antigone – Chapter Summary

1. Consider the conflict between the two main characters. Is Creon wholly wrong in forbidding people to bury Polyneices? What are his reasons for doing so? How does he justify his position to others in the play? Do you think Antigone is a righteous martyr for wanting to bury her brother? What is her justification for breaking the law to do so? What does this tell us about the values of Classical Greece?

2. Discuss the role of gender in the play by addressing the contrast between Ismene as the dutiful Greek woman and Antigone as rebellious and self-willed. Why does Ismene refuse to help Antigone bury their brother? Why does Antigone refuse to let Ismene come to her aid when Antigone is sentenced to execution? What does this tell us about gender roles in Classical Greece?

3. When considering the role of women in classical Greece, what was so unusual about Sophocles' portrayal of the character of Antigone as being the one who was morally "right" over Creon in the end?

4. How do our moral and social values shape our interactions with others?

5. What does our response to conflict teach us about ourselves?

6. To what extent are we defined by our actions?

7. How does the character of Creon from Sophocles' Antigone—a "man of simplicity and banal happiness"—reflect conflicting motivations of political and social order through his decision to sentence Antigone to death in the classical tragedy? Articulate how Creon's commitment to acts he finds loathsome and Antigone's insistence on facing the power of the state both advance the plot of this tragedy and develop themes. Support your statements with examples and quotations from the play.

8. Write a response to literature in which you analyze the nature of Creon's and Antigone's tragic flaw. Identify errors in judgment or weaknesses in character and indicate how this flaw brings about death and affects all of Theban society. Who better fits the definition of a tragic hero, Antigone or Creon? Support your statements with examples and quotations from the play.

Antigone – Chapter Summary

Discussion Questions:

1. How do the geography, climate, and culture of one's homeland affect his or her view of the larger world? How might the geography of Greece have affected the ancient Greek worldview? Do you see any evidence of this perspective within the Antigone?
2. What events in Greek history are happening during the fifth century B.C.E.? How might these events influence the creation of literature during this time?
3. What is a polis?
4. How is Athens different from other city-states? How does democracy work in Athens? How is it different from our current government in the United States?
5. Who are the main deities in ancient Greece, and what are their particular spheres of influence?
6. Why do no gods appear in the Antigone? Even if there are no gods present on stage during the play, are the gods involved in this play at all? What parts of the play support your ideas? This could be a good theme to trace throughout the Antigone while you read. Are there any areas of modern life that combine various cultural elements (e.g. political, religious, social)? What similarities or differences do you see between your culture and that of the ancient Greeks?
7. If you were an ancient Greek person sitting in the Theater of Dionysus, what other buildings or landmarks could you have seen? What effects, if any, do you think these sights would have had on you?
8. What are the parts of the Greek theater? What words are familiar to us in English? How have ~~https://humanities.wisc.edu/~~ these words changed (or not changed) meaning over time?

Antigone – Chapter Summary

1. What were the expectations of elite Athenian females, especially during the fifth-century B.C.E.? What sorts of things could they do and not do? What important roles did they play for the benefit of the oikos (the household, the family)?
2. What was the role of women in ancient Greek burial rites?
3. What is Antigone's dilemma at the beginning of the play? What are her duties to her family (her oikos), and what are her duties to her city (the polis)?
4. Why does the fact that Creon is Antigone's uncle (and last living male guardian) complicate her dilemma?
5. In what terms does Antigone understand her 'crime'? Why does she say that she will "be a criminal—but a religious one"?
6. In what ways is Antigone like a masculine, Homeric hero at the beginning of the play? How is she a doer of deeds and speaker of words? In what ways does Antigone behave or not behave like a traditional elite female? Why do you think that Sophocles would write about such a transgressive female? In what ways could Antigone have been frightening to an ancient Athenian audience?
7. What other elements of Antigone's character do you see?
8. How does Ismene act as a foil to Antigone? What is Ismene like? What are Ismene's reasons for her behavior?
9. How does Antigone treat Ismene? Why does she act like this?
10. Is it strange, according to Greek cultural practice, that Antigone and Ismene meet outside the gates of the palace? How or why?
11. Read the scene in which Ismene reappears during Antigone's confrontation with Creon, beginning around line 530. Why does Sophocles include her in this scene? Is this the same Ismene we saw at the beginning of the play? How should we understand her behavior (throughout the play) in terms of its cultural context?
12. When does Ismene exit the play? Why is her exit not announced or mentioned? What happens to Ismene, do you think? Why do we never find out? Is the silence concerning Ismene and her fate connected to Pericles' comments about women (see above)?
13. How would you define a hero in your own terms? How would you define a hero in terms of Homeric epic (the Iliad and Odyssey)? Does Antigone fit either of these paradigms? Can Antigone, as a female, be a hero? In what ways is Antigone heroic and not heroic? Be sure to create a definition for a hero before judging her.

https://humanities.wisc.edu/

Antigone – Rule of Law Essay or Socratic

1. *"Law and order exist for the purpose of establishing justice, and ... when they fail to do this purpose, they become dangerously structured dams that block the flow of social progress."* (Martin Luther King, Jr.)
2. *"The end of law is not to abolish or restrain, but to preserve and enlarge freedom...where there is no law, there is no freedom."* (John Locke)
3. *"An individual who breaks a law that conscience tells him is unjust, and who willingly accepts the penalty of imprisonment in order to arouse the conscience of the community over its injustice, is in reality expressing the highest respect for the law. "*(Martin Luther King, Jr)
4. "The law isn't justice. It's a very imperfect mechanism. If you press exactly the right buttons and are also lucky, justice may show up in the answer. A mechanism is all the law was ever intended to be." (Raymond Chandler)
5. *"An unjust law is itself a species of violence. Arrest for its breach is more so."* (Mohandas K. Gandhi
6. The concept of law and order. Explain what you think the quotation means in your own words. Agree or disagree with the quotation, explaining your reasoning and providing examples or evidence to clarify or support your argument.
7. Do human beings have an obligation to be disobedient when laws go against our moral conscience?

ELA –12th– Spelling

What Does The Epic Mean To You?

What is Creon's fatal flaw? How does the flaw affect his state? His ability as a leader? His downfall? What does a play that centers on this particular fatal flaw have to say about the qualities that are needed or not needed in a ruler?

What connection between injustice, tyranny, and civil disobedience can be found in Antigone? To uphold the moral law, Antigone breaks the civil law. Down through the ages and into modern times, citizens have used this theme to guide them in redressing their grievances. Can you think of an example? How does it relate to the ideas on this issue expressed in Antigone?

In what ways is Creon responsible for his own downfall? Does Creon suffer from excessive pride? How would you characterize Creon as a ruler? Is Creon deserving of sympathy?

How are women portrayed in the play? What does the play say about the place of women in society?

What does the play Antigone say about absolute power? What does the play say about obligations to family

Antigone – Chapter Summary

Socratic Seminar: Loyalty and Antigone

1. What is loyalty? How does one prove his or her loyalty?
2. What is more important to have loyalty to, yourself, the laws, or some higher power?
3. To whom do you have loyalty? Why?
4. Would you ever betray your best friend? A relative? Your country? Why or why not?
5. What makes people change loyalties?
6. How does hardship affect people's loyalties? Why?
7. What kinds of hardship might affect people's loyalties? Why?
8. What is betrayal? Who can betray a person? What does betrayal look like and feel like?
9. What makes a person betray another?

Antigone Study Guide

1. What new problem is being faced by Oedipus' family?
2. What take to each of the sisters have on it? What do they cite as reasoning?
3. How does Antigone feel about the consequences for her actions?
4. What is the focus of the Chorus' initial speech?
5. What news is brought by the Sentry? What does his dithering about coming to Creon show? How is he received by Creon?
6. Explain the argument of the Chorus concerning mankind. How does their speech apply to Creon and Antigone?
7. Would it be possible for Creon and Antigone to find common ground based on their arguments? Who do you agree with?
8. What makes Ismene decide to take credit along with her sister? How does Antigone react to her "sacrifice?"
9. What information does Ismene bring to light regarding Creon's ties to Antigone?
10. How does the Chorus regard the Oedipus family? Who holds the power in their final admonitions?
11. How does Haemon answer his father regarding his loyalty? How does Creon attempt to prove that his decree is just?
12. Summarize Haemon's side of his argument with his father.
13. How is identity shown to be a motivation behind Creon's decisions?
14. What drives Haemon from his father? What do you think he has run off to do?
15. What sentence will be imposed on Antigone?
16. How does the Chorus interpret the recent events? What does that say about them and their abilities of interpretation?
17. Explain Antigone's view of her punishment vs. the views of the Chorus.
18. What does Tiresias warn Creon about? Based on what proof? What is Creon's initial reaction?
19. What finally causes Creon to change his mind? Justify.
20. How does each of the characters die? Who takes responsibility?
21. What is the final warning provided by the Chorus?

Literary Analysis

Themes and Characters

"All men make mistakes, but a good man yields when he knows his course is wrong, and repairs the evil. The only crime is pride."
— Sophocles, Antigone—

Which is more important to Sophocles—family or authority? Look at Antigone, Ismene, Creon, and Haimon, and at what happens to them and their relationships.

How should we regard the character Antigone? As prideful and reckless? As heroic? As an innocent victim of yranny? As a martyr? As a masochist? As an idealist? In what significant ways are Creon and Antigone similar?

 ETHOS LOGOS VALUE/VIRTUE OF THE MONTH
Silence and Order

Themes To Explore
> **Tragedy**
> **The State vs. Religion**
> **Rivalry**
> **Natural Rights**
> **Fate and Free Will**
> **Rules and Order**

What makes Antigone a tragedy?
The play Antigone is often thought to be a Greek tragedy because each of the tragic heroes is neither extremely good or bad, their fortunes change from good to bad, their misfortunes do not result from their own wrong doings, and they arouse pity within the audience.

Vocabulary

Novel Words – <u>Antigone</u>

Anarchist
Auspicious
Contempt
Counsel
Decree
Defile
Impassively
Insolence
Lamentation
Marshall
Meddle
Penalty
Perverse
Principle
Reverence
Sate
Sententiously
Swagger
Transgress
Welfare

Latin Root Words

Trib - pay
Dign - worthy
Luc - light
Rupt - break
Grat - pleasing
Medi - middle
Soph - wisdom
Curr - run
Tempor - time
Migr - wander
Trans - across
Gamy - marriage
Numer - number

Grade Level Vocabulary

asylum
benevolent
camaraderie
censure
circuitous
clairvoyant
collaborate
compassion
compromise
Condescending
conditional
Conformist

congregation

GREAT MEN & WOMEN

Sophocles
467 - 406 BC

"If you try to cure evil with evil you will add more pain to your fate."
– Sophocles

★ Sophocles was an ancient Greek playwright and storyteller who shaped culture in ancient Greece. Athens in the fifth century B.C. was a golden age of drama for Greece and the world.

★ Sophocles actively participated in Athenian political and cultural life. It was expected for citizens to serve and, Sophocles served as a diplomat, general, and even a priest. Athenian leader Pericles chose Sophocles to be treasurer of the Delian Confederation.

1,5,9 - 5

ETHOS LOGOS

Sophocles – 496-406 BC

- Greatest of Ancient Greek Playwrights
- Known for his dramatic, poetic, and musical talents
- Was a general, political leader, and priest

Sophocles is admired for his Oedipus Trilogy

- Written over a 40 year period
- Began with the last & third part of the trilogy, *Antigone*
- Twelve years later he wrote the first part of series, *Oedipus the King*
- During the last year of his life, he wrote the middle segment, *Oedipus at Colonus*

HISTORICAL SIGNIFICANCE
SOPHOCLES

Sophocles led the Greek literary scene throughout his life and had won a total of 18 competitions throughout his lifetime. He was the Steven Spielberg and JK Rowling of his time. His most famous plays were 'Antigone', 'Oedipus at Colonus', 'Ajax', 'Electra', 'The Women of Trachis'. His plays often involved themes about the relation between man and the Gods, and featured Heroes of his plays had to overcome various obstacles. He tapped into the Hero's Journey ideas that continue today.

Key Dates and Events

Sophocles was born in a prosperous family in Attica and showed his talent as a playwright from an early age. Sophocles was highly educated. Sophocles studied poetry, music, dancing, and gymnastics. We went on to become the most famous playwright in Athens, producing over 120 plays. He lived to be 90 years old. Homer's great Greek epics The Odyssey and The Iliad profoundly influenced Sophocles' work and we see themes borrowed or influenced by the epic poems.

Sophocles lived through amazing ancient times, including the Greek victory in the Persian Wars and the Peloponnesian War.

Key Virtues That Made Them Great

- Creative
- Intelligent
- Organized
- Leadership
- Loyalty
- Patriotic
- Courageous

Sophocles wrote 120 tragedies only 7 survive today

- His plays always contain a moral lesson
- He was a technical innovator for his time
  - added a third character
  - introduced painted sets
  - expanded the size of the chorus to 15
  - made each play a trilogy separate in nature (each play could stand alone)
- Famous Works Include:
  Oedipus Rex
  Oedipus on Colonus
  Antigone

RECITATION – 12TH GRADE

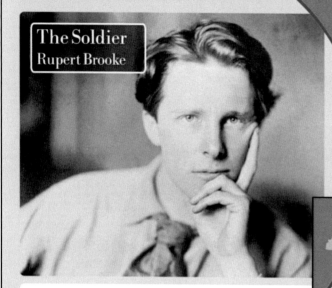

The Soldier
Rupert Brooke

★ **About The Poet**
Rupert Brooke's (1887–1915) was an English poet. Brookes was well traveled an lived and adventurous life before he joined WW1. He saw combat action in the fight for Antwerp in 1914.

★ **About the Poem**
In this poem, Brooks tries to encapsulate the feelings, dangers and emotions of WW1. The poem looks to comfort the survivors but downplay the horrors of w

12-2

ETHOS LOGOS

The Soldier

RUPERT BROOKE

If I should die, think only this of me:
That there's some corner of a foreign field
That is for ever England. There shall be
In that rich earth a richer dust concealed;
A dust whom England bore, shaped, made aware,
Gave, once, her flowers to love, her ways to roam,
A body of England's, breathing English air,
Washed by the rivers, blest by suns of home.
And think, this heart, all evil shed away,
A pulse in the eternal mind, no less
Gives somewhere back the thoughts by England given;
Her sights and sounds; dreams happy as her day;
And laughter, learnt of friends; and gentleness,
In hearts at peace, under an English heaven.

★ **ETHOS LOGOS VALUE/VIRTUE OF THE MONTH** ★
Silence - Order

The values and virtues of the month are
SILENCE and ORDER.

Weave these traits into your novel studies,
other subject areas you are studying and
opportunities to show SILENCE and ORDER in
your daily life.

PRACTICE THESE WAYS TO BRING ORDER TO YOUR LIFE:

- Make your bed neatly every morning.
- Organize your school work and make a list for homework assignments.
- Help clean up after dinner. Do the dishes, put food away, help out.
- Have bedtime and wake up routines. Sleep is important.
- Make to do lists and work through your lists.
- Set your house in perfect order before you criticize the world.
- Take pride in your appearance. Get a haircut, tuck your shirt in.
- Fight procrastination. Make decisions about things when they show up.
- Develop a routine - Consistency is the key to school and life success.

ORDER AROUND YOU CREATES ORDER INSIDE YOU.

Ben Franklin, as a young boy realized that by having
order inhis life, he could pursue new interests and
ideas. He spent his life creating, dreaming, building
business, and starting a new Country. All his dreams
were madepossible by keeping his time, his life, and
his world in order.

READ

- The Bernstein Bears and the Messy Room
- Aunt Minnie McGranahan by Mary Skillings Prigger
- Superheros Don't Clean Their Rooms ... Or Do They?
- A Place For Everything: Habit 3 – Stephen Covey

"... never give in, never, never, never - in nothing, great or small, large or petty - never give in except to convictions of honor and good sense."

Winston Churchill
Oct. 29, 1941

WHEN IT COMES TO GOSSIP, PRACTICE SILENCE

Gossip destroys reputations.
Don't judge people based on gossip.
Gossip makes you look bad.
Gossip actually changes the way we see people.
If you're partaking in gossip, you could be next.
People won't trust YOU if you gossip.
Figure out the problem behind the gossip.
Privately address specific gossipers.
Don't listen to others when they gossip.
Stay away from people who gossip to you, they will gossip about you.

WHAT THE VIRTUE OF SILENCE LOOKS LIKE IN YOUR WORLD

1. Don't talk on your cell phone when you have a captive audience.
2. Never say something to a stranger on the internet that you would not say to a stranger in person.
3. Remember, the internet is forever.
4. Silence may be NOT posting.
5. Don't unload your anger on those who are not at fault for your problem.
6. Don't attack people personally.

10 WAYS TO PRACTICE SILENCE

1. Stop talking – Silence has a purpose in all conversations.
2. Choose your words wisely – Don't rush.
3. Don't react – reflect before you speak.
4. Be mindful - accept silence instead of fighting it.
5. Be outside – Appreciate the silence of nature.
6. Be patient and practice silence.
7. Try to silence the negative thoughts in your mind.
8. Listen more than you speak.
9. Turn off the screens.
10. Breathe deeply.

Historical Pairing

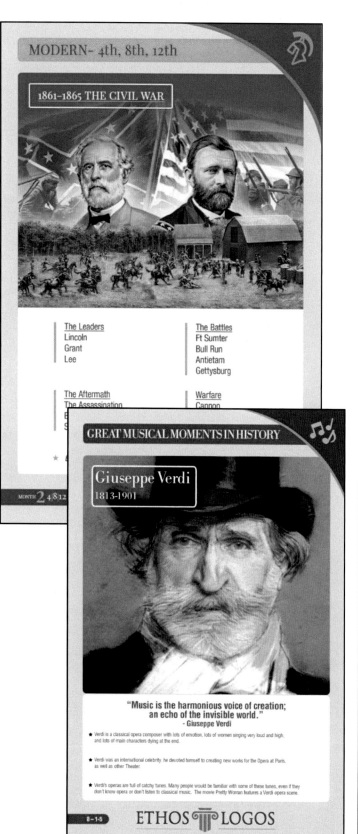

MODERN- 4th, 8th, 12th

1861–1865 THE CIVIL WAR

The Leaders
Lincoln
Grant
Lee

The Battles
Ft Sumter
Bull Run
Antietam
Gettysburg

The Aftermath
The Assassination

Warfare
Cannon

MONTH 2 4|8|12

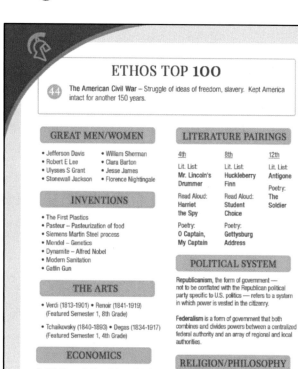

ETHOS TOP 100

44 The American Civil War – Struggle of ideas of freedom, slavery. Kept America intact for another 150 years.

GREAT MEN/WOMEN

- Jefferson Davis
- Robert E Lee
- Ulysses S Grant
- Stonewall Jackson
- William Sherman
- Clara Barton
- Jesse James
- Florence Nightingale

INVENTIONS

- The First Plastics
- Pasteur – Pasteurization of food
- Siemens Martin Steel process
- Mendel – Genetics
- Dynamite – Alfred Nobel
- Modern Sanitation
- Gatlin Gun

THE ARTS

- Verdi (1813-1901) • Renoir (1841-1919) (Featured Semester 1, 8th Grade)
- Tchaikovsky (1840-1893) • Degas (1834-1917) (Featured Semester 1, 4th Grade)

ECONOMICS

By 1860, 90 percent of the nation's manufacturing output came from northern states. The North produced 17 times more cotton and woolen textiles than the South, 30 x more leather goods, 20 x more pig iron, and 32 x more firearms.

LITERATURE PAIRINGS

4th	8th	12th
Lit. List: Mr. Lincoln's Drummer	Lit. List: Huckleberry Finn	Lit. List: Antigone
Read Aloud: Harriet the Spy	Read Aloud: Student Choice	Poetry: The Soldier
Poetry: O Captain, My Captain	Poetry: Gettysburg Address	

POLITICAL SYSTEM

Republicanism, the form of government — not to be conflated with the Republican political party specific to U.S. politics — refers to a system in which power is vested in the citizenry.

Federalism is a form of government that both combines and divides powers between a centralized federal authority and an array of regional and local authorities.

RELIGION/PHILOSOPHY

Churches emphasized that the Union had to be preserved because of the special place that America occupied in world history. With its republican institutions, democratic ideals, and Christian values, the United States supposedly stood in the vanguard

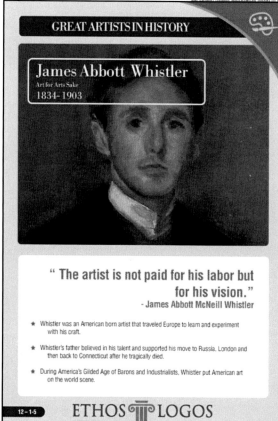

GREAT MUSICAL MOMENTS IN HISTORY

Giuseppe Verdi
1813-1901

"Music is the harmonious voice of creation; an echo of the invisible world."
- Giuseppe Verdi

★ Verdi is a classical opera composer with lots of emotion, lots of women singing very loud and high, and lots of main characters dying at the end.

★ Verdi was an international celebrity, he devoted himself to creating new works for the Opera at Paris, as well as other Theater.

★ Verdi's operas are full of catchy tunes. Many people would be familiar with some of these tunes, even if they don't know opera or don't listen to classical music. The movie Pretty Woman features a Verdi opera scene.

8 – 1-5

ETHOS LOGOS

GREAT ARTISTS IN HISTORY

James Abbott Whistler
Art for Arts Sake
1834- 1903

" The artist is not paid for his labor but for his vision."
- James Abbott McNeill Whistler

★ Whistler was an American born artist that traveled Europe to learn and experiment with his craft.

★ Whistler's father believed in his talent and supported his move to Russia, London and then back to Connecticut after he tragically died.

★ During America's Gilded Age of Barons and Industrialists, Whistler put American art on the world scene.

12 – 1-5

ETHOS LOGOS

Artists and Musicians Pairing

Historical Pairing
Actual Time Period

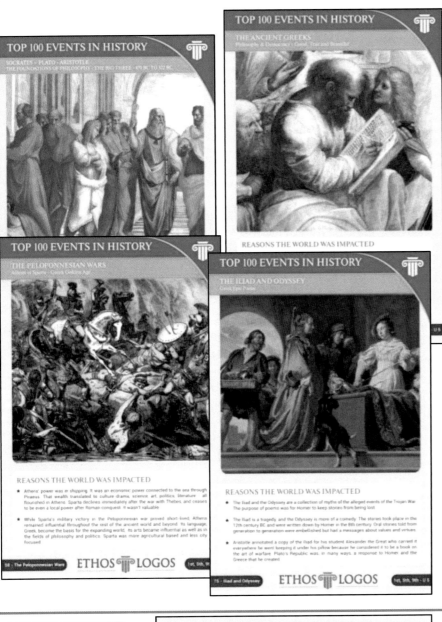

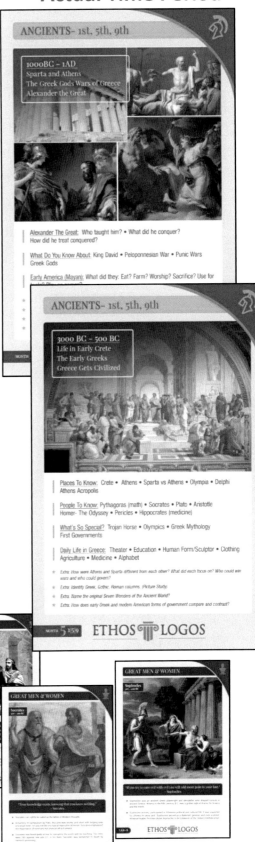

Great Men and Women

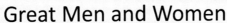

Unit #: 3,4 (Oct. - Nov.)

Novel: The Odyssey

Grade Levels: 12th

History:

1865-1914
Post War MOVEMENT
Transportation, Immigration

1914-1929
EXCESS and ABUNDANCE - 2nd
Industrial Revolution, World War I
The Roaring 20's

Artists - Musician:
Verdi – Whistler

Value/Virtue:
Honor – Citizenship
Truth, Beauty and Goodness

Governance:
Monarchy
Republic/Democracy

Religion:
Christianity

Cultural Saying Unit 3
- Out of the blue,
- When pigs fly
- He who lives by the sword, dies by the sword

Cultural Saying Unit 4
- Pass with flying colors
- Wolf in sheep's clothing
- Head on a Platter

The Odyssey– The Epic

Conventions of an Epic

A hero
Objective (honest) narrator
The Story is serious
Story begins in the middle (Latin: *in media res*) of the story, then goes back in time to explain *exposition*
Long and complicated journey
Vast setting
Land of the dead
Real people and places,
Fictional (make-believe) people and places
A gallery (list) of other heroes
Divine intervention
Prophecy
Fate or destiny
Grand, dramatic speeches
Universal theme about life the Epic Question

Remember that in Greek culture, poetry is considered an aspect of education.

Here are six of the major themes or lessons that the ancient Greeks wanted to teach their children through poetry like the *Odyssey*.

- Respect for the gods and goddesses
- The importance of home and family
- Acts of courage, strength, and leadership
- Concern for the welfare of others
- Displays of intelligence, curiosity, and cleverness
- Obedience to leaders

An **epic** is a long narrative poem that recounts the adventures of an **epic hero**, a larger-than-life figure who undertakes a great journey and performs deeds requiring remarkable strength and cunning

Epic Hero

Possesses superhuman strength, craftiness, and confidence
Is helped and harmed by interfering gods
Embodies ideas and values that a culture considers admirable
Emerges victorious from perilous situation

Epic Plot

Involves a long journey, full of complications, such as strange creatures, divine intervention, large-scale events, treacherous weather.

Epic Setting

Includes fantastic or exotic lands
Involves more than one nation

An epic poem is narrated in predictable ways:
- In an invocation, the poet narrator starts the poem by stating the tale's subject and asking for a poetic inspiration from a guiding spirit.
- The narrator begins telling the tale in the "in the middle of things" ("in medias res") describing what is happening after certain important events that have already occurred.
- The narrative includes speeches by principal characters - including gods and antagonists of the epic hero - which reveal their personalities.
- The narrative's tone and style are formal rather than conversational.
- The use of figurative language makes the narrative vivid and exciting for listeners and readers.

The Odyssey– Chapter Questions

Book I – A Goddess Intervenes (pgs. 1-15)

1. What did Poseidon have against Odysseus?
2. Who tried to help Odysseus get home?
3. Why did the goddess Athena want Zeus to send Hêrmes to Kalypso?
4. What problems did Odysseus' absence cause for his wife and son?
5. Who does Athena disguise herself as in order to help Telémakhos?
6. Why do you suppose Telémakhos hasn't tried to stand up to the suitors so far?
7. Why did Telémakhos go on a voyage?

Book II – A Hero's Son Awakens (pgs. 19-31)

1. Who is Antinoös?
2. According to Antinoös, why was Penélopê to blame for the messy situation in Odysseus' house?
3. What omen does Zeus send?
4. Who was Halithersês and what prediction did he make?
5. Athena, disguised as Mentor, told the suitors, "I am not incensed by all the suitor's plots and violence…Instead my wrath indicts the rest of you, who sit in silence." What does she mean?
6. Does Telémakhos recognize Athena when she's disguised as Mentor?
7. Why didn't Eurýkleia want Telémakhos to leave?
8. What order does Telemakhos give to Eurykleia?
9. What kind of government did the Greek city-state have? How has Homer used that pattern for Ithaka? What questions come to mind as you think of the fact that since Odysseus has been away, no council has been called?
10. Describe Telémakhos' handling of the meeting. What impression do you get of him as a leader?
11. What clever scheme has Penélopê used to delay her marriage?
12. What two people in addition to the goddess Athena have been the major influences in Telémakhos' upbringing? Of what sex are they? Is Homer depicting Telemakhos as immature?
13. Why does Athena see that Telémakhos must go on a journey to find his father? What does she know the journey will accomplish for him personally?

Book III – The Lord of the Western Approaches (pgs. 35-49)

1. Look up the word *mentor*. From what language did it come? What does it mean?
2. What influence might Homer's use of Mentor as a character have had on its present meaning?
3. What steps toward maturity does Telémakhos take in this book?
4. What is the story of Agamémnon? What relationship does it have to Telémakhos' situation?
5. What do we learn about Penélopê by hearing the contrasting story of Klytaimnésta?
6. Who is Nestor? What news of Odysseus does he have?
7. Which of Nestor's sons travels with Telémakhos?

The Odyssey– Chapter Questions

Book IV - The Red-haired King and his Lady (pgs. 53-78)

1. How did Meneláos (Menelaus) treat the two strangers? Why do you think Telémakhos didn't identify himself in the beginning?
2. What did Meneláos tell Telémakhos about the wooden horse?
3. Why didn't Meneláos go right home after the Trojan War?
4. What did Meneláos reveal about Odysseus' whereabouts?
5. What is Helen's story? How does the Helen in this book differ from what she was as a younger person?
6. What does Telémakhos learn about his father's friendship with Meneláos? How are the experiences of the two alike?
7. What encouragement could Meneláos' story give to Telémakhos?
8. Why is this visit valuable in helping Telémakhos mature?
9. Of what importance to Telémakhos is Meneláos telling the story of his encounter with the Old Man of the Sea?
10. What do the suitors plan to do to Telémakhos upon his return to Ithaka?
11. Back in Ithaka, why did Iphthimê appear to Penélopê?
12. How did Iphthimê try to reassure her?
13. What did Penélopê want to hear?

Book V – Sweet Nymph and Open Sea (pgs. 81-95)

1. At the meeting of the gods, how does Athena's view of Odysseus' situation differ from Zeus'? What action does Zeus take?
2. Describe Kalypso's (Calypso's) home.
3. From this passage, what did Greeks value in women and home life?
4. What is Hermês compared to at the beginning of this book?
5. How did Kalypso help Odysseus leave the island – and why?
6. Why did Kalypso help Odysseus? Did she have a choice?
7. Was Odysseus at all unhappy to say good-bye to Kalypso?
8. What is Styx? How do the gods use its name?
9. Why did Poseidon stir up a storm?
10. How did the nymph, Ino, and Athena help Odysseus survive?

Book VI – The Princess at the River (pgs. 99-108)

1. What unusual provision does Athena make for Odysseus to get clothes and shelter?
2. Why are the girls frightened when the see Odysseus?
3. Which goddess does Homer compare Nausikaa with? Why?
4. Why is Nausikaa's reaction different from that of the other girls?
5. What invitation does she give Odysseus?
6. What future event does she consider?
7. How does Odysseus enter the city? Why?
8. Why does Athena not make a face-to-face appearance in answer to Odysseus' prayer?

The Odyssey– Chapter Questions

Book VII – Gardens and Firelight (pgs. 111-121)

Skip this Book
Summary: At the palace of King Alkínoös and Queen Arêtê, Odysseus begs that the Phaiákians conduct him safely home across the sea to Ithaca, which they agree to do – after, of course, the ritual sacrifices and feasting (competitions).

Book VIII – The Songs of the Harper (pgs. 139-142)

Skip to page 139, line 501
Summary: Odysseus is entertained with feasting, athletic games, and song and dances, and is given elaborate parting guest-gifts.

1. Why does Odysseus cry when he hears the story of the Trojan horse?
2. What does the king do about his reaction?
3. What is foreshadowed by King Alkínoös' telling what his father predicted?
4. How have Books V-VIII formed a bridge from Telémakhos' story to the stories that Odysseus is about to tell?

Book IX – New Coasts and Poseidon's Son (pgs. 145-162)

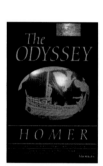

1. Who is the narrator for most of book IX? Why?
2. What is Odysseus' first stop after Troy?
3. Why does he go there?
4. How do Odysseus' men become vulnerable in the land of the Lotos-Eaters?
5. Was Odysseus justified in his actions on the land of the Lotos-Eaters?
6. Why did Odysseus and his men enter the Kyklops' (Cyclops') cave?
7. How did Odysseus lose six men in the land of the Kyklopês?
8. How did Odysseus survive? List important details.
9. How does Odysseus show his cunning in the passage with the Kyklops, Polyphêmos?
10. Odysseus reveals his name and land as he escapes, why is this a foolish move?
11. Is Odysseus' behavior heroic here? What does this show you about him?
12. Do you feel sorry for Polyphêmos? Was Odysseus unfair to him?
13. What action at the end of this book could be considered foreshadowing? What do you know will happen to Odysseus?

The Odyssey– Chapter Questions

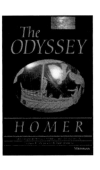

Book X – The Grace of the Witch (pgs. 165-182)

1. Who is Aiolos (Aeolus)?
2. What gift – and instructions – did Aiolos give Odysseus?
3. How did Odysseus and his men end up back in Aiolia soon after leaving it?
4. Why wasn't the king as hospitable toward them on their return as he had been originally?
5. Describe the Laistrygonians' odd appearance and behavior.
6. How did Odysseus lose several men in the Laestrygonians' land?
7. Describe Kirkê's (Circe's) house and the guards in front of it.
8. Why are the men not afraid? What happens when they go in?
9. Who reports the incident to Odysseus and the others?
10. Who protects Odysseus from Kirkê's witchery? How?
11. Before Odysseus will eat with or make love to Kirkê, what does he make her do?
12. Who opposes Odysseus when he tells the men to pull the ship up on land and go to eat at Kirkê's house? Why?
13. How long did Odysseus and his men stay on Kirkê's island?
14. Do you think Odysseus had any affection for her?
15. Did Odysseus make a good decision by compromising his morals/values to save his men from Kirkê?
16. Kirkê decides to let Odysseus leave her island, but tells where he must go next on his journey. Where must he go and what must he do there?
17. Why do you think Homer includes Elpênor in the story? Do you feel sorry for him? How is drinking portrayed in this epic poem?
18. What gift does Kirkê leave for them near the ship?

Book XI – A Gathering of Shades (pgs. 185-206)

1. Where is Ocean Stream? What one quality stands out about it?
2. What does Odysseus do first when he lands? What response does he get?
3. Who is the first person he recognizes? What is his request?
4. Why does Teirêsias drink the blood?
5. What predictions does he make?
6. How will Odysseus die?
7. Why does Odysseus' mother, Antikleía, not look at him the first time he sees her?
8. What four things does he learn from her?
9. What happens when he tries to hug his mother, Antikleía? Why?
10. What experience do the women whom Perséphonê sends have in common?
11. Who is Jocasta (spelled "Epikastê" on pg. 193)? What is the story about her and her son?
12. When Odysseus feels his story has been long enough, about whom does Alkínoös' want to hear?
13. What tragic reception did Agamémnon get when he returned from Troy?
14. What does Akhilleus (Achilles) say about death?
15. Next Odysseus visits those who are tormented in the afterlife. Describe the punishment of the following:
    1. Títyos (pg. 204)-
    2. Tántalos (pg. 204)-
        1. What word that we use today came from his name?
    3. Sísyphos (pg. 204)-
16. What was Heraklês' (Hercules') crime? What was his punishment?
17. Now that he has accomplished peace, why does Heraklês pity Odysseus?
18. Why do Odysseus and his men leave so quickly afterward?
19. Who is Perséphonê? What's her story?
20. Why must she stay in Hades (underworld) six months of every year?
21. What happens on earth while Perséphonê is in the underworld with Hades?

The Odyssey– Chapter Questions

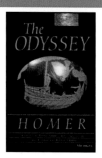

Book XII – Sea Perils and Defeat (pgs. 209-225)

1. What is Odysseus' first act after leaving Hades and returning to Kirkê's island?
2. What two great dangers does Kirkê warn the men about? What advice does she give about meeting them?
3. Describe Skylla (Scylla) and Kharybdis (Charybdis).
4. Which of those two monsters does Kirkê recommend that they sail near? Why?
5. What is her warning about Hêlios' cattle? What will be the consequences to Odysseus? To his men?
6. When Odysseus tells the experience with Skylla and Kharybdis, what does he say was the most pitiful sight?
7. What disagreement do Eurýlokhos and Odysseus have as night approaches?
8. Why do the not stay for just one night as they had planned?
9. What agreement between two gods does Kalypso explain to Odysseus?
10. What impression does this give you of the Greek gods?
11. What danger that he once experienced with his men does Odysseus now face all alone? What are the consequences?
12. In paragraph form, describe how Homer has used the flashback technique and has adapted tales extant at the time to create a poem about an epic hero. What features of theses stories contribute to their continuing popularity?

Book XIII – One More Strange Island (pgs. 229-244)

1. Give an example of *metaphor* that you find in the first two pages of this book.
2. Give an example of *simile* from the first two pages of this book.
3. What is the physical setting for this book? What are Odysseus' plans?
4. How does the parting ceremony show their religious beliefs?
5. How does Homer manage to get Odysseus to Ithaca without his knowing where he is?
6. When Poseidon expresses his anger over not smashing the ship when it first started out, what does Zeus suggest that he do? How does Alkínoös interpret that action?
7. Why do the people prepare a sacrifice to the gods?
8. Why has Athena prepared a mist to cover the beach?
9. How does Athena disguise herself? What does she tell Odysseus? What story does he tell her?
10. How does Athena compliment Odysseus? What does she help him do?
11. Why is it important that Athena has prepared Odysseus for his homecoming by telling him of the situation in Ithaca?
12. What disguise does Athena say she will give to Odysseus? Where does she tell him to go? Why?
13. What motive did Athena have for sending Telémakhos away? What danger to him does she reveal?
14. What specific changes come to Odysseus when Athena passes her wand over him?

The Odyssey– Chapter Questions

Book XIV – Hospitality in the Forest (pgs. 247-264)

Skip this book. *Odysseus goes to the home of his faithful swineherd Eumaios, who does not recognize his master as "the old beggar" tells an elaborate and false tale about his background.*

Book XV – How they Came to Ithaca (pgs. 267-286)

1. How does Athena get Telémakhos to head for home?
2. What do his host, and hostess, insist he must have before he leaves?
3. What good omen appears when they make the parting sacrifice?
4. How does Helen interpret the omen?
5. Why does Telémakhos hurry to leave Meneláos' home?
6. Who asks to go with Telémakhos? Why?
7. What reason does Odysseus give for needing to meet Penélopê?
8. Why does Eumaios feel that Odysseus should wait to see her?
9. What does he hear will happen to the "beggar" if he goes as he is?
10. What do we learn about Eumaios from his story?
11. Because Athena wants Telémakhos to be the only one to meet his father, how does she dispose of the prophet?
12. What good omen accompanies the landing? What is the interpretation?
13. What has Homer accomplished in this book?

Book XVI – Father and Son (pgs. 289-305)
1. How does Odysseus quickly learn that the young man is a special person?
2. How does Telémakhos show that he is a thoughtful, polite man?
3. What interesting answer does Telémakhos give when Odysseus asks him why his brothers don't help him with the suitors?
4. How does Homer get Eumaios out of the way so that father and son can get acquainted?
5. What feature of the gods does Athena reveal when she gets Odysseus' attention?
6. What does Athena tell Odysseus to do?
7. How does Odysseus look after talking to Athena?
8. What is Telémakhos' reaction to the transformation in his father?
9. How many men does Telémakhos figure have been added to the household with the coming of the suitors and their servants?
10. Why do Telémakhos and Odysseus decide not to ask anyone to help them in fighting the suitors?
11. What plans do Odysseus and Telémakhos make for going home? What will be done with the weapons in Odysseus' home?
12. When Odysseus wants to find out which farmhands and servant women are loyal to him, what advice does Telémakhos give?
13. What happens just as Eumaius reaches Odysseus' home? What does he have to add to the news Penélopê receives?
14. How do the suitors feel about the news? For what two reasons must they dispose of Telémakhos?
15. What good advice does Amphínomos of Doulíkhion give? (pg. 302)
16. How did Penélopê find out about the plot against her son? What does she say to Antínoös? What does he owe Odysseus?
17. How does Antínoös respond? What does Eurýmachos say? What do his words reveal about him?
18. What does Athena do just before Eumaios' return? What news does he bring?
19. What do Telémakhos and his father exchange when Eumaios isn't looking? What does this tell you about them? How might this small detail be important to the story?

The Odyssey– Chapter Questions

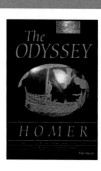

Book XVII – The Beggar at the Manor (pgs. 309-331)

1. How does Telémakhos provide for his father's being able to get to town?
2. Who first sees Telémakhos in town? What is her reaction?
3. How does his mother respond to his return?
4. How has Telémakhos changed since he left home in Book II?
5. Who has been instrumental in making this change?
6. Why does Telémakhos want Peiriaos (pg. 311) to keep the gifts Meneláos has given him?
7. Who is the guest Telémakhos has brought with him? What does he predict? What omen has he seen?
8. How are the suitors acting upon Telémakhos' return?
9. Contrast Eumaios' desire to go to town with Odysseus'.
10. What kind of person in Melánthios, (pg. 316) the goatherd? Give evidence.
11. Who is Argos? (pg. 319) What touching encounter does Odysseus have with him?
12. What is ironic about Odysseus' entrance into his own home?
13. What food does Telémakhos give to his father?
14. What does Athena prompt him to do? What does he learn about the suitors?
15. What does Odysseus predict will happen to Antínoös?
16. How does Telémakhos react? Of what is he thinking?
17. Why does Penélopê send for Eumaios? What does she learn from him? What does she request that she be able to do?
18. What is Penélopê's prediction? How does Telémakhos react? How does she interpret his action?
19. How does Telémakhos show his concern for the swineherd?
20. What has this book accomplished in preparing for the revenge of Odysseus and Telémakhos against the suitors?

Book XVIII – Blows and a Queen's Beauty (pgs. 335-350)
Skip this book. *The suitors and even some of the serving maids continue to abuse Odysseus the beggar and the hospitality of the house.*

Book XIX – Recognitions and a Dream (pgs. 353-372)
1. What task faces Odysseus and Telémakhos?
2. How does Telémakhos get Odysseus' help in storing the weapons without raising the nurse's suspicions?
3. How is the use of *light* continued from Book XVIII into this one?
4. When Melnátho abuses Odysseus again, of what does he warn her? How does Penélopê react? (pg. 355)
5. In Penélopê's conversation with Odysseus, what three things does she reveal that she has used to delay her remarriage?
6. In telling his fictitious background, Odysseus says his name is Aithôn, meaning, "blazes," again referring to light and to consuming fire. What is the background he makes up? (pg. 359)
7. How does he convince Penélopê that he has really seen her husband?
8. What prediction does Odysseus, as Aithôn, make?
9. What does Penélopê believe about hospitality?
10. Why does Odysseus get Eurýkleia to bathe him? What causes her to recognize him? (pg. 365)
11. What does *Odysseus* mean? Why is that name appropriate? (pg. 366)
12. Why doesn't Penélopê react when Eurýkleia drops Odysseus' foot into the basin and splashes the water?
13. What is the nightingale's story?
14. What is Penélopê's dream? How does Odysseus interpret it?
15. Why can't Penélopê accept that interpretation?
16. How has Penélopê decided to pick her next husband?

Book XX – Signs and a Vision (pgs. 375-387)
Skip this book. *The suitors continue to behave outrageously, Odysseus continues to brood on his revenge, and even more omens of what is to come are revealed.*

The Odyssey– Chapter Questions

Book XXI – The Test of the Bow (pgs. 391-405

1. From whom and for what reason did Odysseus receive the bow?
2. Whom does Penélopê get to help her in running the contest? How do Eumaios and Philoitios react when they see the bow?
3. How does Antínoös respond to their reaction? What compliment dos he pay Odysseus? Of what is he sure?
4. How does Telémakhos express his excitement over the contest?
5. Who are the ringleaders? How do they act toward the others? What are their individual actions when they get their turns?
6. To whom does Odysseus reveal himself? Why?
7. After the meal, what request does Odysseus make? What is the general reaction? What specifically does Antínoös say?
8. Who intervenes to allow the beggar to try? Why should the men have no worries about his participating?
9. What is Penélopê's perfect retort to Antínoös' worries about his pride and being shown up by the beggar?
10. Who takes over? Why?
11. What request does he make of Penélopê? Why?
12. What actions do Eumaios and Philoitios take? Why?
13. How does Homer build suspense as the audience waits for Odysseus to string the bow and shoot the arrow?
14. What transpires between father and son at the end of the book? What action does Telémakhos take?

Book XXII – Death in the Great Hall
1. What two things does Odysseus do to start this book?
2. How do the men know they are facing Odysseus? What ishis justification for acting?
3. What does Eurýmakhos do to try to save himself? What other plot does he reveal? What does he promise to Odysseus?
4. Look through book XXII and jot down details that make the fight scene vivid.
5. How does Melanthius help the suitors? Who stops him?
6. How does Athena spur Odysseus on? How does she prove that Odysseus and Telémakhos can fend for themselves?
7. What are the injuries incurred by two of the avengers?
8. When Athena holds her man-shattering aegis-cape over the suitors, how do the react?
9. Many think Homer patterned the minstrel after himself. What reason does the minstrel give to keep himself alive?
10. What causes Odysseus to smile for the first time? Who are Phenius and Medon? What does Odysseus do for them?
11. Cite two similes that Homer uses to describe the aftermath of the battle with the suitors.
12. What must the disloyal women servants do? What simile describes their fate?
13. What modern examples from movie, TV, or literature parallel the maiming and killing of Melanthius?
14. Since Odysseus does not take killing lightly, what does he do to purify the house?
15. What conclusions might one draw about justice in Homer's day? What action can the prince take? What part do the citizens apparently play?

Book XXIII – The Trunk of the Olive Tree
Cite details that show Eurýcleia's eagerness to tell her mistress the news.
1. How does Penélopê react to the news? Why? How does she show that she half believes what she hears?
2. What causes Odysseus to smile for the second time?
3. Of what danger to himself does Odysseus reveal that he is aware? What does this reveal about the law in Homer's day?
4. What deceptions will everyone create to keep the townspeople unaware of what has happened?
5. What details describe Athena's transformation of Odysseus?
6. With what secret dos Penélopê try Odysseus before she will accept him as her husband?
7. What favor does Athena grant to Odysseus and Penélopê? Why?
8. What action does she take to bring morning? How does she help Odysseus and Telémakhos to escape?
9. What repetition does Homer use to refresh the minds of the listeners?
10. What example do you see of the double standard of morality between men and women apparently accepted in Homer's day?
11. What two serious events keep the story from being wrapped up immediately?

The Odyssey– Chapter Questions

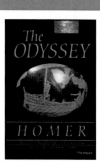

Book XXIV – Warriors, Farewell

1. What is the setting for the beginning of this book?
2. What amazes the dead men?
3. What is Agamemnon's reaction to Odysseus' execution of the suitors? To Penélopê's waiting for her husband? How does he contrast his experience to that of Odysseus?
4. What interesting detail about the funerals of prominent men is mentioned incidentally here?
5. What actions of Odysseus and Penélopê are repeated in this book?
6. To create the picture of Odysseus' father, Homer is said to have recalled the appearance of an old fanner he once saw. List three details that make the picture vivid.
7. What physical characteristic already noticed about Odysseus now identifies him for his father? How does Athena change the older man after his bath?
8. What is happening back at Odysseus' home? Of what does Medon warn them? Of what does Halitherses Mastorides remind them? What is the townspeople's reaction?
9. What happens among the gods regarding the events in Ithaca?
10. What must Odysseus and Telémakhos do next? Who stops it?
11. Who finally brings peace to Ithaca? How?
12. How has Homer tied together the loose ends to bring a happy ending?

The Odyssey– Essay or Socratic Discussion

1. Sooner or later, why must we all leave home?
2. When does a story about Odysseus morph into our story?
3. Almost 5,000 years later, what can the journey of Odysseus teach us?
4. To what extent, if at all, can our greatest strengths also be our greatest weaknesses?
5. What does Odysseus begin to learn about the consequences of his own behavior?
6. What type of knowledge does Odysseus need to acquire to become an effective husband, father, and king?
7. To what extent, if at all, is this entire journey symbolic?
8. To what extent, if at all, does Odysseus evolve as a character?
9. What does this story demonstrate about the effects of war?

In an attempt to persuade Odysseus to stay with her forever, Calypso offers Odysseus immortality in lines 223 to 236 on pages 158-159. He declines the offer, however. Please write a journal entry with the following three paragraphs:

1. What are the advantages and disadvantages of immortality?
2. What would you do if you were offered immortality?

3. How does the wily Odysseus decline the offer in a persuasive way?

Watch *O Brother, Where Art Thou?* -- a very loose version of *The Odyssey* set in the American South during the Great Depression -- and write a short essay that compares and contrasts the plot events, scenes, and characters from the original epic to the modern movie.
George Clooney stars as Ulysses Everett McGill (Odysseus).

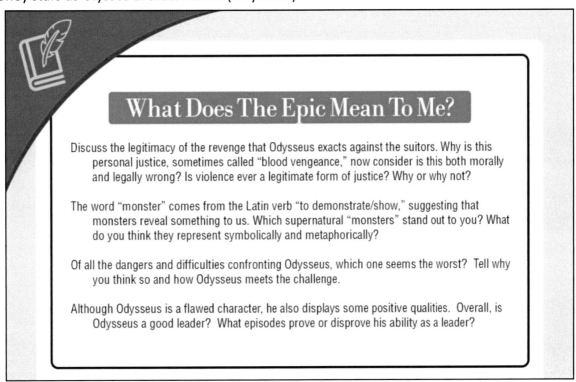

What Does The Epic Mean To Me?

Discuss the legitimacy of the revenge that Odysseus exacts against the suitors. Why is this personal justice, sometimes called "blood vengeance," now consider is this both morally and legally wrong? Is violence ever a legitimate form of justice? Why or why not?

The word "monster" comes from the Latin verb "to demonstrate/show," suggesting that monsters reveal something to us. Which supernatural "monsters" stand out to you? What do you think they represent symbolically and metaphorically?

Of all the dangers and difficulties confronting Odysseus, which one seems the worst? Tell why you think so and how Odysseus meets the challenge.

Although Odysseus is a flawed character, he also displays some positive qualities. Overall, is Odysseus a good leader? What episodes prove or disprove his ability as a leader?

The Odyssey– Projects

1. Create a map of the places Odysseus goes. Include what he encounters, who dies, the length he is there, and how he manages to leave. Use events from our story for some credit. Use events from the full version of the story (which we don't have, and you would need to find online) for huge credit.

2. Create an illustrated and detailed map depicting your odyssey. This can be done on a standard-sized piece of poster board, or you may create some other 3-dimensional map of some kind.
   Your "map" should include the following:
   1. The obstacles you have written about in your essay. You may include others that were not written about. You may use monsters to symbolize your obstacles or other graphics, objects, etc.
   2. A legend that specifies symbols, mileage, etc.
   3. This map should not have any negative or blank space and be very detailed and creative. Feel free to draw, use computer graphics, or magazine cut-outs. It should be neat and professionally presentable.

3. Write an essay on some of the ways Odyssey has influenced cultures for 2,800 years.
4. Index Card Recommendations: After finishing a book, students write a mini-book recommendation detailing story elements, their favorite character/part, and who they think would benefit most from reading the book
5. Book Talks: Similar to index card recommendations, but done orally in front of the class
6. Book Soundtracks: Students create a soundtrack for their book, typically matching one song of their choosing to each chapter, including a sentence explaining their choice
7. Cover Remix: Students re-design the book's cover based on their own interpretation/feelings about the book
8. Cast the Movie: Students assign people they know (famous or not) to play the roles of main characters from their book.
9. Character Convos: Students choose a character from the book they'd like to talk with, and script a phone/text/in-person conversation with that character.
10. Of all the dangers and difficulties confronting Odysseus, which one seems the worst? Tell why you think so and how Odysseus meets the challenge.
11. Although Odysseus is a flawed character, he also displays some positive qualities. Overall, is Odysseus a good leader? What episodes prove or disprove his ability as a leader?
12. A hero is defined as any character admired for his/her courage, nobility, and bold deeds, and thought of as an ideal or model being. According to this definition, is Odysseus a hero?

The Odyssey– The Hero's Journey

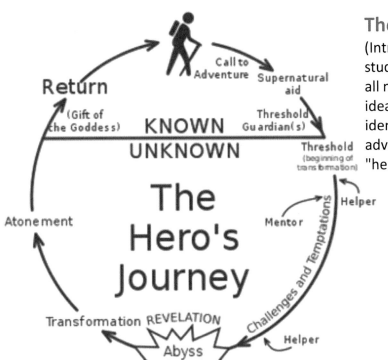

The Heroic Journey:

(Intrigued by mythology, author Joseph Campbell studied the myth and made the) claim that nearly all myths, and some other story types, have similar ideas and the heroes' adventures are almost identical in their format. The different stages of adventure identified have come to be called the "hero's journey."

Hero's Journey's Examples

The Wonderful Wizard of Oz
The Hobbit
Star Wars
The Lion King
The Hobbit
The Matrix

Archetypes Appearing In The Hero's Journey

Joseph Campbell was heavily influenced by the Psychiatrist Carl Jung whose theory of the collective unconscious involved archetypes—recurring images, patterns, and ideas from dreams and myths across various cultures.

Below are several archetypes often found in myths.

HEROES
SHADOWS -Villains, enemies, or the enemy within.
MENTORS
HERALD: The bringer Call to Adventure.
THRESHOLD GUARDIANS: gatekeepers
SHAPESHIFTERS
TRICKSTERS: mischief-makers.
ALLIES .
WOMAN AS TEMPTRESS

The Odyssey– Chapter Questions

The Odyssey

- One of the two major epics from the culture of ancient Greece
- 8th century BC (between 800 BC to 701 BC)
- We're not sure who really composed it. Tradition says that it was composed by the poet Homer.
- Notice how I'm saying "composed," not "wrote." That's because the 8th century BC in Greece, even though they had written language, was still more of an oral culture – stories were passed down by memorization, not by being written down.
- The *Odyssey* was written down in the 6th century, around the year 529 or so.

Other Famous Epics

Iliad and *Odyssey*	Greece
Gilgamesh	Samaria
Aeneid	Rome
Song of Roland	France
Divine Comedy	Italy
Mahabharata, Ramayana	India
Sundiata	Mali

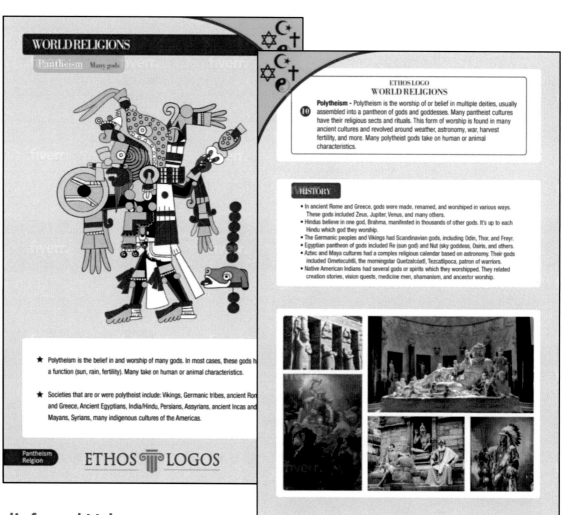

Greek Beliefs and Values

The Greeks believed completely in the existence of <u>gods and goddesses</u>; *polytheism*

 Believed that gods took an <u>active interest in human life</u>

 Gods behaved in <u>human</u> ways (possessed human characteristics

 <u>Respect</u> for the gods was essential for success and survival

Greek culture also known for <u>hero-worship</u>

 Hero might be the town's founder or a historical figure who played a major role in an important battle

Greeks also believed in <u>monsters</u> and mythical creatures

Literary Analysis

Themes and Characters

Aside from being courageous, intelligent, and determined, what qualities and traits make Odysseus an admirable hero? How does this make him a hero? One of the fundamental components of the Hero's Journey is personal transformation. How has Odysseus's character evolved by the end of his journey? Who and/or what affects his growth the most? How?

Why do you think The Odyssey still resonates with us today? Is Odysseus and his hero's journey worthy of our modern esteem and consideration?

In general, does Odysseus control his own destiny, or is his fate determined by the gods?

Explore the themes as you read the story: Reality versus Disguise - Hospitality – Revenge –Determination – Loyalty - Salvation

"A man who has been through bitter experiences and travelled far enjoys even his sufferings after a time".

Homer

Themes To Explore
- **Loyalty/Perseverance**
- **Revenge and Justice**
- **Fate, the Gods, and Free Will**
- **Wisdom over Might**
- **Perils of Temptation**
- **The Long Journey HOME**

 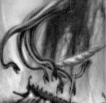  

⭐ **ETHOS LOGOS VALUE/VIRTUE OF THE MONTH** ⭐
Resolution or Perseverance (Grit) and Humility -Cleanliness

The Hero Theme
1. What makes a hero?
2. Are epic heroes brave, smart, or lucky?
3. How have heroes been portrayed throughout history?
4. What are the elements of an epic poem?
5. *What makes Odysseus a hero? What is his "fatal flaw"?*

Greek Values That Were Idealized
- Intelligence
- Glory: equivalent to FAME
    - War stories
    - Souls that achieved glory during life were given privileges in Hades
- Hospitality: Helping others
    - Offered food, shelter, protection to travelers without question
    - Hospitable even when they didn't want to be
    - Brotherly duty or fear of the gods?
- Loyalty: family, community, & gods
- Bravery

What elements of mythology are reflected in the epic?
What is epic poetry?
What is an epic hero?

About The Author

GREAT MEN & WOMEN

Homer
800 – 701 BC

"Hateful to me as the gates of Hades is that man who hides one thing in his heart and speaks another."

1,5,9 -5,6

ETHOS ⫪ LOGOS

Historical Significance of Homer

Homer was an ancient Greek poet who wrote Iliad and Odyssey. Homer is credited as the first and the greatest epic poet and the author of Europe's first known literature.

Homer's two epic poems have become archetypal road maps in world mythology and history. The stories provide an important insight into early human society and illustrate how little has changed.

KEY DATES AND EVENTS

Herodotus, the ancient historian, who lived from 484 BC to 425 BC, placed Homer's year of birth four centuries before his own, making it around 850 BC.

He was the son of Telemachus and Epikaste, and is a professional storyteller and court singer. From Homer's works, we can determine that he must have come from an aristocratic family.

Homer lived in Iona near present day Turkey. It is also believed that Homer was blind. Homer's epic poems Iliad and Odyssey were written during the era of the Trojan War, and his art heavily influenced Greek culture.

Homer was a wandering minstrel, traveling from place to place, singing the stories of 'The Iliad' and 'The Odyssey.' It is said that, in the course of his travelling.

THE ILIAD AND THE ODYSSEY

The Iliad is the story of the siege of Troy. The poem/epic features the Trojan War, Trojan horse, and Paris' kidnapping of Helen, the world's most beautiful woman.

The Odyssey picks up after the fall of Troy. The hero Odysseus is alive and trapped on Calypso's island after years of war. Suitors move into his house to court his wife, who they think is a widow. Antinous and the other suitors prepare an ambush to kill Odysseus when he reaches port. On Mount Olympus, Zeus sends Hermes to rescue Odysseus from Calypso and Poseidon intervenes.

KEY VIRTUES THAT MADE HIS STORIES GREAT

Courage
Honor
Duty
Love and Loyalty
Adventure
Honesty
Justice

★ ETHOS LOGOS VALUE/VIRTUE OF THE MONTH ★

1. Who was Homer?
2. How is the era (Ancient Greece) reflected in the work?
3. How does Homer hook and hold his audience?

Who Was Homer

Both The Iliad and The Odyssey were allegedly written by <u>Homer</u>

- He was Blind
- No official information has been found regarding his birthdate or birthplace.
- Homer did not compose each epic all at once: he told them in a series of short episodes that could be recited in an evening.
- Editors, not Homer himself, organized the epics in 24 books.

The Odyssey - Novel Vocabulary

Muse
Grotto
Malevolent
Morose
Incensed
Versatile
Unstinting
Obstruct
Marauding
Clamor
Citadel
Usurped
Embellish
Astute
Adept
Audacious

Unscathed
Impudence
Quest
Burnished
Vantage
Denounced
Replete
Tribulations
Portents
Vortex
Thwarts
Amok
Shrouded
Scour
Supplication
Libation
Contrived
Contentious

Grade Level Vocabulary

convergence
deleterious
demagogue
digression
diligent
discredit
disdain
divergent
empathy
emulate
enervating
enhance

sagacity
scrutinize
spontaneity
spurious
submissive
substantiate
subtle
superficial
superfluous
suppress
surreptitious
tactful

The Odyssey - Novel Vocabulary

dwindle
tumult
peril
cower
impudence
mortified
rebuke
guise
renowned
commandeer
justification
omen
contemptible
wily
embossed
revelry
jostle
implacable
deflect
revulsion
lavish
aloof
tremulous

plunder
valor
formidable
guile
muster
sustain
prodigious
victuals
civility
appall
brute
ponderous
profusion
carrion
embark
beguile
ardor

Latin Root Words

Fy - make
Ocul - eye
Cur - care for
Ultra - beyond
Oid - appearance
Gest - carry
Apt - fit
Tact - touch
Voc - voice
Rid - laugh
Ped - foot or child
Mort - death
Carn - flesh

Latin Root Words

Anim - mind
Tort - twist
Nym - name
Sanct - holy
Meta - change
Petr - rock
Mir - wonder
Man - hand
Rect - right
Volv - roll
Demi - half
Retro - backward
Sens - feel

Recitation Pairing

RECITATION – 12TH GRADE

The New Colossus
Emma Lazarus

★ **About The Poet**
Emma Lazarus (1849 –1887) was an American author of poetry, pros
translations, as well as an activist for Jewish causes.

★ **About the Poem**
This poem was written in 1883 to raise money for the construction of
the Statue of Liberty (Liberty Enlightening the World). In 1903, the po
onto a bronze plaque and mounted inside the pedestal's lower level. T
of the sonnet were set to music by Irving Berlin as the song "Give Me
Your Poor" for the 1949 musical Miss Liberty

ETHOS ⛫ LOGOS

12-4

The New Colossus

EMMA LAZARUS

Not like the brazen giant of Greek fame With conquering limbs astride from
land to land; Here at our sea-washed, sunset gates shall stand A mighty woman
with a torch, whose flame Is the imprisoned lightning, and her name Mother of Exiles.

From her beacon-hand Glows world-wide welcome; her mild eyes command The
air-bridged harbor that twin cities frame, "Keep, ancient lands, your storied pomp!"
cries she With silent lips. "Give me your tired, your poor, Your huddled masses
yearning to breathe free, The wretched refuse of your teeming shore,

Send these, the homeless, tempest-tossed to me, I lift my lamp
beside the golden door!"

★ **ETHOS LOGOS VALUE/VIRTUE OF THE MONTH** ★
Humility – Cleanliness

RECITATION – 12TH GRADE

Ulysses
Alfred, Lord Tennyson

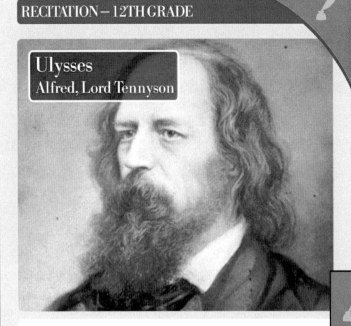

★ **About The Poet**
Alfred, Lord Tennyson (1809-1892) was the Poet Laureate during much of Queen Victoria's reign and remains one of the most popular British poets of all time.

★ **About the Poem**
The poem takes the form of a dramatic monologue spoken by Ulysses, a character who also appears in Homer's Greek epic The Odyssey and Dante's Italian epic the Inferno. Facing old age, mythical hero Ulysses describes his discontent and restlessness upon returning to his kingdom, Ithaca, after his far-ranging travels. Despite his reunion with his wife Penelope and his son Telemachus, Ulysses yearns to explore again.

12-3

ETHOS ⳹ LOGOS

Recitation Pairing

Ulysses

ALFRED LORD TENNYSON

It little profits that an idle king,
By this still hearth, among these barren crags,
Match'd with an aged wife, I mete and dole
Unequal laws unto a savage race,
That hoard, and sleep, and feed, and know not me.

I cannot rest from travel; I will drink
Life to the lees. All times I have enjoy'd
Greatly, have suffer'd greatly, both with those
That loved me, and alone; on shore, and when
Thro' scudding drifts the rainy Hyades
Vext the dim sea. I am become a name;
For always roaming with a hungry heart
Much have I seen and known,-- cities of men
And manners, climates, councils, governments,
Myself not least, but honor'd of them all,--
And drunk delight of battle with my peers,
Far on the ringing plains of windy Troy.
I am a part of all that I have met;
Yet all experience is an arch wherethro'
Gleams that untravell'd world whose margin fades
For ever and for ever when I move.
How dull it is to pause, to make an end,
To rust unburnish'd, not to shine in use!
As tho' to breathe were life! Life piled on life
Were all too little, and of one to me
Little remains; but every hour is saved
From that eternal silence, something more,
A bringer of new things; and vile it were
For some three suns to store and hoard myself,
And this gray spirit yearning in desire
To follow knowledge like a sinking star,
Beyond the utmost bound of human thought.

★ **ETHOS LOGOS VALUE/VIRTUE OF THE MONTH** ★
Perseverance - Resolution (Grit)

Historical Pairing

MODERN– 4th, 8th, 12th

1865-1914 MOVEMENT
Transportation, Immigration, Westward Expansion,
Industrial Society, Gilded Age,
Teddy Roosevelt, Progressivism

<u>What do you know:</u> Roosevelt – Taft • Custe...
American Imperialism • Immigration – Labor

<u>Industrial Revolution</u>
Transcontinental Railroad
Wright Brothers
Henry Ford – Model T
Robber Barons

<u>Reconstruction</u>
Econ-Poli-Social
13th – 14th – 15th Amendment
Plessey v Ferguson

MONTH 3 4|8|12   ETHOS L...

MODERN– 4th, 8th, 12th

1914-1929 SEARCHING FOR MEANING
Industrialization – The Roaring 20's,
Prohibition, Jazz, Entertainment,
Stock Market Crash

<u>Roaring 20's:</u>
Speakeasy
Jazz
Great Gatsby

<u>Events:</u>
Music
Prohibition
Woman's Movement
Inventions

<u>Big Ideas:</u>
Materialism
Mexican Revolution
Hyperinflation

LOGOS

MODERN– 4th, 8th, 12th

1914-1929 SEARCHING FOR MEANING
Industrialization – The Roaring 20's,
Prohibition, Jazz, Entertainment,
Stock Market Crash

$100. WILL BUY THIS CAR. MUST HAVE CASH. LOST ALL ON THE STOCK MARKET

<u>Key Ideas:</u>
Allied v Axis
Important Dates – Start, Finish, America's Entrance
Treaty of Versailles
Woodrow Wilson
League of Nations
Treaty of Versailles
Trench Warfare
Rosie the Riveter
Tank Warfare
Lusitania
Monarchy
Assassination Arch Duke Ferdinand

MONTH 4 4|8|12   ETHOS ⬛ LOGOS

Historical Pairing
Actual Time Period

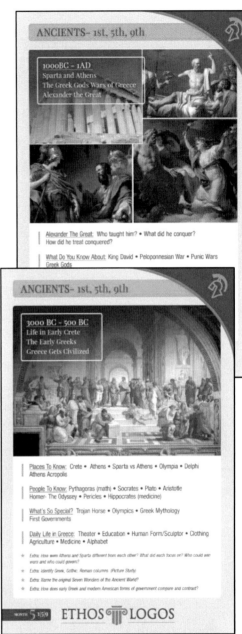

Great Men and Women

Artists and Musicians Pairing

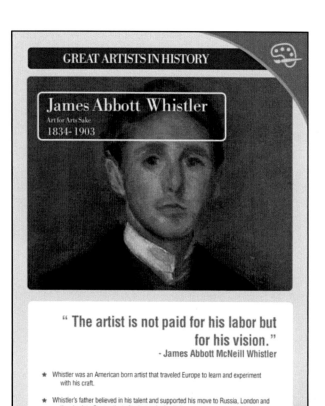

GREAT ARTISTS IN HISTORY

James Abbott Whistler
Art for Arts Sake
1834-1903

" The artist is not paid for his labor but for his vision."
- James Abbott McNeill Whistler

★ Whistler was an American born artist that traveled Europe to learn and experiment with his craft.

★ Whistler's father believed in his talent and supported his move to Russia, London and then b...

★ During A...
on the...

12 - 1 - 5

ETHOS LOGOS
TOP 50 ART WORKS

68 Whistler's Mother – It is one of the most famous works by an American artist. It is an American icon and a Victorian Mona Lisa.

Facts About The Artist

● Whistler's father, a railroad engineer, recognizing his talent, and enrolled in the Imperial Academy of Fine Arts when he was 11 years old.
● As a child he was prone to mood swings and temper tantrums but would calm down when offered the chance to draw and paint.
● James Abbott Whistler applied to the United States Military Academy at West Point and was selected in 1851. He was kicked out for being rebellious.
● In 1871, a model for one of his portraits failed to appear, so Whistler asked his mother to pose for the portrait. He painted what came to be known as 'Whistler's Mother'.

Historical Significance

● During the 1860s, he became fascinated with nocturnal paintings, night scenes primarily set in harbors, painted with a blue or light green palette.
● Whistler was a major artists active during the American Gilded Age, and was a leading proponent of the philosophy of "art for art's sake".

Great Works

★ Portrait of the Artist's Mother
★ The White Girl
★ At the Piano
★ Old Battersea Bridge

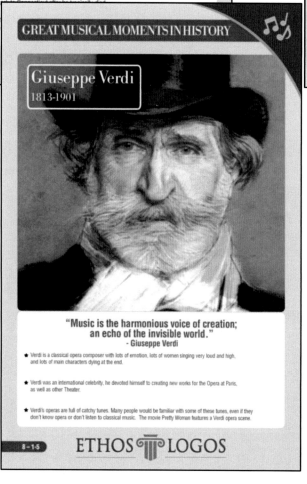

GREAT MUSICAL MOMENTS IN HISTORY

Giuseppe Verdi
1813-1901

"Music is the harmonious voice of creation; an echo of the invisible world."
- Giuseppe Verdi

★ Verdi is a classical opera composer with lots of emotion, lots of women singing very loud and high, and lots of main characters dying at the end.

★ Verdi was an international celebrity, he devoted himself to creating new works for the Opera at Paris, as well as other Theater.

★ Verdi's operas are full of catchy tunes. Many people would be familiar with some of these tunes, even if they don't know opera or don't listen to classical music. The movie Pretty Woman features a Verdi opera scene.

8 - 1 - 5

ETHOS ██ LOGOS

ETHOS TOP 25 MUSIC

09 **Giuseppe Verdi**
Verdi is considered, together with Richard Wagner, the most important opera composer of the nineteenth century. Although the two composers never met, there was a known rivalry between them.

Facts About The Artist

● Verdi's father was an innkeeper who had a small farm. At the age of 9 he played the organ for church services.
● He had no formal musical training but his love of music made him one of the greatest of all time.
● He liked Shakespeare, which is why some of his operas, 'Macbeth', 'Otello', and 'Falstaff' are all based on Shakespeare's plays.
● Giuseppe Verdi's funeral in 1901 remains the largest public assembly of any event in the history of Italy.

Historical Significance

● Verdi was an Italian romantic composer who is regarded as one of the most influential composers of the 19th century.
● The music of Verdi served the audience of the mass public rather than that of the musical elite.
● His works reflected the popular culture of his time.

Great Works

★ Rigoleeto
★ Il Trovatore
★ La Traviate
★ 'Grand March' -opera Aida
★ Requiem

★ ETHOS LOGOS VALUE/VIRTUE OF THE MONTH ★

The values and virtues of the month are
RESOLUTION and PERSEVERENCE.

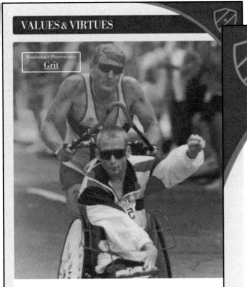

KEY LESSONS TO LEARN FROM PERSEVERANCE THROUGH SETBACKS

- Challenges make you stronger and strengthen your ability to face and conquer more adversity in the future.
- You become more confident from overcoming many difficulties.
- When facing adversity it makes you appreciate the good times.
- You identify new ways to tackle tasks.
- You grow as a person – persevering builds your resilience and strengthens your willpower.
- You become a visionary person who learns what works and what doesn't.

WAYS TO HAVE PERSEVERANCE IN YOUR LIFE

- Don't be afraid to fail
- Be 1% better every day
- View setbacks as learning opportunities
- Believe in yourself
- Learn how to handle powerful emotions
- Practice optimism
- Focus on effort and not outcomes
- Keep your goals in mind.
- Remember your goals
- Never Never Never Give Up

READ

- The Little Engine That Could – Piper
- The Tortoise and the Hair – Aesop
- The Most Magnificent Thing - Spires
- Unbroken – Hillenbrand
- Old Man and The Sea – Hemmingway
- Wonder – Palacio
- Grit – Angela Duckworth

WATCH

- Crossing – PG (1999)
- 12 Angry Men (1957)
- The Ghosts of Mississippi PG13 (1996)
- Rudy PG (1993)
- Castaway PG-13 (2000)
- Apollo 13 PG (1995)
- The Boy Who Harnessed The Wind (2019)
- Shiloh PG (1997)
- Toy Story (1995)
- Remember the Titans PG (2003)
- Hidden Figures PG (2016)
- Mulan (1998)
- Selma - PG13 (2014)

MODELS

- Thomas Edison
- Walt Disney
- Colonel Sanders
- Bethany Hamilton
- JK Rowling
- Abraham Lincoln
- Victor Frankl
- Nick Vujicic

The values and virtues of the month are HUMILITY and CLEANLINESS.

Weave these traits into your novel studies, other subject areas you are studying, and opportunities to show HUMILITY and CLEANLINESS in your daily life.

"Humility is the solid foundation of all virtues."

– Confucius

"Cleanliness and order are not matters of instinct; they are matters of education, and like most great things, you must cultivate a taste for them."

– Benjamin Disraeli

HISTORY AND HUMILITY

For 2500 major Western and Eastern societies have valued humility.

Greek philosopher, Socrates spoke about wisdom, as being 'knowing what you don't know'.

Aristotle understood humility as a moral virtue, and the ideal 'Golden Mean', between the vices of arrogance and moral weakness.

Confucius taught that humility was to be 'other oriented in spirit, and to values social good over individual glory'. By being humble, Confucianism can create stronger societies and a sense of belonging.

In Christianity, one of Jesus' most famous messages was delivered as the Sermon on the Mount. He taught that to live a Christian life, we should forgive, we shouldn't worship money, and we shouldn't hoard things but instead share. He outlined that we should comfort those in sorrow, help the poor, forgive those who hurt us, and treat others as you would like to be treated.

In the Muslim faith, the prophet Mohammed lived humbly all his life and never boasted of his social or political position. He rejected being worshiped and instead believed Humility and courtesy are acts of piety.

In Judaism, Moses, the greatest hero of Jewish tradition, is described by the Bible as "a very humble man, more humble than anyone else on the face of the earth."

Humble people strive to see themselves truthfully.
Humble people have a strong sense of their place in the world.
Humble people see their mistakes, learn and know their limitations.
Humble people are open to new ideas and others.
Humble people have a low focus on themselves
Humble people appreciate the value in all things
Humble people are excited for a friends good fortune
Humble people care more about the rights others before themselves.
Humble people are servants.
Humble people don't care who gets the credit.
Humble people are quick to forgive.
Humble people are thankful.
Humble people are patient and don't get easily frustrated with others.
Humble people ask for help and are they are not know-it-alls.

CLEANLINESS QUESTIONS TO PONDER

- What ways can you help clean your classroom? Your school? Your city?
- How do we keep our environment clean?
- What happens when we show orderliness by putting everything in its proper place?
- How does it feel when our room/desk is neat?
- What does it mean to have a pure and clean heart?
- What does it mean to have a clean mind?
- What does it mean to use clean words?
- What does it mean to have clean and pure actions?
- How can we minimize the chances of germs entering into our bodies? Why should we wash fruits and vegetables before eating them?
- How does cleanliness keep us healthy and strong?

HOW TO ORGANIZE YOURSELF FOR CLEAN LIFE

- Tackle the clutter! If something doesn't bring you joy, get rid of it.
- Make time to organize and clean. Pick up as you go.
- Don't overwhelm yourself; start small.
- Make schedules and deadlines. Use a list.
- Don't Procrastinate, clean it up NOW!
- You are not alone, clean up after yourself, think of your family too.
- Find a spot for your toys, clothes put things back.

PRACTICE PERSONAL HYGIENE

- Regular Showers and Baths
- Wash your hands often
- Brush your teeth, twice a day
- Cover your mouth when you sneeze.
- Keep your clothes neat and washed
- Make sure food is prepared and safe

ENGLISH – 12TH

Hamlet

HAMLET

Time and Place

Hamlet famously declares that "something is rotten in the state of Denmark." What other natural imagery is used to describe the corruption of the Danish court? What "unnatural" events or behaviors preceded the events recounted in the play? What "unnatural" events or behaviors occur during the play?

About The Author

★ Discuss what you already know about Shakespeare and his works. What makes his/her work lasting? Who are some lasting story tellers from your generation (film, books, documentaries)?

12 -5,6

ETHOS 🏛 LOGOS

Unit #:	5, 6 (Dec - Jan)
Novel:	Hamlet
Grade Levels:	12th

History:
1929-1941
THE BUST The Great Depression, Roosevelt's New Deal

1930-1945
NATIONALISM Rise of Dictators World War II Beginning WWII

Artists - Musician:
Verdi – Whistler
Straus - Matisse

Value/Virtue:
Honor – Citizenship
Truth, Beauty, and Goodness

Governance:
Monarchy
Republic

Religion:
Christianity

Cultural Saying Unit 5
- Piece of cake
- You can't teach an old dog new tricks
- How the Mighty Have Fallen

Cultural Saying Unit 6
- Read between the lines
- Horse of a different color
- Jezebel & Delilah

Hamlet– Pre-Read

1. This play was written in the middle of Shakespeare's career and is known as one of his best works.
2. It is a tragedy—meaning that someone *may* die at the end, and the main character *may* have one or two flaws.
3. Shakespeare himself is a circumspect man. Not much is biographically known about him. He was married to Anne Hathaway. He lived in the times of two British rulers, Elizabeth and James. He had stocks in one theatre called the Globe, and this turned out to be a very wise business move.
4. Some critics have suggested that Shakespeare's father was a social climber, and so was he.
5. Shakespeare had three children, but his only son died. His name has Hamnet. See any significance there?
6. Regarding the play, it is good to know that Hamlet is performed always wearing black.
7. You may have seen famous scenes parodying someone holding a skull and talking to it. This is from Hamlet. Also, the famous line "To be or not to be" is in this play.
8. So, after hearing all of the information about Shakespeare and Hamlet, it's time to collaborate and see what we know about the play in total so far, so we're going to make a KWL chart
9. Ask the students what they know about the play, or themes represented in the play. Discuss them as they come up and put the ideas and concepts onto the chart.
10. Discuss what you already know about Shakespeare and his works.
11. Shakespeare was classified by writer Ben Jonson as "not of an age, but for all time."
12. What current writer/filmmaker/producer (last 50 years) do you see as also having this title? What makes his/her work lasting?

Hamlet– Act Questions

Act 1

1.1 The Ramparts of the Castle
1. Describe the prevailing atmosphere of the scene. How is that atmosphere created? What is the irony of the password —Long live the king‖? What is ironic about the guard who is coming on to duty challenging the one who is already on duty?
2. Identify images of sickness or disease. What do these suggest?
3. Why does Marcellus bring Horatio to the ramparts of the castle? What background information does Horatio give about Denmark and about the reasons for the ghost's appearance? What is the political situation in Denmark? What are the present relations with Norway and how did they come about? What reasons does Horatio suggest for the appearance of the ghost?
4. What is the importance of the actual appearance of the ghost in this scene? Explain how the central contrasts between appearance and reality become evident in this scene.

1.2 Meeting of the Royal Court
1. How does Claudius reveal himself to be a capable monarch in this scene? Consider his handling of the explanation of the situation in Denmark (including his justification of the marriage to Gertrude), the Norway affair, Laertes' request, Hamlet's request. Consider also Claudius's advice to Hamlet about grieving for his dead father.
2. What qualities of Hamlet's character are evident a) in his first words of the play? b) in his soliloquy? c) in his comments on his mother's marriage in his soliloquy and his later comments on that marriage to Horatio (lines 137-59 and lines176-81)? d) in his general conversation with Horatio and the sentries? What is Hamlet's relationship with Horatio?
3. What are the contrasts between the characters of Hamlet and Laertes? Why does Claudius grant Laertes' request and refuse Hamlet's?
4. What lines of conflict does this scene establish?
5. Look at Hamlet's reference to the —unweeded garden‖ (lines 135-36). What is the significance of this imagery in terms of the play and the character of Hamlet? What is the garden? Who or what are the weeds?
6. Explain with specific references how this scene develops the motif of appearance versus reality.

1.3 The Advice Scene
1. Why do both Laertes and Polonius warn Ophelia against Hamlet? Explain the specific reasons each one gives to Ophelia to warn her away from Hamlet.
2. Generally, what is Polonius's advice to Laertes? What does his advice to his son tell us about his values? How do Polonius's various bits of advice to his children serve to characterize him and his relationship with his children? What is Shakespeare suggesting about family relationships through this portrait of one family within the court?
3. How do Ophelia's reactions to the advice she receives from both her brother and father serve to characterize her?
4. Identify images of traps or false appearances in this scene. What is their significance?
5. What does Polonius forbid Ophelia from doing? What is the possible significance of this order?

1.4 - 1.5 Meeting the Ghost
1. What is Hamlet suggesting about human nature in lines 23-38 of scene 4? What is the importance of the imagery he uses? Explain what the speech indicates about Hamlet's character.
2. Summarize the Ghost's revelations to Hamlet. How was he murdered? What does he indicate about the horrors of death and his present circumstances? What is the significance of the imagery the Ghost uses and the Ghost's instructions about Gertrude?
3. Compare Hamlet's first reaction to the Ghost's news (ll. 29-30) with his last words of the scene. Explain Hamlet's further reaction to the Ghost's news (1.5.92-112). Explain the contradiction. Consider also Hamlet's emotional state throughout the scene. What does this tell us about his character?

Hamlet– Act Questions

Act 2

Scene I

1. Where is Reynaldo going? What are his instructions from Polonius?
2. Why does Polonius send Reynaldo with such orders? Why is "indirection" (Polonius' plan) a better way to find information?
3. What has Hamlet done to upset Ophelia so greatly? What is a possible cause for his behavior (in your mind)?
4. How does Polonius interpret Hamlet's actions? What does he intend to do with the information?

Scene II:

1. Why have Rosencranz and Guildenstern come to Elsinore?
2. What do Claudius and Gertrude want from these two men? Why?
3. Guess at some other reasons for Claudius/Gertrude to charge Rosencranz and Guildenstern with their orders.
4. How had Fortinbras fooled his uncle? What deal was made between them?
5. What request is made of Claudius on behalf of Fortinbras? What is his reaction?
6. What does Hamlet's letter show to the audience? What does it show the characters in the play?
7. What plan does Polonius suggest to test his theory? Given his plans (both here and before) – what conclusions can we make about Polonius as a character?
8. How does Hamlet use language against Polonius?
9. Is Hamlet toying with Polonius or trying to sincerely insult him? Explain your opinion.
10. What can we figure out about Hamlet's view of the world and his personal situation from his discussion with Rosencranz and Guildenstern?
11. Why do Rosencranz and Guildenstern believe Hamlet sees Denmark as a prison? What do you think is the real reason?
12. Is Hamlet accurate in his explanation of why Rosencranz and Guildenstern were sent for?
13. Is Hamlet honest to his friends regarding his "madness"? Do you believe they understand him?
14. How does Hamlet go about insulting Polonius? May there be some hint from Hamlet in reference to Ophelia considering his chosen example?
15. What speech is requested by Hamlet for the players to recite? How does this speech connect to his situation?
16. What play is requested for performance? What do you believe Hamlet wants added to it? (consider whole section)
17. What upset Hamlet so much about the players and their acting? Is he right in feeling that he's a failure?
18. How does Hamlet intend to "catch" the king? Do you believe this will be effective? Explain why.

Hamlet– Act Questions
Act 3

3.1 (The Nunnery Scene)
1. What is Rosencrantz and Guildenstern's explanation for Hamlet's madness at the beginning of Act 3?
2. Explain how and why Claudius admits his guilt. What might this aside indicate about his character? Explain the significance of Polonius's speech that prompts the aside.
3. Analyze Hamlet's famous "To be, or not to be" soliloquy in scene 1. How does he view death? How does he view life? How does he view an afterlife? Explain the conflicts that Hamlet is experiencing between the honor code and the religious code of response.
4. The scene with Ophelia is known as the Nunnery Scene. Why does Hamlet treat Ophelia as he does? Why does he deny his love for her? Why does he curse himself? Does he know or suspect someone is watching him? How might that knowledge or supposition affect his behavior? How will it affect his interpretation of her actions?
5. Support the idea that Hamlet is becoming more cynical and disintegrating spiritually in the first scene of Act 3.

3.2
1. Summarize in a couple of sentences Hamlet's instructions to the players.
2. What does Hamlet instruct Horatio to do before the play? What qualities of Horatio does Hamlet admire?
3. Describe Hamlet's behavior at the play. How does he speak to his mother, uncle, Polonius, and Ophelia? What might this indicate about Hamlet?
4. Explain why Hamlet compares himself to a musical pipe. Think about how Rosencrantz and Guildenstern are treating him. (lines 370-402)
5. Explain Hamlet's feelings in lines 419-432. How is this soliloquy different from others? Note further images of disease.

3.3
1. Explain the king's soliloquy. Is he sorry he killed his brother? What would he have done in order to repent?
2. Why won't Hamlet kill Claudius and get revenge in this scene? (lines 77-101) Explain Hamlet's rationale. What is the irony of the king's final words in the context of Hamlet's remarks?

3.4 (The Queen's Closet Scene)
1. How and why does Hamlet kill Polonius?
2. Explain what Hamlet says to Gertrude when he compares the portraits of Claudius and Old Hamlet. This sub-scene is called the Portrait Scene.
3. Why does the ghost re-appear? What is the effect of his re-appearance on both Hamlet and Gertrude?
4. What does Hamlet explain to his mother about his madness? (lines 203-218)
5. Note images of sickness or disease.
6. What does Hamlet instruct Gertrude to do and to avoid doing?
7. What does Hamlet suggest he will do on his upcoming trip to England?

Act Three – General
1. What are the similarities and differences between Hamlet's treatment of Ophelia in the Nunnery Scene and his treatment of Gertrude in the Closet and Portrait scene?

Hamlet– Act Questions

Act 4

4.1
1. How does Gertrude seek to shield Hamlet in this scene?
2. What are Claudius's chief concerns about the murder?

4.2
1. How does Hamlet reveal his —antic disposition‖? What else may he reveal about his attitudes to his friends?

4.3
1. What reasons does Claudius give for not proceeding with legal action against Hamlet? What are other reasons?
2. What are the details of the King's plan for Hamlet (ll. 67-77)?
3. Note images of sickness and disease. Why are they significant?

4.4
1. Of what importance is the first appearance of Fortinbras?
2. What are the points of comparison between him and Hamlet?
3. Hamlet talks about, "Some craven scruple/Of thinking too precisely on the event." Comment on this phrase as providing the reason for Hamlet's delay. What conclusion does Hamlet come to about greatness? What is the effect of Fortinbras's appearance in the play on Hamlet?
4. Explain Hamlet's attitude at the end of the act.

4.5
1. What is the dramatic purpose of Ophelia's madness? What are its causes?
2. What are the contrasts between Laertes and Hamlet?
3. How does Claudius show himself to be resourceful, courageous and manipulative?

4.6 – 4.7
1. What qualities of Hamlet does his letter show? What has happened to Hamlet?
2. How does his return affect the plot?
3. Explain how Claudius is able to manipulate Laertes into helping him. Explain the plan they devise. How does Claudius show himself to be unscrupulous and clever at the same time?
4. Explain the significance of the poison imagery.

Act 5

1. What are the purposes of the gravedigger scene? What themes does it bring out? Consider the issues over which the grave-diggers debate and the grave-digger's talk with Hamlet.
2. How does Hamlet show that he has changed in character somewhat? Many people remember the famous lines spoken to Yorick. Explain the significance of this particular speech and Hamlet's other speeches about death, particularly the one about Alexander.
3. What are the dramatic purposes of Ophelia's funeral?
4. What has Hamlet done to Rosencrantz and Guildenstern? What is Hamlet's attitude to his actions? Quote lines to show his attitude.
5. What is the significance of the Osric episode?
6. Why does Horatio warn Hamlet about engaging in the duel with Laertes? Explain Hamlet's response, —Not a whit we defy augury…..‖ (5.2.210).
7. How does nemesis overtake a) Claudius, b) Laertes, c) Gertrude, d) Hamlet?

Personal Relfection

What Does The Play Mean To You?

What is a true friend? How can anyone be "true to themselves" when situations often make it necessary to perform many different roles? Why do we take our frustration out on those we love the most? How does one decide how to live?

Taking revenge for his father's death would be seen as Hamlet "taking the law into his own hands." How do you feel about vigilantism in the play? What about in present day?

Hamlet lists off troubles of the world, not just his own that make him want to die. If he was a present-day character, what other factors of the world do you think would be bothering him? Wars? Corporations? Technology? Religions?

Hamlet insults Ophelia by insulting all women in general. Are the stereotypes and claims he makes towards women still seen now? Have the stereotypes changed? Have they disappeared?

Whom would you prefer to have as a best friend, Horatio or Hamlet? Which of the two would you be more likely to fall in love with? Explain your answer by describing the qualities you admire and those you dislike in each character.

Does Hamlet believe he has a purpose in life? If so, what is it? If not, why is this reasoning? What do you feel your purpose in life is right now?

1. What is a true friend?
2. How can anyone be "true to themselves" when situations often make it necessary to perform many different roles?
3. What is the philosophical basis of existentialism and how can meaning be found?
4. Why do we take our frustration out on those we love the most?
5. How does one decide how to live?

6. How do you deal with your sadness?
7. Why is Hamlet so sad?
8. Do you feel that Hamlet's sadness over his father's death and mother's remarriage is justified? Why or why not? Do you think that this has anything to do with the time and place of the play?
9. What is Hamlet's idea of a perfect marriage? What roles would the husband and wife play? What is your definition of an ideal marriage? What roles should husband and wife play?
10. Is Laertes' advice for Ophelia useful? Is this similar advice that an older brother would give to a younger sister? Is this trait of 'wisdom' something that he may have received from his father? Why or why not?

Personal Reflection

1. Who do you normally go to for advice?
2. Is Laertes' advice for Ophelia useful? Is this similar advice that an older brother would give to a younger sister? Is this trait of 'wisdom' something that he may have received from his father? Why or why not?

3. If your best friend told you that a ghost appeared to them and asked for them to seek out revenge, what would you do?
4. Would you be Hamlet's ally in this scenario? From what you know of his characteristics, why do you think Horatio and Marcellus choose to follow him?
5. Taking revenge for his father's death would be seen as Hamlet "taking the law into his own hands." How do you feel about vigilantism in the play? What about in present day?

6. Have you ever been put in a situation where an authoritative figure has made you go against your personal morals to do something? (i.e.: working at a coffee shop where you must throw away the baked goods at the end of the day, even though there is a homeless man outside who would greatly benefit from having some of the food given to him.)
7. What qualities do you look for in a good friendship? Do you think Rosencrantz and Guildenstern elicit this?

8. Hamlet lists off troubles of the world, not just his own that make him want to die. If he was a present-day character, what other factors of the world do you think would be bothering him? Wars? Homophobia? Corporations? Technology?
9. Claudius mentions that he has a guilty conscience to the audience in this scene. Does this confession change your point of view on his character?
10. Hamlet insults Ophelia by insulting all women in general. Are the stereotypes and claims he makes towards women still seen now? Have the stereotypes changed? Have they disappeared?

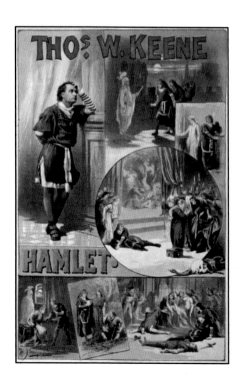

Literary Analysis

Themes and Characters

What do you think Hamlet's tragic flaw is? To what extent does Hamlet correspond to classical notions of tragedy?

You are Horatio. Write a eulogy for Hamlet. Describe his character. Include pictures of things he would have loved. Gently allude to his bad qualities and discuss why his good qualities triumph over these.

From what you know about the characters, which character is most important in Hamlet's life? Most aggravating? Who is the most important person in your life? Why?

Is Hamlet's appearance of madness helping him to enact his revenge on Claudius? Why or why not? How has madness impacted the identity of Hamlet as a character?

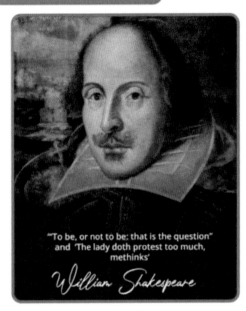

"To be, or not to be: that is the question" and 'The lady doth protest too much, methinks'

William Shakespeare

 ETHOS LOGOS VALUE/VIRTUE OF THE MONTH
Honor-Citizenship and Truth, Beauty and Goodness

Themes to Explore
- **Moral corruption**
- **Revenge**
- **Appearance and reality**
- **Mortality**
- **Madness**
- **Religion**
- **Politics**

Symbolism in Hamlet
- Ghost
- The Skull
- Flowers
- Gravedigger
- The Mousetrap

Hamlet– Essay or Socratic

1. Why does Hamlet delay so long in avenging his father's murder?
2. What is the role of theatre within Hamlet? What is the purpose of the Hecuba speech, the play-within-the-play, and Hamlet's advice to actors? What practical purposes do theatrical moments serve in the plot? What symbolic purposes do they serve? Does theater "hold, as twere, a mirror up to nature"?
3. Hamlet is full of madness, both real and feigned (maybe). What is the difference between the mad and the sane characters in the play, especially in what they say and how they say it? What are the similarities and differences between Hamlet's madness and Ophelia's?
4. The conflicts of Hamlet take place in the context of a single family's domestic problems, and also in the context of political decisions that affect an entire country. How do the family and political levels of Hamlet interact? Where do they reinforce each other, and where, if ever, do they contradict each other?
5. Almost from his opening lines, Hamlet reveals an obsession with suicide. He never carries out the impulse to take his own life, but it remains with him for much of the play. How do Hamlet's reasons for avoiding suicide – and his attitude towards his own death – change throughout the play?
6. One of the more famous lines in Hamlet is, "To thine own self be true, and it must follow, as the night the day, thou canst not then be false to any man". Which of the characters in Hamlet are true to themselves? Does that prevent them from being false to one another? Does the meaning of this quote change for you when you consider that it's spoken by Polonius, one of the play's most frequently mocked characters?
7. It seems like half the characters in Hamlet are foils for Hamlet, and the rest of them are foils for each other. How do the different foils bring out different aspects of Hamlet's character? What other effects does all this doubling produce?
8. Is Hamlet's reaction to his mother's remarriage reasonable, or are his standards of fidelity too high? In the play-within-the-play, which Hamlet himself revised, the player Queen vows never to marry again. "Such love would need be treason in my breast". Does Hamlet expect his mother to remain single for the rest of her life?
9. As he is dying, Hamlet begs Horatio to tell his story. Do you think the story Horatio will tell is the same one the readers or the audience have just experienced? Is Horatio capable of telling Hamlet's true story?

Novel Vocabulary - Hamlet

1.1 (Act – Scene)
assail (36) v.- to attack
fortified (37) v.- shielded; secured; protected
usurp (54) v.- to seize; to confiscate
esteemed (97) v.- to honor; to respect; to prize; to treasure
ratified (99) v.- approved; confirmed; legalized
mettle (108) n.- endurance; bravery
resolute (110) n.- brave; fearless; relentless people
privy (145) adj.- made participant in a secret

1.2
dole (13) n.- sadness
visage (84) n.- the face or facial expression of a person
denote (86) v.- to indicate; to mark; to signal; to mean
countenance (247) n.- appearance; facial expression

1.3
calumnious (42) adj.- slanderous; attacking one's character
precept (64) n.- rule; principle
perilous (111) adj.- dangerous
importuned (119) v.- insistently begged

1.4
traduced (20) v.- to slander; to speak falsely of
pernicious (112) adj.- deadly

2.1
glean (16) v.- to gather; to collect
sovereign (28) adj.- absolute; total undisputed
satirical (214) adj.- sarcastic; biting; mocking
rogue (214) n.- villain; fiend; scoundrel
promontory (322) n.- a cliff high above water
firmament (324) n.- the sky; the heavens
pestilent (326) asj.- deadly; likely to cause an epidemic
paragon (331) n.- perfect example; model; standard

3.1
consummation (71) n.- completion; achievement
calamity (77) disaster; cause of great distress
inoculate (128) v.- to cure by introducing some antigenic material
wantonness (158) n.- immorality; extravagance
dejected (169) adj.- depressed; disheartened

3.2
abominably (37) adv.- detestably; with hatred
occulted (85) adj- hidden [obsolete, outdated usage except in medicine]
clemency (170) n.- leniency; mercy
beguile (249) v.- to deceive; to cheat
contagion (421) n.- the causative agent of a disease

3.3 (Act – Scene)
annex[ment] (22) v.- to add; to join
compelled (66) v.- forced
bulwark (46) n.- anything serving as a defense against an attack
chide (122) v.- to scold; to reprimand
mandate (227) n.- a command; a decree

4.1
discord (46) n. lack of agreement
dismay (46) n.- apprehension; discouragement

4.4
garrisoned (25) v.- assign troops for protection
exhort (49) v.- to urge by strong argument
imminent (63) adj.- about to happen

4.5
conjectures (20) n.- guesses; suppositions
superfluous (103) adj.- extra; beyond what is needed
incensed (141) adj- angered; infuriated
obscure (238) adj.- not well known; hidden

4.7
abate (131) v.- to lessen; to decrease
remiss (152) adj.- negligent; lax in attending to duty

5.1
cudgel (57) v.- to beat with a heavy club
abhorred (193) adj.- hated; disgusting
prate (297) v.- to talk idly; to chatter

5.2
sultry (111) adj.- oppressively hot
perdition (125) n.- eternal damnation; hell
faction (252) n.- a group
carouses (315) v.- drinks merrily
treachery (337) n.- willful betrayal of trust; deception

Grade Level Vocabulary

ephemeral	hackneyed
evanescent	haughty
exasperation	hedonist
exemplary	hypothesis
extenuating	impetuous
florid	impute
fortuitous	incompatible
frugal	inconsequential

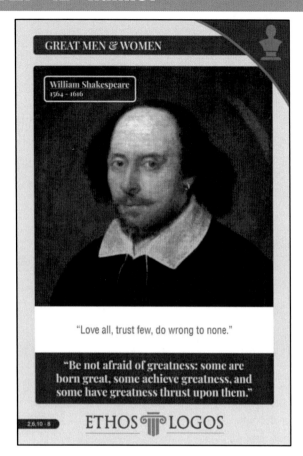

About The Author

- William Shakespeare was an English poet and playwright who was born on April 23, 1564. William was the third child of John Shakespeare and Mary Arden.
- Scholars suspect that he attended the King's New School in Stratford-upon-Avon. This school taught reading, writing, and the classics.
- He lived during the reigns of Elizabeth I and James I and coined hundreds of new words and phrases that we still use today.
- During his lifetime Shakespeare became very famous for writing 154 sonnets and 37 plays.
- He wrote three types of plays, comedies, tragedies, and histories

The English Elizabethan Era is one of the most prominent periods in the History of England. This time period brought about great explorers such as Sir Francis Drake and Walter Raleigh, and the first appearance of theaters in England!

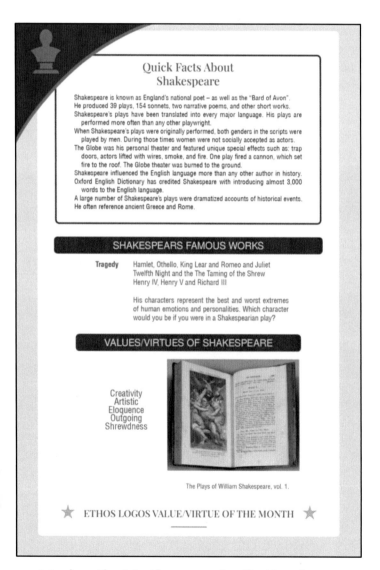

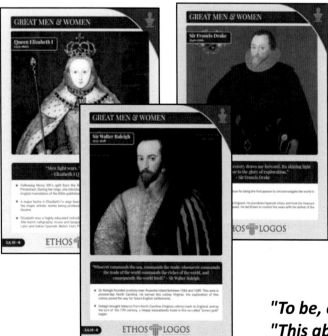

"To be, or not to be: that is the question" - Hamlet
"This above all: to thine own self be true" – Hamlet
"The lady doth protest too much, methinks" - Hamlet

The values and virtues of the month are
HONOR and CITIZENSHIP.

Weave these traits into your novel studies, other subject areas you are studying, and opportunities to show HONOR and CITIZENSHIP in your daily life.

HONOR - DEFINITION

A good character, or a reputation for honesty and fair dealing.

A keen sense of right and wrong; adherence

CONGRESSIONAL MEDAL OF HONOR

The Medal of Honor is the United States' highest award for military valor in action. Each Medal of Honor recipient has a story behind their medal which involves extraordinary, courage, sacrifice, integrity. A deep love of country and a desire to always do what is right.

A distinguished award presented only to the deserving, the Medal tells a story of its own.

The Medal is authorized for any military service member who "distinguishes himself conspicuously by gallantry and intrepidity at the risk of his life above and beyond the call of duty

While engaged in an action against an enemy of the United States;

While engaged in military operations involving conflict with an opposing foreign force;

While serving with friendly foreign forces engaged in an armed conflict against an opposing armed force in which the United States is not a belligerent party."

HONOR WARRIORS FROM HISTORY

10. Maori Warriors
9. Knights of the Roundtable
8. Mongol Warriors – The Khan's
7. Roman Legions and Emperors
6. Apache Warriors in America
5. Ninja and Samurai of Japan
4. Viking Warriors
3. Spartans of Ancient Greece
2. Navy Seals – Green Berets
1. Alexander The Great

Pat Tillman
1976-2004

Left the NFL for the Honor of Serving His County

WHAT IT MEANS TO BE A US CITIZEN

- Have an understanding of the people, history, and traditions that have shaped our local communities, our nation, and the world.
- Have an understanding of our nation's founding documents, civic institutions, and political processes.
- Is aware of issues and events that have an impact on people at local, state, national, and global levels.
- Seeks information from varied sources and perspectives to develop informed opinions and creative solutions.
- Asks meaningful questions and is able to analyze and evaluate information and ideas.
- Uses effective decision-making and problem-solving skills in public and private life.
- Has the ability to collaborate effectively as a member of a group.

NCSS.org

WHAT DOES IT MEAN TO BE A GOOD CITIZEN?

- Take personal responsibility and model values
- Good citizens do their share to help their families and communities to be better.
- They are good neighbors.
- They obey rules, laws, cooperate with others.
- Stay informed about important issues and vote.
- They are responsible for themselves.
- Get involved in community affairs.
- Volunteer to serve the community

MODELS

- Pat Tillman (NFL)
- Audie Murphy
- Harriet Tubman
- Davey Crockett
- Billy Graham

WATCH

- Follow Me Boys (1966)
- 42 (2013)
- Lincoln (2012)
- 1776 (1972)
- All The Presidents Men (1976)
- Boys Town (1938)
- Gettysburg (1993)
- October Sky (1999)

READ

- Her Right Foot – Shawn Harris
- Granddaddy's Turn: A Journey to the Ballot Box – M Bandy
- What Can A Citizen Do? Dave Eggers
- When You Grow Up to Vote: How Our Government Works for You – Eleanor Roosevelt
- See How They Run: Campaign Dreams, Election Schemes, and the Race to the White House – S Goodman

The values and virtues of the month are
TRUTH, BEAUTY, and GOODNESS.

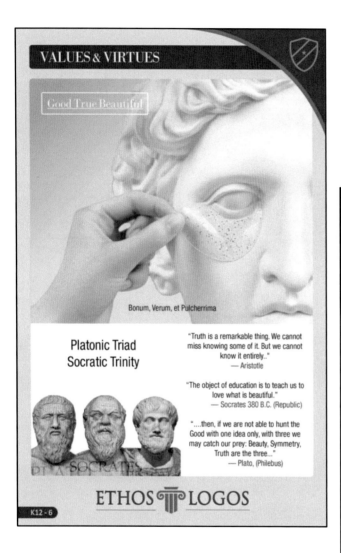

Weave these traits into your novel studies, other subject areas you are studying, and opportunities to show TRUTH, BEAUTY and GOODNESS in your daily life.

QUESTIONS TO PONDER

Good	True	Beautiful
Morals	Science	Art
Culture	Nature	Self
Ethics	Logic	Aesthetics
Education	Arch of Man	Nature
	Mathematics	Forms

ARE THESE FOUNDATIONAL TRUTHS? DEBATE IT!

- Art, music, creativity are pure and unique expressions of being human.
- Society can not have both Equity (Fairness) and Freedom (Liberty). Organizing society between the two is an evolving balance.
- Institutions, Bureaucracies, Mature Companies, Governments all tend towards layers, stagnation and ultimately wither.
- Morality and Virtues are important for democracies to thrive.
- Life's best lessons are taught by tough times. Real discoveries come from chaos, from going to the place that looks wrong, stupid and foolish.
- Most of the things you worry about never happen.
- If you want comfortable journey of life , then reduce the luggage of expectations.
- Everyone is fighting their own battles, so do not judge.

QUESTIONS TO PONDER

How do we measure "good"?
Is it defined by the majority?
Is it measured by self-satisfaction or personal fulfillment?
Why should we be good?
How do we know what is true?
What defines beauty?
Does beauty change over time?
Is beauty in the eye of the beholder or are there universal beautiful things, experiences or moments?

Recitation Pairing

RECITATION – 12TH GRADE

Sonnet 29
William Shakespeare

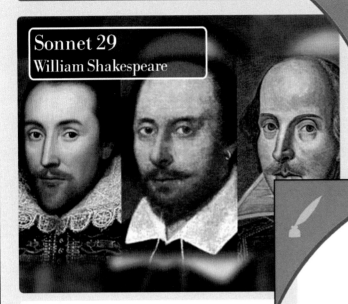

★ **About The Poet**

William Shakespeare (1564-1616) was an English playwright, poe[t] widely regarded as the greatest writer in the English language and [the] greatest dramatist.

★ **About the Poem**

This Shakespearean sonnet, covers profound insights into the em[otions] we experience when in love. As to who Shakespeare was in love w[ith is a] matter. His sonnet sequence is supposedly inspired by the 'lovely [young] lady' but in truth we may never know, or need to know who he is [with.]

12-6

ETHOS ⚭ **LOGOS**

Sonnet 29

WILLIAM SHAKESPEARE

When, in disgrace with fortune and men's eyes,
I all alone beweep my outcast state,
And trouble deaf heaven with my bootless cries,
And look upon myself, and curse my fate,
Wishing me like to one more rich in hope,
Featur'd like him, like him with friends possess'd,
Desiring this man's art and that man's scope,
With what I most enjoy contented least;
Yet in these thoughts myself almost despising,
Haply I think on thee, and then my state,
Like to the lark at break of day arising
From sullen earth, sings hymns at heaven's gate;
For thy sweet love remember'd such wealth brings
That then I scorn to change my state with kings.

★ **ETHOS LOGOS VALUE/VIRTUE OF THE MONTH** ★
Truth, Beauty, and Goodness

RECITATION – 12TH GRADE

The Second Coming
William Butler Yates

★ About The Poet

William Butler Yeats (1865-1939) is considered one of the gre[at]
English language. Yates received the 1923 Nobel Prize for Lite[rature]
greatly influenced by the heritage and politics of Ireland.

★ About the Poem

This poem was written in the early 1900s. There were many n[ew]
technologies– the motorcar, small aircraft, but the world was [ ]
the Russian Revolution of 1917, the Easter Uprising of 1916, a[nd]
War (1914-1918). With all these events behind, it was no won[der]
writers, and artists of all kinds felt as though that there was a [ ]
world happening, and that it would soon come to an end. .

12-5

ETHOS 🏛 LOGO[S]

Recitation Pairing

The Second Coming

WILLIAM BUTLER YATES

Turning and turning in the widening gyre
The falcon cannot hear the falconer;
Things fall apart; the centre cannot hold;
Mere anarchy is loosed upon the world,
The blood-dimmed tide is loosed, and everywhere
The ceremony of innocence is drowned;
The best lack all conviction, while the worst
Are full of passionate intensity.

Surely some revelation is at hand;
Surely the Second Coming is at hand.
The Second Coming! Hardly are those words out
When a vast image out of Spiritus Mundi
Troubles my sight: somewhere in sands of the desert
A shape with lion body and the head of a man,
A gaze blank and pitiless as the sun,
Is moving its slow thighs, while all about it
Reel shadows of the indignant desert birds.
The darkness drops again; but now I know
That twenty centuries of stony sleep
Were vexed to nightmare by a rocking cradle,
And what rough beast, its hour come round at last,
Slouches towards Bethlehem to be born?

★ ETHOS LOGOS VALUE/VIRTUE OF THE MONTH ★
Honor - Citizenship

Historical Pairing

MODERN– 4th, 8th, 12th

1930–1945: NATIONALISM
Rise of Dictators World War II
Beginning WWII

The Rise of Dictators: What was their Rise to Power, Early Life, Economic and Political Beliefs?
• Hitler • Hirohito • Stalin • Mussolini

Why Did These Dictators all Rise At The Same Time?

What political ideology did Hitler embrace? What is the basics of this ideology?

How does Hyperinflation affect people?

How did Treaty of Versailles lead to WW2?

★ Extra: "To the victor goes the spoils" Compare the way the winners of the Civil War and WW1 treated the losers and how each turned out.

MONTH 6 4|8|12 ETHOS LOGOS

MODERN– 4th, 8th, 12th

1929–1941 HEARTACHE
The Great Depression
Roosevelt's New Deal

The Repair:
The New Deal
"We have nothing to fear..."
New Deal Programs We Have Today
Government Overreach- packing the court

People:
Hoovertown
Roosevelt – Fireside Chats

★ Extra: What were the major causes of the Great Depression? How long did it last? How did the Great Depression affect ordinary Americans?

★ Extra: What was life like for rich and poor Americans during the Great Depression?

MONTH 5 4|8|12 ETHOS LOGOS

115

Artists and Musician Pairing

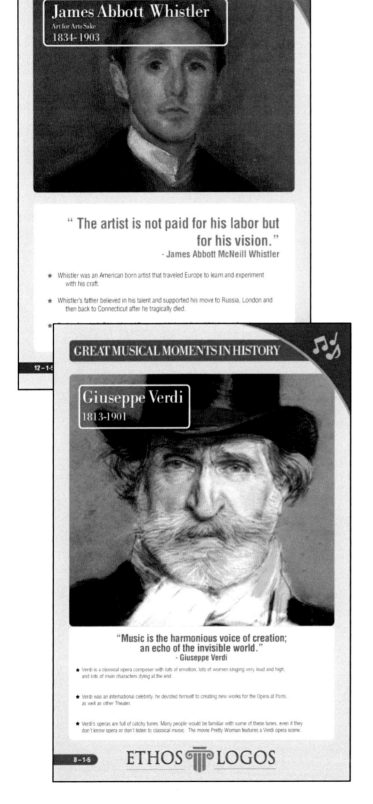

GREAT ARTISTS IN HISTORY

James Abbott Whistler
Art for Arts Sake
1834-1903

" The artist is not paid for his labor but
for his vision."
- James Abbott McNeill Whistler

★ Whistler was an American born artist that traveled Europe to learn and experiment with his craft.

★ Whistler's father believed in his talent and supported his move to Russia, London and then back to Connecticut after he tragically died.

GREAT ARTISTS IN HISTORY

Henri Matisse
Beginning Avante Garde
1869-1945

"When I put down a green, it doesn't mean
grass; and when I put down a blue,
it doesn't mean the sky."
- Matisse

★ Matisse had a friendship, that was rocky, with Pablo Picasso. The mutual respect that they developed for each other would move both artists to great things. How were their works similar? Different?

★ Matisse was close with Cezanne. How were there works similar? Different?

GREAT MUSICAL MOMENTS IN HISTORY

Giuseppe Verdi
1813-1901

"Music is the harmonious voice of creation;
an echo of the invisible world."
- Giuseppe Verdi

★ Verdi is a classical opera composer with lots of emotion, lots of women singing very loud and high, and lots of main characters dying at the end.

★ Verdi was an international celebrity, he devoted himself to creating new works for the Opera at Paris, as well as other Theater.

★ Verdi's operas are full of catchy tunes. Many people would be familiar with some of these tunes, even if they don't know opera or don't listen to classical music. The movie Pretty Woman features a Verdi opera scene.

ETHOS LOGOS

GREAT MUSICAL MOMENTS IN HISTORY

Richard Strauss
1864-1949

"The human voice is the most beautiful instrument of all,
but the most difficult to play"
- Richard Strauss

★ Strauss was one of the greatest German composers that ever lived. He completely changed the technical and expressive aspects of the orchestra during the 19th century. He rose to prominence in the wake of the Second World War, at a time when Germany had been devastated by the effects of the war

★ Strauss' famous work, Don Juan, a tone poem about the renowned philanderer, was the third of his first five symphonic poems. A tone poem, also commonly referred to as a symphonic poem, is an orchestral work that tells a story so they are often dramatic and free form.

★ Sprach Zarathustra, is a Strauss composition which was used as the main theme of the movie 2001 A Space Odyssey directed by Stanley Kubrick.

ETHOS LOGOS

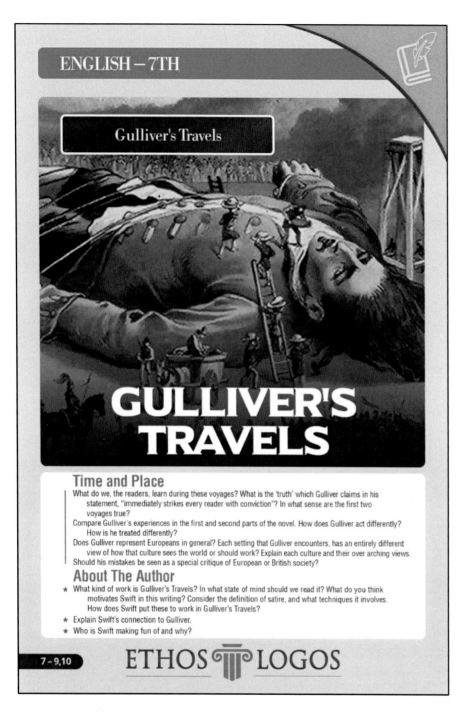

Unit #: 7, 8 (Feb, March)

Novel: Gulliver's Travel

Grade Levels: 12th

History:

1941-1945
WORLD WAR II America enters - Pacific theater Hiroshima Marshall Plan

1945-1961
COLD WAR - Baby Boom, Suburbs, Automobiles, Korean War Civil Rights Movement The Cold War, Eisenhower

Artists - Musician:
Strauss, Matisse

Value/Virtue:
Justice – Service
Moderation - Generosity

Governance:
Republic
Democracy

Religion:
Christianity

Cultural Saying Unit 7
- Second to none
- Night owl
- Kiss of Death

Cultural Saying Unit 8
- Busy as a bee
- Pig out
- Let There Be Light

Gulliver's Travels– Chapter Questions

Adventure 1

1. The man seems to have a flashback to which place?
2. What do the 2 beach combers find one day?
3. What do the small people, the Lilliputans do to the giant Lemuel Gulliver?
4. The Lilliputan soldiers first believe that Gulliver is a what?
5. How long has Gulliver been gone from home?
6. Who do the soldiers think has sent the giant?
7. How do the Lilliputans transport Gulliver?
8. Evaluate the emperor as a ruler. Whose advice does he rely on?
9. Why are Bigenders the enemies of the Lilliputans? What is the origin of their feud?
10. For what purposes do the Lilliputans learn "leaping and creeping"?
11. Compare the Lilliputans' form of government to Englands '. Is it better or worse? How?
12. Who now owns Lemuel and Mary's fine house? Why?
13. Where does Dr. Bates want to take Gulliver?
14. How does Gulliver prove to be a hero to the Lilliputans?
15. After Gulliver embarrasses the empress (by extinguishing the fire), how does the king consider punishing him?
16. How does Gulliver hide from the Lilliputan army while trying to escape?
17. How does Gulliver make a raft?
18. Where does Dr. Bates take Gulliver? How does he convince him to go?

Adventure 2

1. What is unusual about the land of the Brobdingnags?
2. Who finds Gulliver?
3. How does the family try to make money off of Gulliver?
4. Who purchases Gulliver, and how much does he sell for?
5. Who accompanies Gulliver after he is sold?
6. What position does the queen give to Gulliver?
7. How is he transported while he is at the palace?
8. What do you notice about the ruler of the Brobdingnags?
9. How do the Brobdingnags govern themselves?
10. Is this method of government better or worse than England 's, or not comparable?
11. What do you notice about the place of science and education in the land of the Brobdingnags?
12. Why is the queen's dwarf mean to Gulliver?
13. Where does Gulliver live while at the palace?
14. How old is Glumdalclitch, and how would you describe her relationship with Gulliver?
15. Why does Gulliver introduce gunpowder to the Brobdingnags, and how is this demonstration received?
16. What does Tom find in his father's knapsack back home?
17. How does Gulliver defend himself against the wasps?
18. What happens to Gulliver one day while he is at the beach with Glum?
19. When the bird drops Gulliver, where do he and the box land?

Gulliver's Travels– Chapter Questions

Adventure 3

1. What is unusual about Laputa?
2. How does Gulliver get transported to Laputa?
3. How big is the floating island? How many people live on it?
4. What nationality do these people remind you of? Why might Swift include these people in a book?
5. What seems to characterize the people of Laputa?
6. Who is Prince Munodi?
7. What does Dr. Bates do with Mary's letter?
8. What is a "flapper"? What is its use?
9. What is the Rajah predicting will happen?
10. How is the island controlled (in scientific terms)?
11. What is the problem with the way the island navigates?
12. What is Tom Gulliver drawing?
13. Why does Gulliver want to "reverse the lodestone"?
14. Where does Gulliver fall?
15. How does Munodi's mother view intellectualism?
16. Why does Gulliver want to find the "Academy"? What type of place is it?
17. What might the "Academy" represent in real-life societies?

At this point, Gulliver travels around the land of Luggnagg . **These places represent societies intrigued with the Period of Enlightenment: Love of intellectual and scientific attitudes and practices.**

1. Why is the old man mashing cucumbers?
2. Who does Gulliver meet in the Room of Answers? Why is this appropriate?
3. Back in England , where is Gulliver placed?
4. Gulliver ends up being a prisoner at the palace of the Glubbubdribs. It's like a scene out of the movie Groundhog Day. Why?
5. When Gulliver is drugged and sleeping at night, what does the king do to him?
6. Who does Gulliver end up summoning through a mirror? Why?
7. In the land of the Struldbrugs, a lady speaks to Gulliver from a golden eye. What is unusual about the Struldbrugs?
8. What is wrong with the people near the waters of immortality?
9. Back in England , how is Dr. Bates caught in a lie?
10. Does Gulliver drink from the waters of immortality? Why or why not?
11. While Mary is trying to get Gulliver off his addiction to laudanum, what ship experience does he tell her about?
12. How does he leave the ship?

Adventure 4

1. Gulliver, back in England , is taken to a court hearing. What does he call the people there?
2. Describe the real Yahoos. What do you think they represent?
3. Describe the Houyhnhms. What do you think they represent?
4. In the world of Adventure 4, the Houyhnhms act like _____ and the Yahoos act like _____.
5. Who is "Mistress"?
6. What do the Yahoos dig on the beaches for?
7. What does Gulliver find by digging on the beaches? What does he do with his findings?
8. What does the Houyhnhm Council decide about Gulliver?
9. How does he plan to leave the Houyhnhms?
10. Why does Gulliver throw his food overboard?
11. Who rescues him?
12. How does Mary answer when Dr. Bates asks her if Mary believes Gulliver's stors?
13. Why does Tom appear at the court hearing?
14. What does Tom's evidence prove?
15. Lem, Mary, and Tom return home. How does life continue for the Gullivers?
16. Why does Lem like to visit the stables at his home?

Essay or Socratic – Gulliver's Travels

1. Choose *one* land in *Gulliver's Travels*. Who/what does Swift critique within the land and/or people?
2. Gulliver changes throughout this novel and in each land he seems to take on a new persona. How does his character in the first few voyages compare to his last one? What do you think of Gulliver?
3. Which among the four places from Gulliver's travels would you like to go to and why?
4. How does Swift introduce and develop the Lilliputians? What does this say about what Swift is attempting to communicate?
5. How do Swift's descriptions of the Lilliputian's warlike nature and political processes convey his true intent?
6. What do we, the readers, learn during these voyages? What is "the truth" which Gulliver claims in the Letter "immediately strikes every reader with conviction"? In what sense are the first two voyages true?
7. What perspective on human life and human society does Gulliver gain in Lilliput and Brobdingnag? Are the things that Gulliver learns during his first voyage consistent, contradictory, or complementary to what he learns during the second? Do the two experiences shed light on one another?
8. Which society does Gulliver admire more—that of Lilliput, or of Brobdingnag? Why does he prefer it? In which society is he better off?
9. What kind of work is Gulliver's Travels? In what state of mind should we read it? What do you think motivates Swift in this writing? Consider the definition of satire, and what techniques it involves. How does Swift put these to work in Gulliver's Travels?
10. Gulliver's Travels shifts through a series of opposing theories and cultures. Each setting that Gulliver encounters, has an entirely different view of how that culture sees the world and thinks that it does, or should work

1. Some would argue that Swift was a misanthrope and that *Gulliver's Travels* proves his hatred of mankind. Agree or disagree with this assessment and support your opinion with examples from the text.
2. In his satire, Swift makes a correlation between size and morality. Explain how this works in the *Travels*, paying particular attention to Gulliver in Lilliput and in Brobdingnag.
3. Why do you think that Gulliver insists on traveling, especially after he faces hardships on his journeys?
4. Which historical figures do you think Gulliver represents?
5. Who do you think was the intended audience for *Gulliver's Travels*?
6. At the end of the novel, what hope does Gulliver have for human nature?
7. Why does Swift utilize base body functions to symbolize the actions of humans?

Literary Analysis

Conflicts

man v man,
Gulliver faces countless creatures, some who befriend him and others who capture and inflict harm onto him, like the Lilliputians or pirates.

man v self,
Gulliver must put aside his own understand of how things work in order to survive during his travels as well as face his own flaws and failures.

man v society,
When Gulliver returns to England, he realizes his family are much like the hate yahoos.

man v nature,
Gulliver often arrives on these strange island because the winds or sea too him there. He often doesn't know how or plan of going home, but nature provides a way.

man v technology
Laputa is full of music and math but the people who live there fail to make practical use of their knowledge therefore making it useless.

Themes

Might Versus Right
Gulliver experiences the advantages of physical power on both ends, the one who has it and the one who is without it. There are those who claim to rule based of morals, but no single person can rule off these, some amount of physical force must be executed. Where is the line drawn from brutality and what is necessary to maintain control?

The Individual Versus Society
Gulliver Travels explores the idea of a utopia as well as relating back to our own dystopian society. On Gulliver solo adventures he is able to visit these perfect utopia society but upon his return to England surround by society all he see is his financial failure.

The Limits of Human Understanding
The idea that humans are not meant to know everything and that all understanding has a natural limit is important in Gulliver's Travels. We can see this through the strange new things Gulliver experiences and although Gulliver is intelligent, he is very naive. This is an important lesson to humanity that no matter how smart you are you are always going to be a little naive, because one can not simple experience everything.

Novel Words – Gulliver's Travels

Conscience - conformity to one's own sense of right conduct
Passage - a journey usually by ship
Latitude - an imaginary line around the Earth parallel to the equator
Tide - the periodic rise and fall of the sea level
Abate - become less in amount or intensity
Diminutive - very small
Prodigious - great in size, force, extent, or degree
Countenance - the appearance conveyed by a person's face
Victuals - any substance that can be used as food
Proclamation - a formal public statement
Expedient - a means to an end
Candid - openly straightforward and direct without secretiveness
Momentous - of very great significance
Inured - made tough by habitual exposure
Debate - think about carefully; weigh
Subsidy - a grant paid by a government to an enterprise
Incessant - uninterrupted in time and indefinitely long continuing
Latter - the second of two or the second mentioned of two
Contrived - showing effects of planning or manipulation
Ponderous - having great mass and weight and unwieldiness
Auspicious - auguring favorable circumstances and good luck
Daunt - cause to lose courage
Divert - occupy in an agreeable, entertaining or pleasant fashion
Apprehensive - in fear or dread of possible evil or harm
Contend - compete for something

Latin Root Words

Caco - bad
Hetero - different
Sci - know
Graph - write
Lat - side
Lith - rock
Tract - pull
In - in or not
Co - together
Phile - love
Ine - nature of
-ar - relating to
Hexa - six

Scripps Spelling– Gulliver's Travels

Manuscript - the form of a literary work submitted for publication –
Taboo - a ban resulting from social custom or emotional aversion
Accomplishment - the action of achieving something
Empirical - derived from experiment and observation rather than theory
Quantitative - expressible as an amount that can be measured
Forensics - scientific tests or techniques used in the investigation of crimes
Fantastically - exceedingly; extremely
Recyclable - capable of being used again
Disparage - express a negative opinion of
Subsequent - following in time or order
Unforeseeable - incapable of being anticipated
Extant - still in existence; not extinct or destroyed or lost

Grade Level Vocabulary

Novel Words – Gulliver's Travels

Provocation - unfriendly behavior that causes anger or resentment
Prostrate - lie face downward, as in submission
Stipulate - make an express demand or provision in an agreement
Encompass - include in scope
Solicitation - an entreaty addressed to someone of superior status
Philosopher - a specialist in the investigation of existence and knowledge
Edict - a formal or authoritative proclamation
Foment - try to stir up
Quell - suppress or crush completely
Schism - the formal separation of a church into two churches
Embargo - a government order imposing a trade barrier
Prow - the front part of a vessel
Encomium - a formal expression of praise
Grandeur - the quality of being magnificent or splendid
Lilliputian - a very small person
Treatise - a formal exposition
Deficient - inadequate in amount or degree
Maxim - a saying that is widely accepted on its own merits
Levy - impose and collect
Husbandry - the practice of cultivating the land or raising stock
Extenuate - lessen or to try to lessen the seriousness or extent of
Impediment - something immaterial that interferes peruse
examine or consider with attention and in detail
Descry - catch sight of
Insatiable - impossible to satisfy

inevitable
integrity
intrepid
intuitive
jubilation
lobbyist
longevity
mundane
nonchalant
novice
opulent
orator
ostentatious
parched

Latin Root Words

Fract - break
Platy - flat
Theo - god
Fin - end
Hedron - Sided Object
Ambul - walk
Ous - full of
Topo - place

About The Author

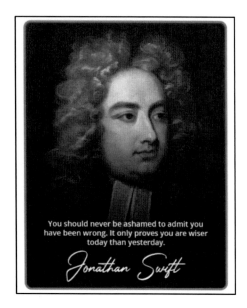

You should never be ashamed to admit you have been wrong. It only proves you are wiser today than yesterday.

Jonathan Swift

Jonathan Swift (30 November 1667 – 19 October 1745) was an Anglo-Irish satirist, essayist, political pamphleteer (first for the Whigs, then for the Tories), poet and Anglican cleric who became Dean of St Patrick's Cathedral, Dublin, hence his common sobriquet, "Dean Swift".

Swift is remembered for works such as A Tale of a Tub (1704), An Argument Against Abolishing Christianity (1712), Gulliver's Travels (1726), and A Modest Proposal (1729). He is regarded by the Encyclopedia Britannica as the foremost prose satirist in the English language,[1] and is less well known for his poetry. He originally published all of his works under pseudonyms—such as Lemuel Gulliver, Isaac Bickerstaff, M. B. Drapier—or anonymously. He was a master of two styles of satire, the Horatian and Juvenalian styles.

His deadpan, ironic writing style, particularly in A Modest Proposal, has led to such satire being subsequently termed "Swiftian"

Jonathan Swift was born on 30 November 1667 in Dublin in the Kingdom of Ireland. He was the second child and only son of Jonathan Swift (1640–1667) and his wife Abigail Erick (or Herrick)

He attended Trinity College, Dublin, the sole constituent college of the University of Dublin, in 1682,[14] financed by Godwin's son Willoughby. The four-year course followed a curriculum largely set in the Middle Ages for the priesthood. The lectures were dominated by Aristotelian logic and philosophy. The basic skill taught the students was debate, and they were expected to be able to argue both sides of any argument or topic. Swift was an above-average student but not exceptional, and received his B.A. in 1686 "by special grace."

Travels into Several Remote Nations of the World, in Four Parts, by Lemuel Gulliver, first a surgeon, and then a captain of several ships, better known as **Gulliver's Travels**. Much of the material reflects his political experiences of the preceding decade. For instance, the episode in which the giant Gulliver puts out the Lilliputian palace fire by urinating on it can be seen as a metaphor for the Tories' illegal peace treaty; having done a good thing in an unfortunate manner. In 1726 he paid a long-deferred visit to London, taking with him the manuscript of Gulliver's Travels.

Wikipedia

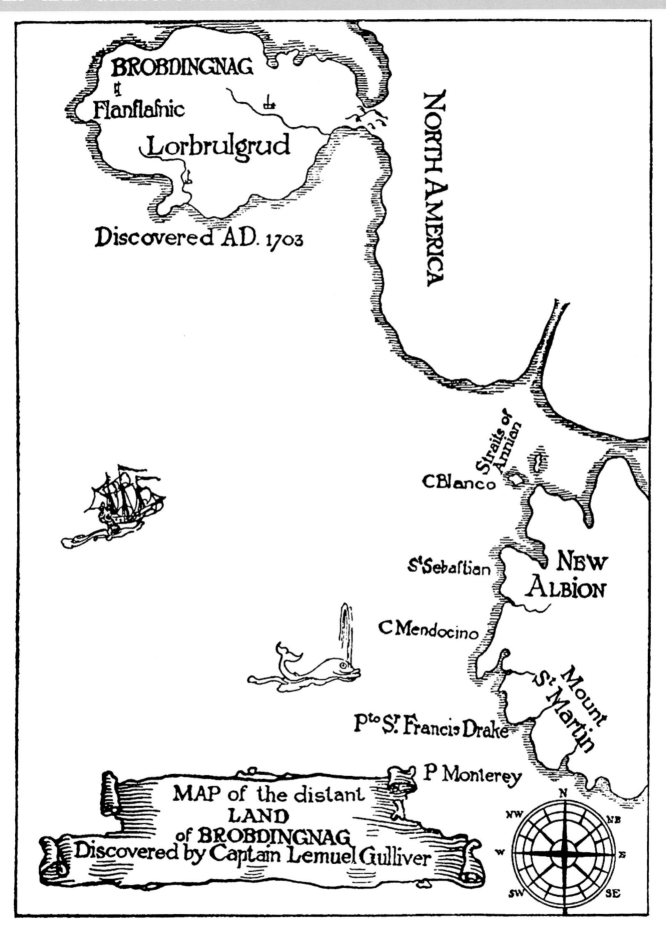

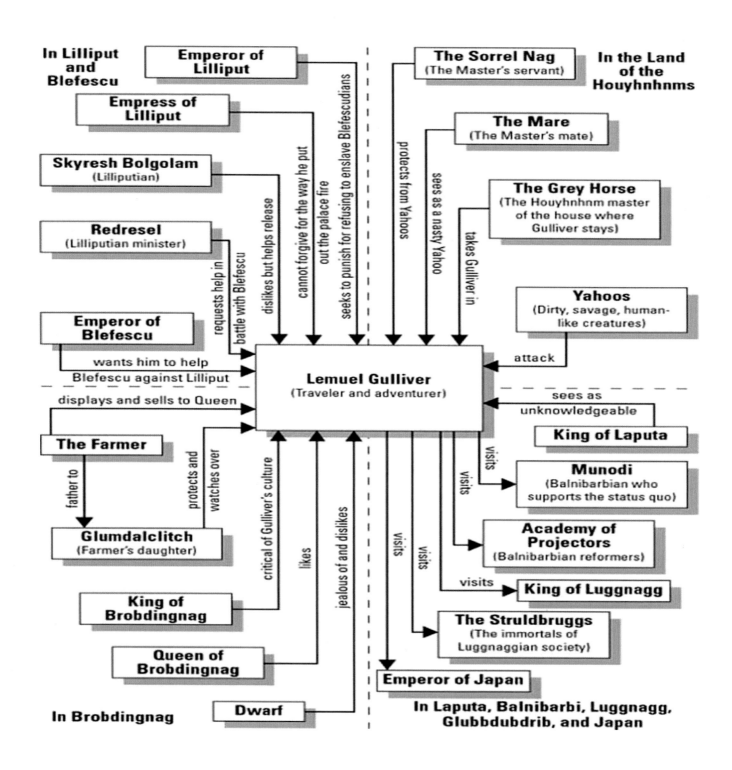

In Lilliput and Blefescu

Emperor of Lilliput

Empress of Lilliput

Skyresh Bolgolam (Lilliputian)

Redresel (Lilliputian minister)

Emperor of Blefescu

requests help in battle with Blefescu

dislikes but helps release

cannot forgive for the way he put out the palace fire

seeks to punish for refusing to enslave Blefescudians

wants him to help Blefescu against Lilliput

displays and sells to Queen

The Farmer

father to

protects and watches over

Glumdalclitch (Farmer's daughter)

critical of Gulliver's culture

King of Brobdingnag

likes

Queen of Brobdingnag

Dwarf

jealous of and dislikes

In Brobdingnag

Lemuel Gulliver (Traveler and adventurer)

The Sorrel Nag (The Master's servant)

The Mare (The Master's mate)

The Grey Horse (The Houyhnhnm master of the house where Gulliver stays)

protects from Yahoos

sees as a nasty Yahoo

takes Gulliver in

In the Land of the Houyhnhnms

Yahoos (Dirty, savage, human-like creatures)

attack

sees as unknowledgeable

King of Laputa

visits

Munodi (Balnibarbian who supports the status quo)

visits

Academy of Projectors (Balnibarbian reformers)

visits

King of Luggnagg

The Struldbruggs (The immortals of Luggnaggian society)

visits

visits

Emperor of Japan

In Laputa, Balnibarbi, Luggnagg, Glubbdubdrib, and Japan

The values and virtues of the month are
JUSTICE and SERVICE.

Weave these traits into your novel studies, other subject areas you are studying, and opportunities to show JUSTICE and SERVICE in your daily life.

SERVANT LEADERSHIP CHARACTERISTICS

Robert K. Greenleaf
1977

Listening More
Showing Empathy
Healing not Dividing
Awareness of others
Persuade don't Dictate
Conceptualization of your plan
Foresight with Vision
Stewardship and Ownership
Committed to Growth of People
Building Community.

NATIONAL HONORS SOCIETY AS A STUDENT WHO:

- Is willing to uphold scholarship and maintain a loyal school attitude.
- Participates in some outside activity: 4 H; volunteer for the aged, poor, or disadvantaged; family duties.
- Volunteers is dependable and well-organized assistance; is gladly available.
- Works well with others and is willing to take on difficult tasks.
- Cheerfully and enthusiastically renders any requested service to the school.
- Is willing to represent the class or school in inter-class and inter-scholastic competition.
- Does committee and staff work like student council.
- Shows courtesy by assisting visitors, teachers, and students.

ROTARY
SERVICE Above Self

1. Is it the TRUTH?
2. Is it FAIR to all?
3. Will it build GOODWILL and BETTER FRIENDSHIPS?
4. Will it be BENEFICIAL to all?

JUSTICE THROUGH TIME AS TOLD BY PHILOSOPHERS

Plato, justice is a virtue establishing rational order (The Republic).
Aristotle says justice refers to what is lawful and fair. Equitable distribution.
Augustine, the cardinal virtue of justice requires that we try to give all people their due.
Aquinas, justice is that rational mean between equal distributions and even transactions.
Hobbes believed justice is an artificial virtue, necessary for civil society, important for a social contract.
Hume, justice essentially serves public utility by protecting property and individuals against the state.
Kant, argues justice is the virtue where we respect others' freedom, individuality, and dignity by not interfering with their voluntary actions, so long as those do not violate others' rights.
Mill said justice is a name for the most important social goal of protecting human liberty.

JUSTICE IS THE VIRTUE THAT PERFECTS THE WILL.

Justice = Common good of society
Justice = Fair laws for all citizens
Justice = Citizens follow laws passed
Justice = Respect contracts between individuals
Justice = Our role as citizens to the Government
Justice = The Governments role towards citizens
Justice = The right to plead your case in court
Justice = Fair consequences for breaking a rule/law
Justice = Clear consequences for breaking the law
Justice = Everyone treated the same by the state
Justice = Leaders act fairly to the people
Justice = State honoring citizens Bill of Rights

The values and virtues of the month are
MODERATION and GENEROSITY.

Weave these traits into your novel studies, other subject areas you are studying, and opportunities to show MODERATION and GENEROSITY in your daily life.

MODERATION – ALSO KNOWN AS (AKA):

Self-restraint, "taking the middle road", temperance, harmony.

Plato, in "The Republic", described moderation as the harmony between reason, spirit, and desire.

Gluttons, fanatics, and the weak willed self-destruct by refusing to make the tradeoffs necessary to lead a good life.

Weigh tradeoffs mindfully.

Unruly thoughts, attractions of the senses, desires, anger, covetousness, and avarice constantly arise in the mind of the person who has no mental discipline; and these impel him to do evil deeds.

Moderation in all things, finding the mean, or middle ground, between excess and lack.

When King Midas was granted his wish that everything he touched turned to gold, he got what he wished for, including turning his own daughter into gold.

If you don't make your own tradeoffs, they will be made for you by nature, by chance, or by other people.

Be aware of your moderation triggers, like advertising, celebrities, undealt with feelings.

No food, one problem. Too much food, many problems. We are a society of too much 'food'.

MODERATION HISTORY

In ancient Greece moderation was a very important value. At the Temple of Apollo at Delphi there are two phrases, one of them very famous and the other completely forgotten. "Gnóthi seautón", which means "know yourself" and "Medèn ágan", which is "nothing in excess". Even 2500+ years ago, society aimed at the moderation of the senses, actions and words..

WAYS TO PRACTICE GENEROSITY

- Give some words of encouragement.
- Spend some time with the elderly.
- Say "yes" when someone asks for help.
- Tell someone they made a difference in your life.
- Be willing to help complete strangers.
- Give freely without expecting anything in return.
- Even small acts count.
- Donate your books.
- Donate 5-10% of your income.
- Pick up garbage.
- Pay the animal shelter a visit.
- Carry someone's bags.
- Give up your seat.
- Participate in a cleanup day.
- Become someone's mentor.
- Offer your services for free.

WHAT DOES GENEROSITY LOOK LIKE IN ACTION?

- When we give generously of our time, our attention, our energy, our work, our skills and talents, our knowledge, our experience, our physical space, and our emotional involvement.
- When we give a compliment, a kind word, a smile, a pat on the back.
- When we give credit, we give recognition, we give validation.
- When we give the benefit of the doubt, and are quick to acknowledge the good in those who falter. We give reassurance.

Generosity is the virtue that can go on mirroring itself until the end of time.

TIPS ON WHAT GENEROSITY IS

Tip 1 – Share or give something that has meaning for you

Tip 2 – Do not expect anything in return: you do not want any attention or a reward for giving

Tip 3 – Don't enquire how your gift is used

Tip 4 – Live with the belief that there is more than enough for everyone

Tip 5 – Take the opportunity to give something

Tip 6 – It's just nice to give something

Tip 7 – Give with all your heart: don't hold back

Tip 8 – Call upon your ability to be considerate and considerate

RECITATION – 12TH GRADE

Still I Rise
Maya Angelou

★ **About The Poet**

Maya Angelou (1928 –2014) was an American poet, memoir[...]
activist. She published seven autobiographies, three books o[...]
books of poetry, and is credited with a list of plays, movies, a[...]
spanning over 50 years. She received dozens of awards and [...]
honorary degrees.

★ **About the Poem**

The poem takes the reader through a series of statements the[...]
herself. Angelou praises, her body, and her ability to rise up a[...]
personal and historical past.. She is going to "rise" above and[...]
that seeks to control her.

12-8

ETHOS ⊤ LOGO[S]

Recitation Pairing

Still I Rise
MAYA ANGELOU

You may write me down in history
With your bitter, twisted lies,
You may trod me in the very dirt
But still, like dust, I'll rise.

Does my sassiness upset you?
Why are you beset with gloom?
Cause I walk like I've got oil wells
Pumping in my living room.

Just like suns and like moons,
With the certainty of tides,
Just like hopes springing high,
Still I'll rise.

Did you want to see me broken?
Bowed head and lowered eyes?
Shoulders falling down like teardrops,
Weakened by my soulful cries?

Does my haughtiness offend you?
Don't you take it awful hard
Cause I laugh like I've got gold mines
Diggin' in my own back yard.

You may shoot me with your words,
You may cut me with your eyes,
You may kill me with your hatefulness,
But still, like air, I'll rise.

Does my sexiness upset you?
Does it come as a surprise
That I dance like I've got diamonds
At the meeting of my thighs?

Out of the huts of history's shame I rise
Up from a past that's rooted in pain I rise
I'm a black ocean, leaping and wide,
Welling and swelling I bear in the tide.

Leaving behind nights of terror and fear I rise
Into a daybreak that's wondrously clear
I rise
Bringing the gifts that my ancestors gave,
I am the dream and the hope of the slave.
I rise
I rise
I rise.

★ **ETHOS LOGOS VALUE/VIRTUE OF THE MONTH** ★
Moderation - Generosity

RECITATION – 12TH GRADE

What Has Meaning
David Foster Wallace

★ About The Poet
David Foster Wallace was an American author of novels, short
and a university professor of English and creative writing. Wal
for his 1996 novel Infinite Jest, which Time magazine cited as
English-language novels from 1923 to 2005.

★ About the Poem
This apple poem for early readers, makes a great first poem. T
repetition in the sentence structure, which will support them a
about concepts of print.

12-7 ETHOS ⬚ LOGO

Recitation Pairing

What Has Meaning
BY DAVID FOSTER WALLACE
2005 COMMENCEMENT SPEECH
KENYON COLLEGE

Because here's something else that's weird but true: in the day-to day trenches of adult life, there is actually no such thing as atheism. There is no such thing as not worshipping. Everybody worships. The only choice we get is what to worship. And the compelling reason for maybe choosing some sort of god or spiritual-type thing to worship -- be it JC or Allah, be it YHWH or the Wiccan Mother Goddess, or the Four Noble Truths, or some inviolable set of ethical principles – is that pretty much anything else you worship will eat you alive.

If you worship money and things, if they are where you tap real meaning in life, then you will never have enough, never feel you have enough. It's the truth.

Worship your body and beauty and sexual allure and you will always feel ugly. And when time and age start showing, you will die a million deaths before they finally grieve you. On one level, we all know this stuff already. It's been codified as myths, proverbs, clichés, epigrams, parables; the skeleton of every great story.

The whole trick is keeping the truth up front in daily consciousness.

Worship power, you will end up feeling weak and afraid, and you will need ever more power over others to numb you to your own fear.

Worship your intellect, being seen as smart, you will end up feeling stupid, a fraud, always on the verge of being found out.

But the insidious thing about these forms of worship is not that they're evil or sinful, it's that they're unconscious. They are default settings. They're the kind of worship you just gradually slip into, day after day, getting more and more selective about what you see and how you measure value without ever being fully aware that that's what you're doing.

And the so-called real world will not discourage you from operating on your default settings, because the so-called real world of men and money and power hums merrily along in a pool of fear and anger and frustration and craving and worship of self. Our own present culture has harnessed these forces in ways that have yielded extraordinary wealth and comfort and personal freedom. The freedom all to be lords of our tiny skull-sized kingdoms, alone at the center of all creation.

★ ETHOS LOGOS VALUE/VIRTUE OF THE MONTH ★
Justice - Service

Historical Pairing

MODERN– 4th, 8th, 12th

1941-1945 WORLD WAR II
America enters – Pacific theater
Hiroshima – Marshall Plan

People:
• Hitler • Churchill • Neville Chamberlain • Hirohito • Stalin • Mu

Events:
• Germany invades Poland • Battle of Britain • Russia

Terms:
• Appeasement • Fascism • German Nationalism • Arian Nation
• Nazi • SS Troopers

Holocaust:
• How It Started
• Life in the Camps
• Liberation
• Story of Survivors

Aftermath:
• Yalta Conference
• League of Nations

MONTH 7 4:8:12 ETHOS LOGOS

MODERN– 4th, 8th, 12th

THE AFTERMATH
OF WORLD WAR II
Hiroshima
Marshall Plan

Aftermath Globally:
• United Nations
• Marshall Plan builds Japan into economic power
• Iron Curtain
• Containment – US Policy

★ Extra: What was the cause and effect of the Marshall Plan?

ETHOS LOGO

MODERN– 4th, 8th, 12th

1941-1945
WORLD WAR II
America enters – Pacific theater
Hiroshima – Marshall Plan

Eisenhower • Churchill • Gen Patton • MacArthur

Harbor • D Day

Midway • Okinawa • Naval – Destroyers - Carriers
Atomic Bomb • Kamikaze Pilots

Industrial mobilization • War Bonds • Enlisted Men
er 9066 – Internments • Newsreels from the front

drop the bomb at Hiroshima?

ETHOS LOGOS

MODERN– 4th, 8th, 12th

1945-1961 – COLD WAR
Baby Boom, Suburbs, Automobiles,
Korean War Civil Rights Movement
The Cold War, Eisenhower

Post War America:
• GI Bill
• Baby Boom • Suburbs
• Superpower
• Interstate System
• Military Industrial Complex
• Middle Class • The Television!

★ Extra: How did the Baby Boom generation impact the 1950's, 60's 70's 80's and today?

★ Extra: Describe life (e.g., transportation, communication, technology, medical, entertainment, growth of suburbs) in the U.S. during the Post War Boom.

MONTH 8 4:8:12 ETHOS LOGOS

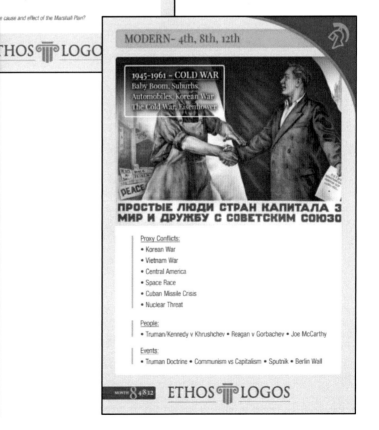

MODERN– 4th, 8th, 12th

1945-1961 – COLD WAR
Baby Boom, Suburbs,
Automobiles, Korean War
The Cold War, Eisenhower

ПРОСТЫЕ ЛЮДИ СТРАН КАПИТАЛА З
МИР И ДРУЖБУ С СОВЕТСКИМ СОЮЗО

Proxy Conflicts:
• Korean War
• Vietnam War
• Central America
• Space Race
• Cuban Missile Crisis
• Nuclear Threat

People:
• Truman/Kennedy v Khrushchev • Reagan v Gorbachev • Joe McCarthy

Events:
• Truman Doctrine • Communism vs Capitalism • Sputnik • Berlin Wall

MONTH 8 4:8:12 ETHOS LOGOS

Artists and Musicians Pairing

GREAT ARTISTS IN HISTORY

Henri Matisse
Beginning Avante Garde
1869-1945

"When I put down a green, it doesn't mean grass; and when I put down a blue, it doesn't mean the sky."
- Matisse

★ Matisse had a friendship, that was rocky, with Pablo Picasso. The mutual respect that they developed for each other would move both artists to great things. How were their works similar? Different?

★ Matisse was close with Cezanne. How were there works similar? Different?

★ Think about the journey from Rembrandt and Caravaggio to Matisse. Art changes and is influenced by technology (photographs), culture, society tastes, world events, wealth. Explain.

12 – 6 -10

ETHOS LOGOS

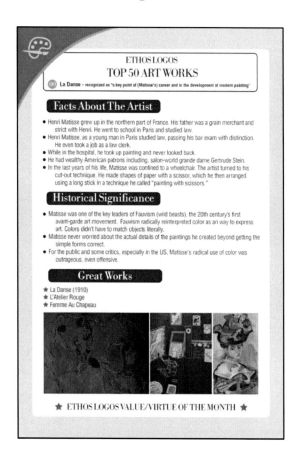

ETHOS LOGOS
TOP 50 ART WORKS

La Danse - recognized as "a key point of (Matisse's) career and in the development of modern painting"

Facts About The Artist

• Henri Matisse grew up in the northern part of France. His father was a grain merchant and strict with Henri. He went to school in Paris and studied law.
• Henri Matisse, as a young man in Paris studied law, passing his bar exam with distinction. He even took a job as a law clerk.
• While in the hospital, he took up painting and never looked back.
• He had wealthy American patrons including, salon-world grande dame Gertrude Stein.
• In the last years of his life, Matisse was confined to a wheelchair. The artist turned to his cut-out technique. He made shapes of paper with a scissor, which he then arranged using a long stick in a technique he called "painting with scissors."

Historical Significance

• Matisse was one of the key leaders of Fauvism (wild beasts), the 20th century's first avant-garde art movement. Fauvism radically reinterpreted color as an way to express art. Colors didn't have to match objects literally.
• Matisse never worried about the actual details of the paintings he created beyond getting the simple forms correct.
• For the public and some critics, especially in the US, Matisse's radical use of color was outrageous, even offensive.

Great Works

★ La Danse (1910)
★ L'Atelier Rouge
★ Femme Au Chapeau

★ ETHOS LOGOS VALUE/VIRTUE OF THE MONTH ★

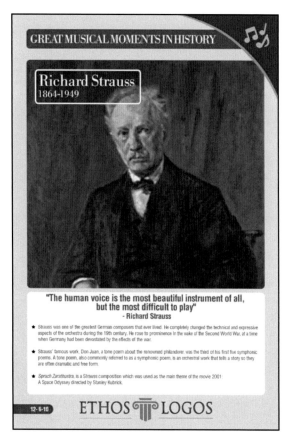

GREAT MUSICAL MOMENTS IN HISTORY

Richard Strauss
1864-1949

"The human voice is the most beautiful instrument of all, but the most difficult to play"
- Richard Strauss

★ Strauss was one of the greatest German composers that ever lived. He completely changed the technical and expressive aspects of the orchestra during the 19th century. He rose to prominence in the wake of the Second World War, at a time when Germany had been devastated by the effects of the war.

★ Strauss' famous work, Don Juan, a tone poem about the renowned philanderer, was the third of his first five symphonic poems. A tone poem, also commonly referred to as a symphonic poem, is an orchestral work that tells a story so they are often dramatic and free form.

★ Sprach Zerathustra, is a Strauss composition which was used as the main theme of the movie 2001: A Space Odyssey directed by Stanley Kubrick.

12 – 6 -10

ETHOS LOGOS

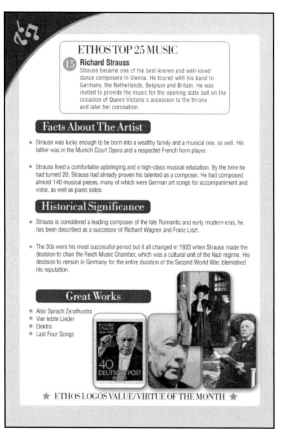

ETHOS TOP 25 MUSIC

15 Richard Strauss
Strauss became one of the best-known and well-loved dance composers in Vienna. He toured with his band to Germany, the Netherlands, Belgium and Britain. He was invited to provide the music for the opening state ball on the occasion of Queen Victoria's accession to the throne, and later her coronation.

Facts About The Artist

• Strauss was lucky enough to be born into a wealthy family and a musical one, as well. His father was in the Munich Court Opera and a respected French horn player.

• Strauss lived a comfortable upbringing and a high-class musical education. By the time he had turned 20, Strauss had already proven his talented as a composer. He had composed almost 140 musical pieces, many of which were German art songs for accompaniment and voice, as well as piano solos.

Historical Significance

• Strauss is considered a leading composer of the late Romantic and early modern eras, he has been described as a successor of Richard Wagner and Franz Liszt.

• The 30s were his most successful period but it all changed in 1933 when Strauss made the decision to chair the Reich Music Chamber, which was a cultural unit of the Nazi regime. His decision to remain in Germany for the entire duration of the Second World War, blemished his reputation.

Great Works

★ Also Sprach Zerathustra
★ Vier letzte Lieder
★ Elektra
★ Last Four Songs

★ ETHOS LOGOS VALUE/VIRTUE OF THE MONTH ★

ENGLISH – 10TH

Don Quixote

Time and Place
Why is Don Quixote by Miguel de Cervantes considered the first modern novel?

Don Quixote, was a Spanish novel written in 1605, the story has a message that individuals can be correct while society is wrong was considered radical for its day. Can you think of examples of this in modern society? Is the plot still relevant today?

About The Author
★ Many authors over the centuries have talked about life being no more than a dream. What do you think they mean? Why would they say something like this?

★ Sancho cannot read, and yet the people think that he is as wise as Solomon. What do you think? What do you think the author might be trying to tell us?

★ The author has used Sancho, who seems stupid at first, to make some criticisms of the Spanish government at that time. What are some of his complaints? Are there any problems like these in our country or in other countries today?

10 - 5

ETHOS LOGOS

Unit #: 9,10 (April, May)

Novel: Don Quixote

Grade Levels: 12ᵗʰ

History:

1961-1973
TURBULENT 1960'S Kennedy, Space Race, Vietnam War, Woodstock, Civil Rights

1973 -To 9/11
AGE of TERRORISM - 1970's, Watergate, terrorism Iran Hostage Crisis, Reagan 9/11

Artists - Musician:
Strauss - Matisse

Value/Virtue:
Integrity - Loyalty
Courage - Trust

Governance:
Republic
Democracy

Religion:
Christianity

Cultural Saying Unit 9
- Cat got your tongue?
- Put a bug in his ear,
- Land of Milk & Honey

Cultural Saying Unit 10
- Cry crocodile tears
- Raining cats and dogs
- Call Me Ishmael

Don Quixote– Pre-Read

Don Quixote was published in two parts in 1605 and 1615. The book took the world by storm and has now been translated into more than 145 languages. But, before it was the best-selling novel of all time, it was just a book by a man named Cervantes.

How can we describe the importance of the author Miguel de Cervantes in Spanish culture?

Don Quixote chose a squire, a "steed" or "charger," and a "lady love," like every good knight should have. But his was really a farmer, a broken-down old horse, and a simple farm girl. Why did Cervantes make these things so silly-looking?

Don Quixote– Chapter Questions

Comprehension Questions:

Chapter One:
1. Where is Don Quixote from? What is his real name? Describe his life, financial situation, and social class.
2. What has Don Quixote been reading? What effect do the things he reads have on him?
3. What does Don Quixote decide to do? How does he prepare himself? Who or what is Rocinante?
4. Who is Dulcinea del Toboso? Why does Don Quixote need to choose her? What is her real name?

Chapter Two:
1. Why does Don Quixote blame himself for waiting so long to ride out? Is this reality or illusion?
2. What is the first place Don Quixote stops, and who are the people he encounters there? How do they treat him?

Chapter Three:
1. Whom does Don Quixote ask to dub him a knight? (The ceremony in which someone becomes a knight involves a light tap on the shoulder with a sword, and this is referred to as "dubbing" someone a knight.) Why does the person he asks agree to such an inappropriate request? What good advice does he give Don Quixote? (Why do you think he does this?)
2. Knights in romances stayed up all night before the ceremony in which they were made knights to watch over or "keep vigil" over their armor in the chapel of the castle. What does Don Quixote substitute for a chapel and an altar, and what happens during the night?

Additional Questions:
1. In chapter 1, from whose point of view is the story told: the narrator's or Don Quixote's? Is the point of view ever confusing? Give examples of places where the point of view seems to shift. What is the effect of this shift in terms of the question of truth vs. fiction?
2. Relate the shifts in point of view in chapter 1 to the use of the narrator's friend in the prologue and to Don Quixote's encounters at the inn in terms of the question of truth vs. fiction and reality vs. illusion.

Essay Question: Using specific evidence from chapters 1-3, write a short essay defending, challenging, or qualifying this statement: **Don Quixote successfully creates or shapes a reality to fit his illusions.**

https://humanities.wisc.edu/

Don Quixote– Chapter Questions

Questions about the presence of part I of *Don Quixote*
in part II, and about the relationship between
Avellaneda's second part and Cervantes' second part

Part II, prologue

1. In 1614, while Cervantes was fairly close to finishing the second part of *Don Quixote*, another second part appeared under the pseudonym of Avellaneda. How does Cervantes respond to Avellaneda in the prologue?
2. What happens in the two stories about a madman and a dog? And what analogy is there between each of these two stories and the fact that Avellaneda wrote a continuation of *Don Quixote*?

Part II, chapter 1

1. Read just the first sentence of this chapter. Who is the fictional author of the second part of *Don Quixote*? How much time has passed in the lives of the characters between the end of the first part (when Don Quixote returned home) and the beginning of the second part?
2. Historically speaking, how many years separate the publication of the first part and the second part of Cervantes' *Don Quixote*?

Part II, chapter 2

1. According to Sancho, what do people in the village say about Don Quixote, and how does Don Quixote respond to this?
2. 2. What's the big news that Sancho tells Don Quixote? What book is he talking about, and who has written it?
3. How would you feel if you suddenly found out that, without your knowing it, an enormously popular movie appeared around everything you'd recently been doing, saying, thinking – about things that happened even when you were alone? What would you ask someone who had seen the movie?

Part II, chapter 3

1. Why is it hard for Don Quixote to believe that there's a book about him? What doesn't he like about the fact that it was written by a Moor?
2. According to Sansón Carrasco, what's the difference between a poet (i.e., a fiction writer) and a historian? Which of these two is Cide Hamete? [And which of the two is Cervantes?]. Did Sansón read the book as truth (history) or fiction (novel)?
3. What do readers say about this book? What sorts of people read it?

Part II, chapter 4

1. Has the author promised a second part? What problem is there in writing one?
2. What does Sancho want to do now that he knows that the author wants to write a second part?
3. What does Don Quixote decide to do when he hears Rocinante's neighing?

Part II, chapter 72

1. How does Don Quixote know who Álvaro Tarfe is when he hears his name?
2. Can there be two Don Quixotes and two Sanchos? If so, can one of these Don Quixotes or Sanchos be more real or authentic than the other?
3. What does Don Quixote ask Álvaro to do? And what good will that do? What sensations does Álvaro have after all this?

Part II, chapter 74, last page or so

1. What does Cide Hamete do with his pen, and why?
2. What relationship is there between the pen and Don Quixote?

https://humanities.wisc.edu/

Don Quixote– Essay or Socratic Discussion

Questions to think about and prepare for discussion, related to the 'Curioso Impertinente'

1. What happens when fictional characters read a novel while we read it? Consider the question of placing a fiction within a fiction, and these confusing levels of being.
2. How does the narrator tell his story, and what attitudes does he show the readers? Otherwise put, is this narrator the mouthpiece of the author Cervantes, or something quite different?
3. How does the interruption of Don Quixote's battle with the wine skins affect the reading of the novella? What is the influence of the acts Don Quixote performs in his sleep, and what happens while he sleeps in the inn?
4. What types of relationships are depicted in this novella? how do they evolve, how do they conflict, and how are they differently valued by the characters?
5. How do each of the three main characters (Anselmo, Lotario, Camila) experience what happens?
6. Why does the enigmatic Anselmo act the way he does, from beginning to end?
7. How do men speak about women and marriage, as opposed to how these are actually shown in the novella?
8. Cervantes' treatment of "adultery" and the "adulteress" in this novella, what do we see? What do we make of Camila's emergence as protagonist, and her talents as improviser?
9. Who's to blame? Is there no fault, shared fault, weighted fault?
10. How does **domestic** space effect the unfolding of the story: a plot that essentially takes place in one house (and in Renaissance Florence, no less!)?
11. What are we to make of aristocrats and their servants: how Leonela messes things up, or does she?
12. Who are the voyeurs in this story: (1) Anselmo, (2) the reader and listeners in the inn, (3) us?

https://humanities.wisc.edu/

Don Quixote– Chapter Questions

Don Quixote chapter 4 Journal Entries: In your journal, answer numbers 1, 2, 3, and 4.
Please do this question before reading chapter 4.

1. There is an expression, dating probably from the 16th Century, but still in common use, that claims that "the road to Hell is paved with good intentions." What do you think this phrase means? Can you think of examples from your own life or from current events to illustrate it?

2. After reading chapter 4, go back to your journal entry and add your reflections on how that phrase applies to Don Quixote's actions concerning the slave boy and his master.

3. What is ironic about the situation with the slave boy and his master? Why do you think the situation occurs in the way that it does?

4. There is also a second incident in chapter 4. Compare the two incidents. In what ways are they similar? In what ways do they differ? What light do they shed on Don Quixote's perception of reality versus other people's perceptions of reality? Try to distill the problem down to a single phrase: in what way can you explain the essential problem in these two incidents? (Don't be simplistic and say, "it's because Don Quixote is crazy." Instead, try to come up with a statement of the problem that shows insight and thought.)

5. On page 37, when Don Quixote is explaining that it is possible for the owner of the slave boy to be both a wealthy farmer and a noble knight, he says, ". . . each man is the child of his deeds." What do you think that phrase means? How does it relate to Don Quixote's particular choices in life? Do you think it is true? Under what circumstances might it be untrue?

6. Don Quixote is trying to force the merchants to praise the beauty of Dulcinea without seeing a picture of her. He says, "The significance lies in not seeing her and believing, confessing, affirming, swearing, and defending that truth. . . . ." What does he mean? How does this phrase relate to Don Quixote's choices in life? Who is in the right here: the merchants, who want proof of Dulcinea's beauty, or Don Quixote, who asks for their belief without proof? In what areas might this statement apply to your life? Are there instances in which you are willing to accept "truth" without proof and to defend that truth? How are the instances in your life similar to Don Quixote's perspective on life? Is he any less "realistic" than you are?

7. In the incident with the merchants, Don Quixote exhibits strong emotions—as does the muledriver. Explain the reasons that each reacts as he does. Taking into account their unique points of view and using quotations from the chapter, explain their actions and attitudes. Why does Don Quixote respond to the situation as he does? Why do the merchants and muledriver feel and act as they do? What is their perspective? Where does your sympathy lie? Why?

https://humanities.wisc.edu

Don Quixote– Chapter Questions

Don Quixote by Miguel de Cervantes

Directions: Read the following excerpt from *Don Quixote* and answer the questions that follow.

Although the age of chivalry had long passed, stories about knights-errant were still popular in the early 1600s. The heroes of these stories were brave knights who traveled far and wide performing noble deeds. Miguel de Cervantes's novel Don Quixote satirizes such romances. His hero, the elderly Don Quixote, has read too many tales of chivalry. Imagining himself a knight-errant, he sets out across the Spanish countryside with his practical servant, Sancho Panza. In this famous excerpt, Don Quixote's noble motives give dignity to his foolish battle with the windmills.

Just then they came in sight of thirty or forty windmills that rise form that plain, and no sooner did Don Quixote see them than he said to his squire: "Fortune is guiding our affairs better than we ourselves could have wished. Do you see over yonder, friend Sancho, thirty or forty hulking giants? I intend to do battle with them and slay them. With the spoils we shall begin to be rich, for this is a righteous war. . . "

"What giants?" asked Sancho Panza.

"Those you see over there," replied his master, "with the long arms; some of them have well-nigh [nearly] two leagues in length."

"Take care, sir," cried Sancho. "Those over there are not giants but windmills, and those things that seem to be armed are their sails, which when they are whirled around by the wind turn the millstone."

"It is clear," replied Don Quixote, "that you are not experienced in adventures. Those are giants, and if you are afraid, turn aside and pray whilst I enter into fierce and unequal battle with them."

Uttering these words, he clapped spurs to Rozinate, his steed, without heeding the cries of his squire, Sancho, who warned him that he was not going to attack giants, but windmills. But so convinced was he that they were giants that he neither heard his squire's shouts nor did he notice what they were, though he was very near them. Instead, he rushed on, shouting in a loud voice: "Fly not, cowards and vile caitliffs [cowardly person]; one knight alone attacks you!" At that moment a slight breeze arose and the great sails began to move. . .

He ran his lance into the sail, but the wind twisted it with such violence that it shivered the lance in pieces and dragged both rider and horse after it, rolling them over and over on the ground, sorely damaged.

Questions:
What values of chivalry motivated Don Quixote's attack on the windmills?
1. How does Cervantes show the noble side of Don Quixote in this excerpt
2. How does Cervantes show the foolish side of Don Quixote in this excerpt?
3. The phrase "tilting at windmills" literally means "jousting at windmills," like Don Quixote did. Figuratively, this phrase means foolishly attacking imaginary or perceived enemies. It was inspired from this story. Underline in the excerpt where you think this phrase came from.
4. A word in English has been adapted from Don Quixote's name. "*Quixotic*" means idealistic, romantic, or impractical. Based on what you know about Don Quixote, where do you think this word's meaning came from?

https://humanities.wisc.edu/

Don Quixote

1. What causes Don Quixote's delusion about becoming a knight?
2. How does Don Quixote's appearance parody that of a knight in a medieval romance?
3. How does Don Quixote's horse contrast with the horse of a real medieval knight?
4. Why does Don Quixote change his name and that of his horse?
5. What element of chivalric romance does Cervante's parody with the character of Dulcinea del Toboso?
6. Why does Sancho Panza agree to accompany Don Quixote?
7. What aspect of medieval romance does the scene with the windmills parody?
8. What does the reader learn about Don Quixote's character from the passage in Ch. VII of *Don Quixote*
9. Which of the following most accurately describes the contrast between Don Quixote's and Sancho Panza's view of the windmills in Chapter VIII of *Don Quixote?*
10. How would you compare Don Quixote's thirst for adventure to the theme of *Don Quixote?*
11. What was the Spanish Inquisition about, and what effects did it have on the people? How is the literary work Don Quixote affected by events of the Spanish Inquisition? Who was Miguel de Cervantes and what inspired him to write Don Quixote?

Why Do We Admire Dreamers?

Think of people you know or have heard of who have pursued their dreams even when the dreams seemed foolish or impossible to achieve. Which of their qualities do you admire the most? In these two selections, you will meet a character whose devotion to an impossible dream has inspired countless readers.

With a small group, generate a list of people who have been considered dreamers—Mahatma Gandhi, for example. Then discuss these questions: What traits do these individuals share? How have their actions affected the way you look at the world?

Different Types of Love

First: drawing from your own experiences in this area, choose one of the following love-related topics and write a journal entry about how you see it:

1. Jealousy: Is jealousy a positive or negative force in a relationship? Explain.
2. Trust: How important is trust in a relationship? What constitutes a violation of trust?
3. What is forgivable and what is not?
4. Opposites attract: Maybe so, but does the relationship last? How important to a successful relationship is it that two people have similar social status and backgrounds?
5. What is true love?
6. Religion: How important is it that two people in a relationship share the same faith?
7. Friends and lovers: Which do you trust more? Which do you confide in? If your friend tells you that your lover has been unfaithful, but your lover denies it, whom do you believe? Why?
8. Do you want to know EVERYTHING about your significant other? Or would you like to preserve some mystery, a fantasy element? Do you want your significant other to know everything about you? Why or why not?
9. Love at first sight: fact or fiction?

Independently, go back to the question you chose for your journal entry (or choose a different question if another one seems more interesting for this part of the assignment) and answer it from the perspective of one or more characters in one of the couples or groups you chose. Use specific examples from the text to support and illustrate the opinions of the character(s) you chose.

Don Quixote– Essay or Socratic

What Does the Novel Mean To You?

In the novel, Don Quixote has a dream that he insists really happened. Have you ever had a dream that was so real, when you woke up you couldn't tell what was real and what was the dream? What was your dream? Have you had that dream more than once?

A theme in the novel is that Don Quixote fails to see things as they really are. What do you think Don Quixote might see instead of reality if he were to visit your life?

Just as Don Quixote is to meet the duchess, he makes a fool of himself. Have you ever made a fool of yourself in front of someone who was important to you? Were you nervous? Frightened? Embarrassed?

What do you think was the most difficult part of being governor for Sancho? What would have been the most difficult part for you, given those times and troubles? What do you think would be the pros and cons of serving as governor of your own state in these current times?

Why do you think that wealthy people wanted to pretend to be poor shepherds in Cervantes' day? What activities do you think they might have had at their picnics? Do people today do anything like this?

Discuss your own experience (like Quixote's) of being influenced to feel--or feeling you ought to feel--a certain way through television or movies.

Essential Questions

1. What role do dreams, and fantasy play in our lives? Is escaping into our dreams or fantasies a good thing?
   How might it be destructive?
   How can it be positive?
   How can immersing ourselves in fantasy lead to physical problems?
2. Why do people seek escape?
3. Are there dangers in immersing ourselves in the coping strategies of the world?

Supporting Questions

1. Why does Alonso Quixano decide to become Don Quixote? Are his reasons similar to others who immerse themselves in dreams and fantasies?
2. How is Alonso's interest in romantic fantasy similar to today's fascination with escaping online? Is this a good thing?
3. To this point many of the protagonists we have studied have been on a journey. How is Don Quixote's journey similar or different them?
4. How does Don Quixote mock books of chivalry and how does it defend them?
5. Discuss the theme appearance vs. reality.

Literary Analysis

WHAT IS SATIRE?

Satire allows the author to argue a point by taking examples to the extremes to show the flaw in what they are mocking.

Don Quixote is a satire of the Romantic Genre. For example, by pointing out the absurdities in the genre of chivalry, Cervantes also points out the silliness of the belief that reading them will cause someone to go mad. No one ever read a about being a knight and decided that was the life for them. Modern satire often takes on the similar task of playing fantasy games does not make someone loose their grip on reality.

Themes and Characters

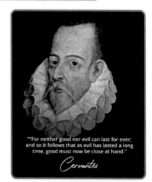

Why do you think that Sancho cares so much for Don Quixote, even though he has suffered because of him? Why do you think that the duke and duchess want to make fun of Sancho and Don Quixote?

Many characters in Don Quixote serve as foils, or opposites, of other characters. What role do these opposed pairs play in developing the novel's themes?

Cervantes explores the complexities of fact and fantasy, truth and lies, justice and injustice. At the heart of Quixote's disagreement with the world around him is the question of truth in chivalry books.

With their "long arms" and tall frames, they work as caricatures of giants. Another possible interpretation is that the windmills represent technology, the destruction of the past, and the loss of knightly values. One of the main themes of the novel is that Don Quixote is a relic.

"For neither good nor evil can last for ever; and so it follows that as evil has lasted a long time, good must now be close at hand."

Cervantes

⭐ **ETHOS LOGOS VALUE/VIRTUE OF THE MONTH** ⭐
Honor and Citizenship

Satire Terms

Satire: the use of humor, irony, exaggeration, or ridicule to expose or criticize people's stupidity or vices
Chivalry: medieval knightly system with it's religious, moral, and social code
Knight Errant: medieval wandering knight in search of chivalrous adventure

Irony: This can mean different things depending on the type. Here are three types of irony.
>   **Dramatic Irony:**
>   **Situational Irony:**
>   **Socratic Irony:**

Parody In Don Quixote

A parody is a comic imitation of another work or of a type of literature. *Don Quixote* and *Man of La Mancha* are parodies of medieval romances, rambling tales of heroic knights and their fearless search for adventure.

Romance heroes were devoted to the ideals of chivalry, the knightly code of honor. Conventions of medieval romance include:

- idealized noble characters
- exaggerated or larger-than-life behavior
- a hero's quest, which is motivated by love, religious faith, or a desire for   adventure
- supernatural or magical elements
- unusual or exotic settings
- incidents involving hidden or mistaken identity

About The Author

- Son of a poor apothecary
- Part of *hidalgo*, noble class
- Spotty education
- Fought with the Spanish-Venetian-Papal fleet
- Cervantes was wounded in battle- left hand maimed for life (1571)
- Lost left hand "for the greater glory of his right hand"
- Captured by Turkish pirates and held in Algiers (1575)
- Known for his daring escapes attempts
- Finally ransomed, depleting his family's wealth (1580)
- Deep debt = begin a literary career!
  - Verse was uninspired
  - Plays were unsuccessful
  - Pastoral romance mundane
- Commissary for the Spanish Armada
- Tax collector
- Applied to go to New World

Miguel de Cervantes was born in 1547 and died in 1616. His first passion was to be an exemplary soldier and was in the Spanish Navy until he was capture by pirates in 1575. He was held captive for five years before being released, where he returned to Madrid and his family. He wrote his first novel, *La Galatea*, in 1585, but it was *Don Quixote* that solidified him as one of the world's best novelists.

Don Quixote– Novel Vocabulary

- **Bewitched**- To place under one's power by or as if by magic; cast a spell over
- **Bravery**- the quality of not being afraid, being able to face danger
- **Chivalry**- the noble qualities of a knight, such as courage, honor, and readiness to help and protect the weak
- **Destiny**- an inevitable outcome that the future will bring
- **Excalibur**- the magic sword of King Arthur
- **Feeble**- physically weak, as from age or sickness; frail
- **Honor**- high regard or great respect given, a keen sense of right and wrong
- **Illusion**- something that deceives by producing a false or misleading impression of reality
- **Joust**- a combat with lances between knights
- **King Arthur**- a legendary king of the Britons; said to have led the Knights of the Round Table at Camelot
- **Knight errant**- a knight traveling in search of adventures in which to exhibit military skill, bravery, and generosity
- **La Mancha**- a plateau region in central Spain: famous as the birthplace of Don Quixote, the hero of Cervantes' novel Don Quixote de la Mancha
- **Peasant**- any person of the class of farmer or farm laborer
- **Quest**- a journey in pursuit of adventure
- **Siesta**- a midday or afternoon rest or nap, esp. as taken in Spain and Latin America
- • **Spain**- A country of southwest Europe comprising most of the Iberian Peninsula and the Balearic and Canary Islands.
- **Squire**- a young man who served a medieval knight as an attendant
- **Steed**- a spirited riding horse
- **Tournaments**- large events at which jousts, and free-for-alls were held
- **Virtue**- general excellence, right action and thinking, goodness

Grade Level Vocabulary

perfidious
precocious
pretentious
procrastinate
prosaic
prosperity
provocative
prudent
querulous
rancorous
reclusive
reconciliation
renovation
Resilient

restrained

Latin Root Words

Alt - high
Ics - art
Iso - equal
Vert - turn
Ate - cause
Cor - heart
Ess - female
Muta - change
Fug - flee
Path - feeling
A - not
Nomy - law
Fid - faith

Recitations Pairing

RECITATION – 12TH GRADE

The Negro Speaks of Rivers
Langston Hughes

★ About The Poet
James Mercer Langston Hughes (1901-1967) was an American poet, activist, novelist, playwright, and columnist from Joplin, Missouri. One earliest innovators of the literary art form called jazz poetry, Hughes is as a leader of the Harlem Renaissance.

★ About the Poem
The poem heavily uses biblical imagery and language to convey its m the connection between African Americans to America and Africa. The mentioned in the poem show an epic journey of African Americans an history has forever connected black Americans to their roots.

12-9

ETHOS LOGOS

The Negro Speaks of Rivers
LANGSTON HUGHES

I've known rivers:
I've known rivers ancient as the world and older than the
flow of human blood in human veins.
My soul has grown deep like the rivers.
I bathed in the Euphrates when dawns were young
I built my hut near the Congo and it lulled me to sleep.
I looked upon the Nile and raised the pyramids above it.
I heard the singing of the Mississippi when Abe Lincoln
went down to New Orleans, and I've seen its muddy
bosom turn all golden in the sunset.
I've known rivers:
Ancient, dusky rivers.
My soul has grown deep like the rivers.

★ ETHOS LOGOS VALUE/VIRTUE OF THE MONTH ★
Integrity - Loyalty

Historical Pairing

MODERN– 4th, 8th, 12th

1961-1973: TURBULENT 1960s
Civil Rights, MLK,
Vietnam War

Events:
- Brown v. Board of Education • Civil Rights Act of 1964
- Martin Luther King Jr.
  Montgomery Bus Boycott
  "I Have A Dream" significance and impact
  Letter From A Birmingham Jail
- The Civil Rights Movement

MODERN– 4th, 8th, 12th

1961-1973: TURBULENT 1960s
Kennedy, Space Race,
Vietnam War, Woodstock

Vietnam War:
- Why? Which Presidents?
- Who Won?

Kennedy to LBJ:

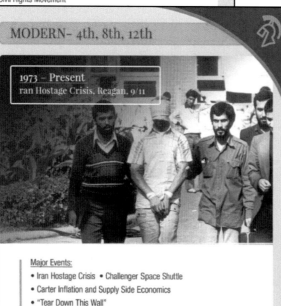

MODERN– 4th, 8th, 12th

1973 – Present
ran Hostage Crisis, Reagan, 9/11

Major Events:
- Iran Hostage Crisis • Challenger Space Shuttle
- Carter Inflation and Supply Side Economics
- "Tear Down This Wall"
- The Microchip and Computer Age and Internet
- Aids Epidemic

Themes:
- It's morning again in America

Patriotism:
- ★ Extra: How did leadership styles differ among Presidents Lyndon Johnson, Jimmy Carter, and Ronald Reagan?
- ★ What did the Reaganomics do? What was the point of Reagan Trickle Down Economics?

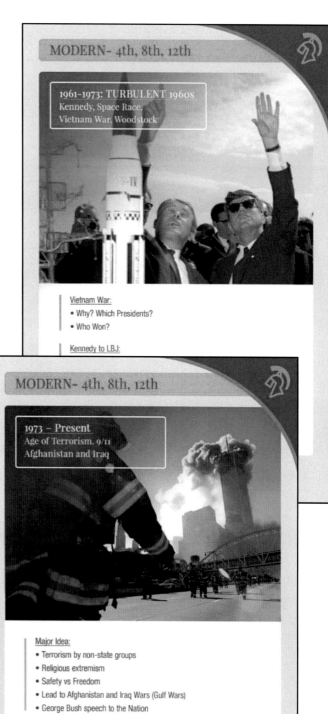

MODERN– 4th, 8th, 12th

1973 – Present
Age of Terrorism, 9/11
Afghanistan and Iraq

Major Idea:
- Terrorism by non-state groups
- Religious extremism
- Safety vs Freedom
- Lead to Afghanistan and Iraq Wars (Gulf Wars)
- George Bush speech to the Nation

★ Extra: What was life like before 9/11? How did it change after 9/11? Do you think the events of 9/11 justified this change? Why or why not?

★ Extra: Why do you think that debate surfaced between advocates of public safety and civil liberties in the months that followed 9/11? What is your position in this debate?

Historical Pairing
Actual Time Period

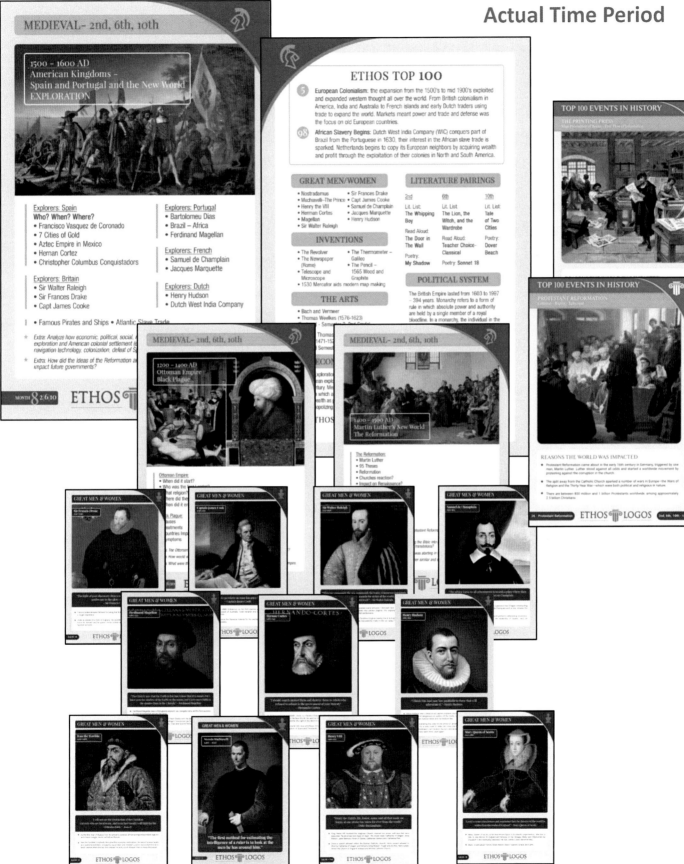

Artists and Musicians Pairing

GREAT ARTISTS IN HISTORY

Henri Matisse
Beginning Avante Garde
1869-1915

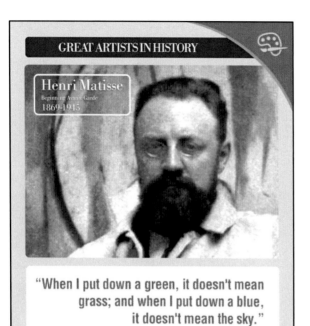

"When I put down a green, it doesn't mean grass; and when I put down a blue, it doesn't mean the sky."
- Matisse

★ Matisse had a friendship, that was rocky, with Pablo Picasso. The mutual respect that they developed for each other would move both artists to great things. How were their works similar? Different?

★ Matisse was close with Cezanne. How were there works similar? Different?

★ Think about the journey from Rembrandt and Caravaggio to Matisse. Art changes and is influenced by technology (photographs), culture, society tastes, world events, wealth. Explain.

12 – 6-10

ETHOS LOGOS
TOP 50 ART WORKS

12 La Danse - recognized as "a key point of (Matisse's) career and in the development of modern painting"

Facts About The Artist

● Henri Matisse grew up in the northern part of France. His father was a grain merchant and strict with Henri. He went to school in Paris and studied law.
● Henri Matisse, as a young man in Paris studied law, passing his bar exam with distinction. He even took a job as a law clerk.
● While in the hospital, he took up painting and never looked back.
● He had wealthy American patrons including, salon-world grande dame Gertrude Stein.
● In the last years of his life, Matisse was confined to a wheelchair. The artist turned to his cut-out technique. He made shapes of paper with a scissor, which he then arranged using a long stick in a technique he called "painting with scissors."

Historical Significance

● Matisse was one of the key leaders of Fauvism (wild beasts), the 20th century's first avant-garde art movement. Fauvism radically reinterpreted color as an way to express art. Colors didn't have to match objects literally.
● Matisse never worried about the actual details of the paintings he created beyond getting the simple forms correct.
● For the public and some critics, especially in the US, Matisse's radical use of color was outrageous, even offensive.

Great Works

★ La Danse (1910)
★ L'Atelier Rouge
★ Femme Au Chapeau

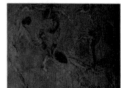

★ ETHOS LOGOS VALUE/VIRTUE OF THE MONTH ★

GREAT MUSICAL MOMENTS IN HISTORY

Richard Strauss
1864-1949

"The human voice is the most beautiful instrument of all, but the most difficult to play"
- Richard Strauss

★ Strauss was one of the greatest German composers that ever lived. He completely changed the technical and expressive aspects of the orchestra during the 19th century. He rose to prominence in the wake of the Second World War, at a time when Germany had been devastated by the effects of the war.

★ Strauss' famous work, Don Juan, a tone poem about the renowned philanderer, was the third of his first five symphonic poems. A tone poem, also commonly referred to as a symphonic poem, is an orchestral work that tells a story so they are often dramatic and free form.

★ Sprach Zarathustra, is a Strauss composition which was used as the main theme of the movie 2001: A Space Odyssey directed by Stanley Kubrick.

12- 6-10

ETHOS [][] LOGOS

ETHOS TOP 25 MUSIC

15 Richard Strauss
Strauss became one of the best-known and well-loved dance composers in Vienna. He toured with his band to Germany, the Netherlands, Belgium and Britain. He was invited to provide the music for the opening state ball on the occasion of Queen Victoria's accession to the throne, and later her coronation.

Facts About The Artist

● Strauss was lucky enough to be born into a wealthy family and a musical one, as well. His father was in the Munich Court Opera and a respected French horn player.

● Strauss lived a comfortable upbringing and a high-class musical education. By the time he had turned 20, Strauss had already proven his talented as a composer. He had composed almost 140 musical pieces, many of which were German art songs for accompaniment and voice, as well as piano solos.

Historical Significance

● Strauss is considered a leading composer of the late Romantic and early modern eras, he has been described as a successor of Richard Wagner and Franz Liszt.

● The 30s were his most successful period but it all changed in 1933 when Strauss made the decision to chair the Reich Music Chamber, which was a cultural unit of the Nazi regime. His decision to remain in Germany for the entire duration of the Second World War, blemished his reputation.

Great Works

★ Also Sprach Zarathustra
★ Vier letzte Lieder
★ Elektra
★ Last Four Songs

★ ETHOS LOGOS VALUE/VIRTUE OF THE MONTH ★

Recitation Pairing

The Builders
LONGFELLOW

All are architects of Fate,
Working in these walls of Time;
Some with massive deeds and great,
Some with ornaments of rhyme.

Nothing useless is, or low;
Each thing in its place is best;
And what seems but idle show
Strengthens and supports the rest.

For the structure that we raise,
Time is with materials filled;
Our to-days and yesterdays
Are the blocks with which we build.

Truly shape and fashion these;
Leave no yawning gaps between;
Think not, because no man sees,
Such things will remain unseen.

In the elder days of Art,
Builders wrought with greatest care
Each minute and unseen part;
For the Gods see everywhere.

Let us do our work as well,
Both the unseen and the seen;
Make the house, where Gods may dwell,
Beautiful, entire, and clean.

Else our lives are incomplete,
Standing in these walls of Time,
Broken stairways, where the feet
Stumble as they seek to climb.

Build to-day, then, strong and sure,
With a firm and ample base;
And ascending and secure
Shall to-morrow find its place.

Thus alone can we attain
To those turrets, where the eye
Sees the world as one vast plain,
And one boundless reach of sky.

★ ETHOS LOGOS VALUE/VIRTUE OF THE MONTH ★
Courage - Trust

MCMCXIX5.211

RECITATION – 12TH GRADE

The Builders
Henry Wadsworth Longfellow

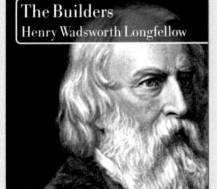

★ About The Poet

★ About the Poem
This poems helps to describes how a nation is built from the contributions of each and every individual of the country. The people from both the past and present collectively work for a nation's advancement.

12-10

ETHOS ⬛ LOGOS

The values and virtues of the month are
INTEGRITY and LOYALTY.

A Proclamation

One of the great treasures of America is the unity of its people. No nation is composed of citizens with such diverse cultural, racial and religious backgrounds as is the United States of America. And while this unique contributions of each segment of our population are important, the significant fact remains that each of us, whatever background, remains loyal to the Nation and to the ideals of freedom for which it stands.

Proclamation 4836— Loyalty Day, 1981

ETHOS LOGOS

Weave these traits into your novel studies, other subject areas you are studying, and opportunities to show INTEGRIY and LOYALTY in your daily life.

"Integrity is doing the right thing even when no one is watching."

- C.S. Lewis

ETHOS LOGOS

WHAT DOES IT MEAN TO BE LOYAL?

Understand what being loyal means-putting someone or something above yourself.
Be willing to sacrifice.
Take time to know who and why you are giving your loyalty.
Decide what or who you are offering your loyalty to is worthy of the investment.
Consider the benefits of loyalty in friendship, to your family to your community.
Weigh the costs of being loyal. How far will you go to be loyal?
Balance your loyalties and prioritize.

QUALITIES OF A LOYAL FRIEND

1. Take a genuine interest in others.
2. Be a giver, not a taker.
3. Be loyal. Be empathetic. Be a good listener.
4. Be a positive person.
5. Appreciate the differences in others.
6. Build on common interests.
7. Be open, honest, and real.
8. Avoid gossip or talking behind friends backs.
9. Make your friendship unconditional.
10. Set healthy boundaries.
11. Celebrate your friends successes.

LOYALTY TO A FRIEND?

"Romans, countrymen, and lovers! Hear me for my cause, and be silent that you may hear. Believe me for mine honor. . . If then that friend demand why Brutus rose against Caesar, this is my answer: not that I loved Caesar less, but that I loved Rome more."

Julius Caesar – Shakespeare

AMERICAN'S CREED

I believe in the United States of America as a government of the people, by the people, for the people; whose just powers are derived from the consent of the governed, a democracy in a republic, a sovereign Nation of many sovereign States; a perfect union, one and inseparable; established upon those principles of freedom, equality, justice, and humanity for which American patriots sacrificed their lives and fortunes.
I therefore believe it is my duty to my country to love it, to support its Constitution, to obey its laws, to respect its flag, and to defend it against all enemies.

INTEGRITY FROM HISTORY

GOOD	BAD
• Aristides (Greek)	• Nero (Rome)
• Marcus Aurelius (Roman)	• Vlad the Impaler (Transylvania)
• Abe Lincoln "Honest Abe"	• Ivan the Terrible (Russia)
• George Washington cutting down the cherry tree	• Robespierre (France)
• Ghandi	• Heinrich Himmler (Germany)
• Martin Luther King Jr.	• Pol Pots (Cambodia)
• Biblical – Abraham, Joseph, David	• Mao Ze Dong (China)
	• Joseph Stalin (Russia)
	• Biblical – King Herod, King Ahab, Judas, Cain

HOW TO LIVE A LIFE OF INTEGRITY

1. Value other people's time.
2. Give credit where it is due.
3. Be authentic.
4. Always be honest.
5. Never take advantage of others.
6. Do not argue over disagreements.
7. Give people the benefit of the doubt.
8. Believe in others.
9. They apologize first.
10. Be kind to those who need it.

READ

Elementary School
• Ruthie and the Not So Teeny Tiny Lie – Ranking
• The Empty Pot – Demi
• The Boy Who Cried Wolf – Giles
• The Lying King – Beard
• Honest Abe – Kunhardt

Middle School
• Lincoln: A Photo biography – Freedman
• Through My Eyes – Bridgest
• Robin Hood – Early
• The Giver – Lowery

WATCH

• Pinocchio
• Willie Wonka and The Chocolate Factory
• It's A Wonderful Life
• Rudy
• 12 Angry Men
• Quiz Show
• Dead Poets Society
• Selma

The values and virtues of the month are
COURAGE and TRUST.

Weave these traits into your novel studies, other subject areas you are studying, and opportunities to show COURAGE and TRUST in your daily life.

WHICH ACTION IS COURAGEOUS AND WHICH IS FOOLISH?

1. Fighting or walking away from a fight?
2. Doing something dangerous that others are doing or not participating even if someone calls you "chicken"?
3. Teasing and bullying someone or standing up for someone who is being mistreated?
4. Blaming others for your mistakes or accepting responsibility?
5. Ignoring a new student or making friends with a new student?
6. Only looking out for yourself or helping others?
7. Following the crowd or doing what's right?
8. Quitting when things get tough or working hard, even when it's difficult?

WHAT IS COURAGE IN ACTION

- The courage to speak up when something doesn't feel or seem right.
- The courage to stand up to their peers when they are mistreating others.
- The courage to stand up for one's beliefs and one's sense of right and wrong.
- The courage to try new things and stick with challenges.
- The courage not to follow the crowd and go along with peer pressure.
- The courage to be a leader with your friends, to be a role model who encourages others build their courage too.
- The courage to tell an adult when something uncomfortable happens.
- The courage to have unique interests, independent thoughts, and to be themselves.

WHAT ARE SOME WAYS YOU CAN SHOW COURAGE?

1. Do the right thing, even if others are not.
2. Bravely deal with your daily challenges.
3. Be willing to try new things, even if you might fail.
4. Tell the truth regardless of the consequences.
5. Face your fears and work to overcome them.
6. Admit your mistakes and learn from them.
7. Do not give into negative peer pressure.

TRUST IN INSTITUTIONS

Why is it important to trust cultural, political, faith based and educational institutions in our society? What happens we we lose that trust?

Research institutional trust and discuss some reasons why some groups have high trust and others low? Is trust in institutions trending up or down?

The Military	Supreme Court	Big Business
Small Business	Medical	Media
Police	Universities	Social Media
Religion	Banks	TV News
President	Science	Congress
	Public Schools	

WHEN A TRUSTING FRIENDSHIP MAY BE BAD FOR YOU:

- The friendship is consistently one-sided
- They make you feel worse, not better
- They bail on you all the time
- They want you to be someone else
- They are overly negative and pessimistic
- You have little or nothing to talk about
- They are passive-aggressive when you say "no" to them
- They dismiss it when you raise a concern
- They betray your trust
- They're a bad influence on you
- They say mean things
- They are always jealous of you
- They don't keep your secrets
- They create or attract drama
- They take advantage of you

HOW TO BE A PERSON TO TRUST

1- Be true to your word and follow through with your actions.
2- Take time to make decisions and think before acting too quickly.
3- Value the relationships that you have—and don't take them for granted.
4- Always be honest.
5- Don't always self-promote.
6- Admit your mistakes.

Trust takes YEARS to build, SECONDS to break and FOREVER to repair.

Text structure refers to the ways that authors organize information in text. Teaching students to recognize the underlying structure of content-area texts can help students focus attention on key concepts and relationships, anticipate what's to come, and monitor their comprehension as they read.

As readers interact with the text to construct meaning, their comprehension is facilitated when they organize their thinking in a manner like that used by the author. Readers who struggle with text comprehension often do so because they fail to recognize the organizational structure of what they are reading, and they are not aware of cues that alert them to text structures (Cochran & Hain).

Fiction texts typically have literary elements such as characters, setting, problem/ solution, and plot. Hearing stories told and read aloud helps children internalize the elements of fiction. When they begin to read, they expect that there will be characters and that some will be more important than others. They also expect a resolution, a satisfying ending.

For 12th grade, below are the following literary skills that you should be mastered by the end of the school year. We encourage you to visit iXL.com for practice exercises on these subject areas. The goal of this year's efforts is to take every opportunity you can find to implement these skills into your novel assignments.

- **Main idea**
  - Determine the main idea of a passage
- **Theme**
  - Match the quotations with their themes
  - Determine the themes of short stories
  - Author's purpose and tone
  - Identify author's purpose
  - Which sentence is more formal?
  - Compare passages for tone
- **Text structure**
  - Compare and contrast in informational texts
  - Match causes and effects in informational texts
  - Match problems with their solutions
  - Identify text structures
- **Literary devices**
  - Identify sensory details
  - Identify the narrative point of view
  - Interpret the meaning of an allusion from its source
  - Recall the source of an allusion
  - Interpret figures of speech
  - Classify figures of speech

- **Analyzing literature**
  - Analyze short stories
  - Vocabulary review: Analyze short stories
  - Label the rhyme scheme
- **Analyzing informational texts**
  - Read and understand informational passages
  - Vocabulary review: Read and understand informational passages
  - Trace an argument
  - Vocabulary review: Trace an argument
- **Comparing texts**
  - Compare information from two texts
  - Compare two texts with different genres
- **Visual elements**
  - Compare illustrations of literary and historical subjects

The Basics

Plot
Setting
Narration/point of view
Characterization
Symbol
Metaphor
Genre
Irony/ambiguity

Other key concepts

Historical context
Social, political, economic contexts
Ideology
Multiple voices
Various critical orientations
Literary theory

Text Structure

1. What type of text is this?
2. How do you know?
3. What text features has the author used to help you understand what you are reading?
4. How do they help you?
5. How do you think the author organized the information?
6. Why do you think the author chose to organize the information in this way?

Literary Analysis In Middle School English

1. Describe characters based on speech, actions, or interactions with others.
2. Demonstrate knowledge of authors, characters, and events of works of literature.
3. Identify, analyze, interpret, and discuss the following elements of literature: – character traits and motivations – allusions – conflict and resolution – irony – figurative language, imagery, and sensory language – point of view – author's attitude or tone – climax
4. Identify, analyze, and discuss elements of a drama.
5. Identify, analyze, and discuss elements of a short story.
6. Identify, analyze, and discuss theme in literary works.
7. Identify cause-and-effect relationships.
8. Make inferences and draw conclusions.
9. Recognize the effect of setting or culture on a literary work.
10. Recognize use of language to convey mood.
11. Discuss author's purpose and analyze literary devices used to accomplish it, including language, organization, and structure.
12. Compare and contrast literary characters and selections.

Typical Literary Analysis Prompts

(Writing Assignments, Identify and Describe, Socratic Discussion, Project and Reports)

1. How does the author's use of diction, imagery, details, language, syntax, and sentence structure contribute to the meaning of the work?
2. How are the various parts of the work interconnected? (For example, do they all contribute to a theme or other statement?)
3. How does the work use imagery to develop its own symbols?
4. How do paradox, irony, ambiguity, and tension work in the text?
5. How does the author resolve apparent contradictions within the work?
6. Is there a central or focal passage that can be said to sum up the entirety of the work?
7. How do the rhythms and/or rhyme schemes of a poem contribute to the meaning or effect of the piece?
8. How the various components of an individual work relate to each other?
9. How two separate literary works deal with similar concepts or forms?
10. How concepts and forms in literary works relate to larger aesthetic, political, social, economic, or religious contexts?

Basic Reading Comprehension Questions

1. Could this story be true? Why or why not?
2. Where is the setting of this story?
3. Who is this story about? Tell about him or her.
4. What words would you use to describe the main character?
5. Do you like the main character? Why or why not?
6. Does the main character have a problem? What is it?
7. How is the problem solved? (What is the solution?)
8. What is the scariest, funniest, saddest, most interesting, or most funny part of the story? Read it aloud.
9. Do you like this story? Why or why not?
10. Do you know any real people who are like the characters in this story? Who are the people? How are they the same? How are they different?
11. Did anything in the story happen that has happened to you? Tell about it.
12. Who is telling this story? Is there a narrator?
13. Why do you think the author chose the title for this story? How does it relate to the story?
14. Would you like to be a character from the story? Why or why not?
15. Would you recommend this book to a friend? Why or why not?

Application Questions

1. Give an example of someone you know who is like one of the characters in the story.
2. If you could have a conversation with one of the characters in the story, which character would you choose, and what would you talk about?
3. Has anything in your life happened that is similar to the things that happened in the story?
4. What events in the story could not happen in real life?
5. Construct an illustration that shows the main characters in the story in a real-life situation.
6. Find words or phrases in the story you do not currently use and write a short story using these words or phrases.

Evaluation Questions

1. Was the main character(s) in the story good or bad? Support your opinion with words from the text.
2. What is your opinion of the story? Did you enjoy reading it? Explain.
3. Do you agree with all of the facts in the story? Explain.
4. Compare this story with other stories you have read in the past. Give evidence from the texts.
5. Would you read other stories like this story? Justify your opinion.
6. Rate the story on a scale of 1-10, with 10 being the highest. Defend your rating.

Knowledge From Text – Based Questions

1. Identify the characters in the story by making a list of all the characters.
2. When and where does the story take place?
3. Tell what the story is about.
4. Locate facts in the story and list the main facts.
5. Find the two most interesting sentences in the story.
6. Make a list of the words in the story you do not know.

Comprehension Questions

1. Describe the characters in the story.
2. Describe how you think the main character feels at the beginning of the story. Describe the main character's feelings at the end of the story.
3. Explain the main idea of the story by retelling it in your own words.
4. Summarize the main facts in the story and discuss how they relate to the main idea of the story.
5. Locate sentences or phrases in the story you do not understand and infer the meanings.

Analysis Questions

1. Explain what part of the story was the most exciting to read and why.
2. Explain what part of the story was the funniest or the saddest and why.
3. Compare and/or contrast the facts in this story to facts in another story.
4. Examine and analyze the main character(s)' feelings at the beginning, middle, and end of the story.
5. Classify and/or categorize these feelings as the same or different.
6. Write a critique of the story and highlight the main facts or main idea of the story.

Synthesis Questions

1. What changes would you make to the story?
2. Predict how your changes would transform or change the story.
3. Generate a new title for the story. Explain your new title.
4. Create a new ending for the story.
5. Combine two characters in the story in order to invent a new character and write a short story with this new character as the main character in your story.
6. Rearrange or change one main fact in the story. Does this change the entire story? How?

Literary Terms for High School Students

alliteration - the repetition of similar initial consonant sounds in order to create a musical or rhythmic effect, to emphasize key words or to imitate sounds. Example: "He was reluctant to return to the room he called home."

allusion - a reference to a well-known person, place, event, literary work, or work of art, often used to help make a comparison.

antagonist - a character or force in conflict with a main character, or protagonist.

autobiography – the story of a person's life narrated by that same person.

biography - a form of non-fiction in which a writer tells the life story of another person.

character - refers to what someone is like – what their qualities are
    (Someone's character refers to their character traits.)

character trait – the quality of a character; what a character is like.

climax – the highest point of action in a story, often the turning point.

conclusion – the outcome of a series of events

conflict – a problem or struggle between two or more forces

denouement – see definition under *plot*

direct characterization – the writer directly states the character's traits or characteristics.

drama – writing meant to be performed by actors on a stage. This form includes dialogue and stage directions.

dynamic character – a character who changes over the course of a story

exposition – see definition under *plot*

external conflict – a problem or struggle between a character and an outside force:
    character vs. character
    character vs. group
    character vs. nature
    character vs. society
    character vs. fate

fable - a brief story, usually with animal characters, that teaches a lesson or a moral.

falling action – see definition under *plot*

fiction – writing that tells about imaginary characters and events. This form uses sentences and paragraphs.

first person point of view - the events are told by a character in the story.

flashback - a section in a literary piece that interrupts the sequence of events in order to relate an earlier incident or set of events.

folk tale – a story composed orally and then passed down from person to person by word of mouth.

foreshadowing – an author's use of hints or clues to give a reader an idea of what may happen next.

free-verse - poetry that has irregular lines and may or may not rhyme.

generalization – a vague or indefinite statement that is made to cover many cases. Example: "All human beings hope for something."

hyperbole – use of extreme exaggeration.

idiom - a word or phrase which means something different from what it says – it is usually a metaphor. An idiom is an expression peculiar to a certain group of people and/or used only under certain circumstances.

imagery – words or phrases that appeal to one or more of the five senses and help to create a vivid description for the reader.

inciting incident – see definition under *plot*

indirect characterization – the writer allows the reader to draw his/her conclusions as to what a character is like, based on the appearances, words, actions, and interactions with other characters.

internal conflict – a problem *within* a character (character vs. self).

introduction – the location of the story where the reader first learns about the main characters, the setting, and the storyline.

Literary Terms for Middle School Students

irony - a situation where the opposite of what is expected to occur or exist *does* occur or exist.

metaphor - a figure of speech in which something is described as if it were something else; a comparison made *without* using "like" or "as".

mood – the atmosphere or feeling an author creates within the piece of writing.

moral – a lesson taught by a literary work.

motivation – a reason that explains or partially explains a character's thoughts, feelings, actions, or speech.

myth – a fictional tale that explains the actions of gods or heroes or the origins of elements of nature.

narrative – writing or speech that tells a story.

narrative poetry – poetry that tells a story

narrator – the speaker or character who is telling the story.

non-fiction - writing that tells about real people, places, objects, or events. This form includes sentences and paragraphs.

objective details – details that are factual and true to life.

onomatopoeia - is a word that imitates or suggests the source of the sound that describes.

oxymoron – the close placement of words having opposite or near opposite meanings in order to create a unique description.

parable – a short tale that illustrates a universal truth, a belief that appeals to all people of all civilizations.

personification – a type of figurative language in which a non-human subject is given human characteristics.

plot – the sequence of events in a literary work. The plot is the writer's plan for what happens, when it happens, and to whom it happens. A plot is built around a *central conflict* – a problem or struggle involving two or more opposing forces. *Plot complications* are events or problems that arise and make it more difficult to resolve the conflict.

(stages of plot)

Exposition provides background for the story. Characters are introduced, the setting is described, and the tone is set.

Inciting Incident is the point where the action or conflict begins, sometimes referred to as the "narrative hook".

Rising action occurs next. The plot "thickens" as the central conflict begins to unfold. Complications are introduced and suspense builds.

Climax is the greatest interest or suspense in the story. At this point the main character has to deal with the conflict directly. It is often the turning point, when the action reaches a peak and the outcome of the conflict is decided. The climax may occur because of a decision the characters reach or because of a discovery or an event that changes the situation. The climax usually results in a change in the characters or a solution to the conflict.

Falling action - the effects here are a result of the climax.

Resolution – the character or character's problems are solved. (note: neither the character nor the reader may necessarily like or agree with how the problems are resolved!

Denouement – this is the time when all the final mysteries and/or questions are answered.

poetry – expressive writing that may use rhythm and rhyme to convey emotion. Poetry uses stanzas or groups of lines.

point of view – the perspective from which a story is told.

protagonist – the main character in a literary work.

pun – a humorous play on words.

repetition – the repeated use of words or phrases in order to emphasize a point.

resolution – see definition under *plot*.

rhyme – a close similarity in the final sounds of two or more words or lines of verse in a poem

rhyme scheme – a regular pattern of rhyming words in a poem. (To indicate the rhyme scheme of a poem, one uses lower-case letters. Each rhyme is assigned a different letter. The rhyme scheme of a poem, for instance, might be *ababcd*.)

Literary Terms for High School Students

rhythm – a flow in music or poetry of regular accented beats

rising action – see definition under *plot*

satire—A work that reveals a critical attitude toward some element of human behavior by portraying it in an extreme way. Satire usually targets groups or large concepts rather than individuals; its purpose is customarily to inspire change.

second person p.o.v. - In second person point of view, the narrator tells the story to another character using "you," so that the story is being told through the addressee's point of view. Second person is the least commonly used p.o.v. in fiction.

setting – the time and location of the events described in a literary work.

simile – a comparison between two things, using "like" or "as".

speaker – the imaginary voice assumed by the writer of a poem, the one describing the events in a poem.

stanza – a group of lines in a poem.

static character – a character who does *not* undergo a change over the course of a story

subject – who or what the story is about; the topic

subjective details – details that reveal the author's feelings, attitudes, or judgments.

symbol /symbolism – anything that stands for or represents something else.

theme – a central message, idea, or concern that expressed in a literary work.

third person point of view - the events are told by someone outside the story.

third person limited p.o.v. - Third person limited point of view is a method of storytelling in which the narrator knows *only* the thoughts and feelings of a single character, while other characters are presented externally. (Third person limited grants a writer more freedom than first-person, but less than third person omniscient.)

tone – the attitude of an author toward the subject that he/she is writing about.

tragic flaw —Tragic error in judgment; a mistaken act which changes the fortune of the tragic hero from happiness to misery.

Poem Literary Terms and Devices

Rhyme: the repetition of sounds of words (ground/found)

Rhyme scheme: a pattern of end rhyme (abab cdcd ee)

Slant rhyme: words that "almost " rhyme, forced rhymes (orange/aren't)

End rhyme: words that rhyme at the end of lines of a poem

Internal rhyme: words that rhyme inside a line of poetry (Once upon a midnight dreary while I pondered weak and weary)

Stanza: a formal division of lines in a poem, considered a unit

Concrete Poem: entire poem is written on the page in a manner that suggests the shape of the subject matter.

Lyric Poem: short, musical poem which expresses a single speaker's strong emotion

Free Verse: poem with no definite rhyme, rhythm, or set form

Narrative Poem: a poem which tells a story

Epic Poem: a long narrative poem about a person of high position who sets out on a great journey

Haiku: 3 lines (5, 7, 5 syllables) usually about nature, always strong imagery, Japanese orgin

Limerick: 5 lines (aabba rhyme scheme) stupid, nonsense humor

Sonnet: 14 lines, definite rhyme and rhythm, often love poems or set in nature, usually very emotional

For 12th grade, below are the following grammar skills that you should be mastered by the end of the school year. We encourage you to visit iXL.com for practice exercises on these grammar categories. The goal of this year's efforts is to take every opportunity you can find to implement these skills into your novel assignments.

- **Sentences, fragments, and run-ons**
  1. Is the sentence declarative, interrogative, imperative, or exclamatory?
  2. Identify the complete subject or complete predicate of a sentence
  3. Identify the simple subject or simple predicate of a sentence?
  4. Identify the compound subject or compound predicate of a sentence
  5. Is it a complete sentence or a fragment?
  6. Is it a complete sentence or a run-on?
  7. Is it a complete sentence, a fragment, or a run-on?

- **Phrases and clauses**
  1. Is it a phrase or a clause?
  2. Identify appositives and appositive phrases
  3. Identify dependent and independent clauses
  4. Is the sentence simple, compound, complex, or compound-complex?
  5. Combine sentences using relative clauses

- **Nouns**
  1. Form and use plurals of compound nouns
  2. Identify plurals, singular possessives, and plural possessives
  3. Form the singular or plural possessive
  4. Identify and correct errors with plural and possessive nouns

- **Pronouns and antecedents**
  1. identify pronouns and their antecedents
  2. Use the pronoun that agrees with the antecedent
  3. Identify vague pronoun references
  4. Identify all of the possible antecedents
  5. Correct inappropriate shifts in pronoun number and person

- **Verb types**
  1. Identify transitive and intransitive verbs
  2. Identify linking verbs, predicate adjectives, and predicate nouns
  3. Subject-verb agreement
  4. Correct errors with subject-verb agreement
  5. Correct errors with indefinite pronoun-verb agreement
  6. Use the correct verb – with compound subjects

- **Verb tense**
  1. Irregular past tense: review
  2. Simple past, present, and future tense: review
  3. Identify and correct inappropriate shifts in verb tense
  4. Form the progressive verb tenses
  5. Form the perfect verb tenses
  6. Identify gerunds and their functions
  7. Identify infinitives and infinitive phrases

- **Adjectives and adverbs**
  1. Identify adjectives
  2. Order adjectives
  3. Identify adverbs
  4. Choose between adjectives and adverbs
  5. Is the word an adjective or adverb?
  6. Form and use comparative and superlative adjectives
  7. Good, better, best, bad, worse, and worst
  8. Form and use comparative and superlative adverbs
  9. Well, better, best, badly, worse, and worst

For 12th grade, below are the following grammar skills that you should be mastered by the end of the school year. We encourage you to visit iXL.com for practice exercises on these grammar categories. The goal of this year's efforts is to take every opportunity you can find to implement these skills into your novel assignments.

- **Prepositions**
  1. Identify prepositional phrases
- **Direct and indirect objects**
  1. Is it a direct object or an indirect object?
- **Conjunctions**
  1. Use the correct pair of correlative conjunctions
  2. Misplaced modifiers
  3. Misplaced modifiers with pictures
  4. Select the misplaced or dangling modifier
  5. Are the modifiers used correctly?
- **Restrictive and nonrestrictive elements**
  1. What does the punctuation suggest?
- **Commas with nonrestrictive elements**
  1. Commas with series, dates, and places
  2. Commas with compound and complex sentences
  3. Commas with direct addresses, introductory words, interjections, and interrupters
  4. Commas with coordinate adjectives
- **Semicolons, colons, and commas**
  1. Use semicolons and commas to separate clauses
  2. Use semicolons, colons, and commas with lists
- **Dashes, hyphens, and ellipses**
  1. Use dashes
  2. Use hyphens in compound adjectives
  3. Decide whether ellipses are used appropriately

- **Pronoun types**
  1. Choose between subject and object pronouns
  2. Compound subjects and objects with "I" and "me"
  3. Compound subjects and objects with pronouns
  4. Choose between personal and reflexive pronouns
     a. Use reflexive pronouns
  5. Is the pronoun reflexive or intensive?
  6. Use relative pronouns: who and whom
  7. Use relative pronouns: who, whom, whose, which, and that
- **Capitalization**
  1. Correct capitalization errors
  2. Capitalizing titles
- **Formatting**
  1. Formatting titles
  2. Formatting and capitalizing titles: review
  3. Formatting street addresses
  4. Formatting quotations and dialogue

Cause and Effect T-Chart

Cause	Effect

Chain of Events

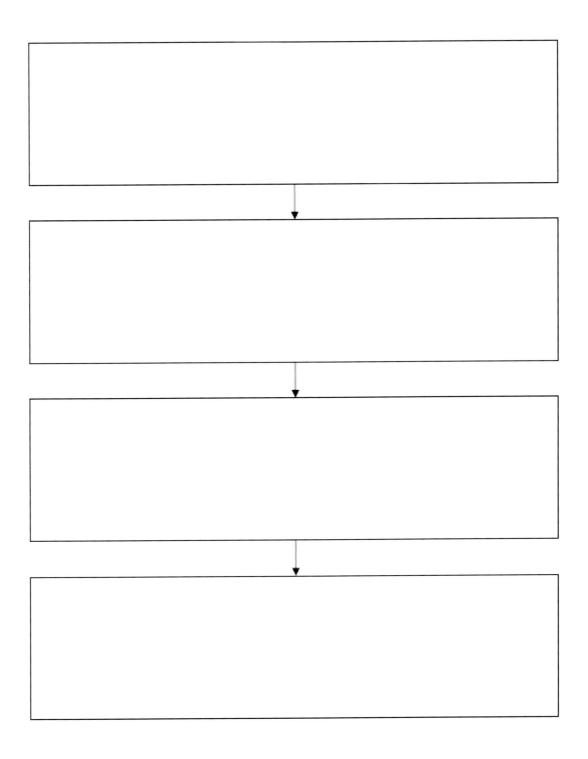

Problem/Solution

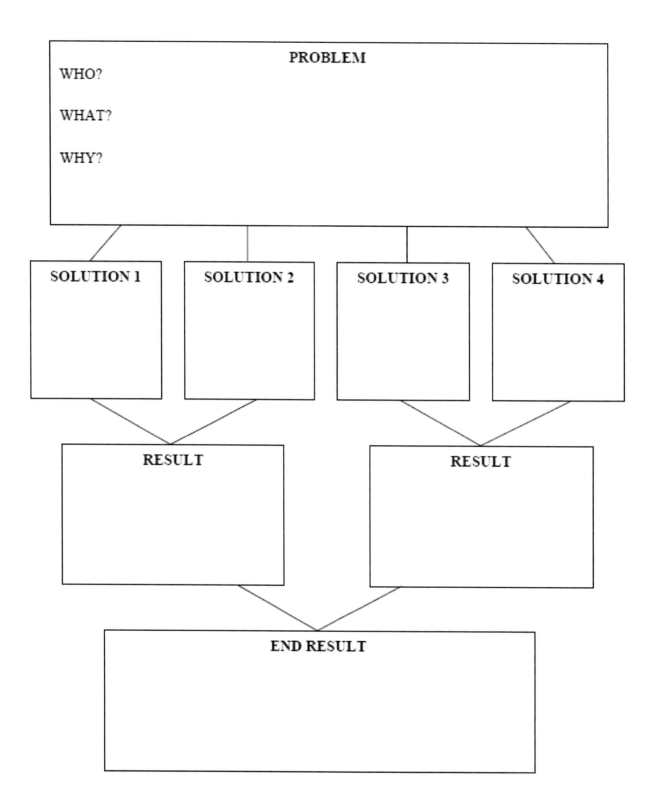

Creative Ways To Learn Vocabulary

1. Provide students with sentences, each containing a blank where a vocabulary word belongs. Have students Use Context Clues to fill in the blanks with the correct vocabulary words.

2. Have students create an Illustrated Class Dictionary of the vocabulary words using a flip chart.

3. On the chalkboard, list five vocabulary words to be Words of the Day. When students come into the classroom, have them use dictionaries to find the meanings of these words. Then have them share and discuss the meanings.

4. Have students work in cooperative learning groups to Write a Story using as many of the vocabulary words as possible.

5. Have students work with a partner to Write Riddles using the vocabulary words as the answers to the riddles. Ask students to share their riddles with the class. • Challenge your students to a Vocabulary Bee. This is similar to a spelling bee, but in addition to spelling each word correctly, the game participants must correctly define the words as well.

6. Ask students to create Crossword Puzzles or Wordsearch Puzzles using the vocabulary words from the story. Then puzzles can be duplicated so they can be shared with the entire class.

7. Play Twenty Clues with the vocabulary words. In this game, a student gives clues about a vocabulary word, and the other students have twenty chances to guess what that word is. The student who correctly guesses the word gets to give the next set of clues.

8. Have students make a Part of Speech Categories Chart with headings, such as Noun, Verb, Adjective, and Adverb. Under the appropriate heading, have them write each word in the context of a sentence, correctly showing its use as that part of speech.

9. Play Vocabulary Charades. In this game, a student acts out the meaning of a vocabulary word while others try to guess what the word is.

These generic forms can be used in your English instruction for each novel.

Close Reading Template	
Text: (Is this text worthy of a close read?) **Focus chunk/portion for close read:** [Photocopy or mark section]	1. **FIRST READ** *(Key Ideas & Details)* Students read text silently. Check for Understanding Strategy:
Complex ideas that require close reading: ☐ Text language ☐ Vocabulary ☐ Implied Meanings ☐ Text Structure ☐ Text Features ☐ Author's purpose	2. **SECOND READ** *(Craft & Structure)* Reread selected chunk focusing on text dependent question #2. Reread Structure: ☐ Independent Reading ☐ Read Aloud ☐ Think Aloud ☐ Shared ☐ Paired Reading
Text Dependent Questions: Develop 2-3 high cognitive level questions that will require students to stay in the text to answer. Be sure that students need to use text evidence in their responses and prompt them to do so.	Students use pencils, post-it or highlighters to mark text portions of text that will aid in citing evidence. Discuss:
1. Key Ideas and Details:	3. **THIRD READ** *(Integration of Knowledge and Ideas)* Reread selected chunk focusing on text dependent question #3. Discuss:
2. Craft and Structure:	
3. Integration of Knowledge and Ideas:	Integration Task:

Purpose of the Frayer Model
For Vocabulary Instruction

The purpose of the Frayer Model *(Frayer, 1969; Buehl, 2001)* is to identify and define unfamiliar concepts and vocabulary. Students define a concept/word/term, describe its essential characteristics, provide examples of the idea, and suggest nonexamples of the idea (knowing what a concept doesn't help define what it is).

This information is placed on a chart that is divided into four sections to provide a visual representation for students. The model prompts students to understand words within the larger context of a reading selection, as it asks students to analyze the concept/word (definition and characteristics) and then synthesize or apply this information by thinking of examples and nonexamples.

It also activates prior knowledge of a topic and builds connections. Explicitly teaching the Frayer Model:

Step 1 Explain the Frayer model chart to the class by using a common word to demonstrate the various components. Model the type and quality of desired answers when giving examples. Think out loud as you try to come up with examples and non examples, etc. Pictures/symbols can also be used.

Step 2 Then review a preselected list of key concept words with the class before reading about the topic in the textbook. Read the text selection. Step 2 Choose a key concept word from the topic read and have students help you complete the Frayer chart.

Step 3 Pass out blank copies of the Frayer Model or have students create a chart in their copies.

Step 4 Then, students practice the strategy in pairs or in small groups with the key concepts and key vocabulary from the topic. (Each group could also be given different key concept words).

Step 5 The groups share their completed charts with each other. Students can then add additional words/images/symbols to the Frayer chart until all four categories are substantially represented.

Example of the Frayer Model

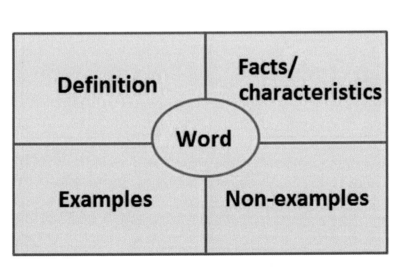

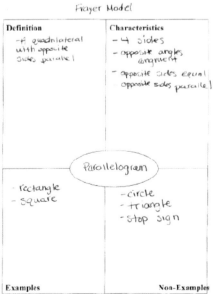

Examples of the Frayer Model

Definition: *(from textbook pg xx)*

Democracy *is the* government of the people, by the people, *for the* people.

Definition: *(in your own words)*

When you vote for people you want to make laws for the country.

Characteristics:

Not ruled by one person
Free elections
Elected TDs
Majority decides
People of the country can take part in the government

Keyword
_____

Democracy

Examples:

Ireland
UK
France
Germany
USA
Australia

Non Examples:

China
North Korea

Definition:

A short poem of 14 lines with rhymes arranged according to a certain scheme. The poem is divided into a major group of 8 lines (the octave) followed by a minor group of 6 lines (the sestet).

Facts:

Three main types of sonnets named after the poets that used them: Shakespearean, Spenserian and Petrarchan.
A strict rhyme scheme - Shakespearean sonnet is ABABCDCDEFEFGG.
Written in iambic Pentameter, a poetic meter with 10 beats per line

Sonnet

Examples:

How do I love thee? Let me count the ways.
I love thee to the depth and breadth and height
My soul can reach, when feeling out of sigh
For the ends of Being and ideal Grace...
Elizabeth Barrett Browning

Shall I compare thee to a summer's day?
Thou art more lovely and more temperate.
Rough winds do shake the darling buds of May,
And summer's lease hath all too short a date...
William Shakespeare

Non Examples:

Ode to a Grecian Urn by John Keats

Mid-Term Break by Seamus Heaney

Back in the Playground Blues by Adrian Mitchel

Blank Forms for the Frayer Model

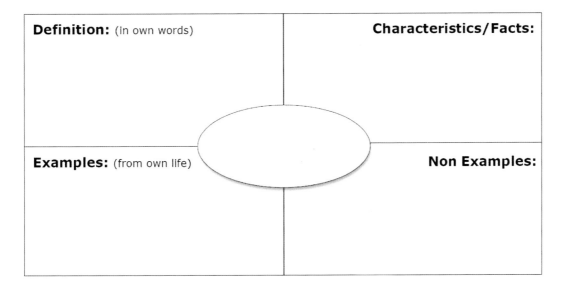

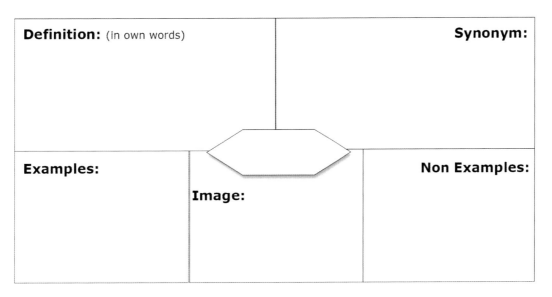

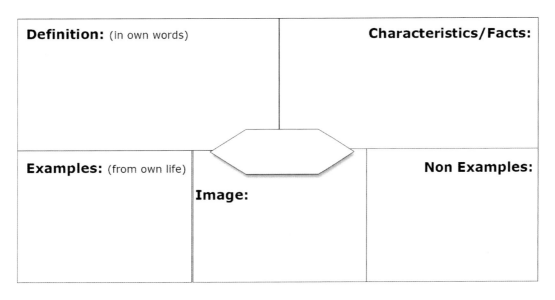

169

Blank Forms for the Frayer Model

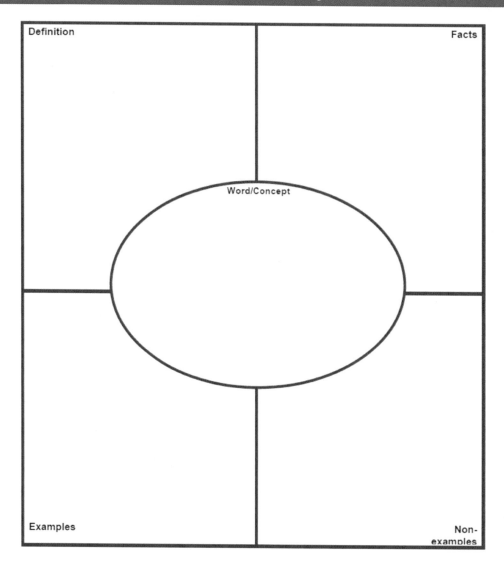

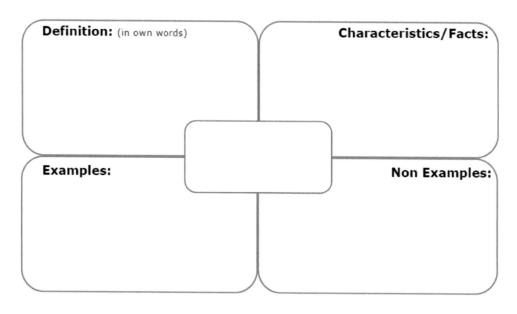

Semantic Mapping/Webbing
Vocabulary Instruction Model

Word webs (also known as semantic mapping) illustrate how key words or concepts are related to one another through graphic representations. Creating word webs can be done as a whole-class, small-group, or individual activity. A word web is a graphic organizer created by students to help them learn vocabulary.

How to Use Word Webs
1. Begin with a word. This strategy works well using words from expository texts.
2. Students free-associate other words, terms, or phrases they associate with the chosen word. The teacher writes these on the board in the order in which they are shared next to the targeted word. This is done until students run out of ideas.
3. Students categorize associations and label the categories. This can be done as a class, in small groups or pairs, or individually.
4. Students can present and explain their maps to others or to the class, with assistance from the teacher, if necessary.
5. When using this as a before reading activity, have students add to the categories after reading.
6. When students are familiar with the strategy, they can produce their own maps for words from independent reading.

Sample Semantic Web

Word Box
Vocabulary Instruction Exercise

1. List vocabulary words for a text or topic in the Word Box.
2. Include both words that are known and unknown.
3. Discuss the words briefly.
4. Have students create sentences with the words, using 2 or 3 words in one sentence to display connections. Then, while reading the text, encourage students to discover how the author used the words. Have the student put a checkmark in front of the sentences in which the student feels s/he used the words correctly.
5. Engage students in discussion and have them revise sentences if necessary.

Word Box

_____ 1. _____

_____ 2. _____

_____ 3. _____

_____ 4. _____

Writing Styles

EXPOSITORY	ARGUMENTATIVE	INSTRUCTIONAL	NARRATIVE
Textbooks (science)	Opinion/Editorial Pieces	Training Manuals	(Auto)Biographies
Textbooks (humanities)	Speeches (including those from seated politicians)	Contracts	Histories
Reports	Advertisements	User Guides/Manuals	Correspondence
Tourism Guides	Political Propaganda	Legal Documents	Curriculum Vitae
Product Specifications	Journal Articles	Recipes	Memoirs
Product/Service Descriptions	Government Documents	Product/Service Descriptions	News Articles
Magazine Articles	Legal Documents		Essays
Company Profiles	Tourism Guides		Interviews
Legal Documents	Correspondence		Agendas
Agendas	Essays		
Correspondence	Reviews		
Essays	Memoirs		
Interviews			
Government Documents			
News Articles			

Standard	Grade(s)												
	K	1	2	3	4	5	6	7	8	9	10	11	12
Differentiate pictures from writing.													
Use available technology for reading and writing.													
Generate ideas.													
Focus on one topic.													
Revise writing.													
Use complete sentences in final copies.													
Begin each sentence with a capital letter and use ending punctuation in final copies.													
Use correct spelling for commonly used sight words and phonetically regular words in final copies.													
Organize writing to include a beginning, middle and end for narrative and expository writing.													
Expand writing to include descriptive detail.													
Identify intended audience.													
Use a variety of prewriting strategies.													
Write a clear topic sentence focusing on the main idea.													
Write a paragraph on the same topic.													
Use strategies for organization of information and elaboration according to the type of writing.													
Include details that elaborate the main idea.													
Recognize different modes of writing have different patterns of organization.													
Write two or more related paragraphs on the same topic.													
Use transition words for sentence variety.													
Utilize elements of style, including word choice and sentence variation.													
Write multiparagraph compositions.													
Compose a topic sentence or thesis statement if appropriate.													
Select vocabulary and information to enhance the central idea, tone, and voice.													
Expand and embed ideas by using modifiers, standard coordination, and subordination in complete sentences.													
Use clauses and phrases for sentence variety.													
Distinguish between a thesis statement and a topic sentence.													
Communicate clearly the purpose of the writing using a thesis statement where appropriate.													
Arrange paragraphs into a logical order.													

1

Narrative Writing Outline

Narration is the retelling of an event with specific details, told through 1st or 3rd person point of view that maintains a distinct author's voice, and has a clear purpose.

Writing Process

Pre-Writing
>Free-writing
>Planning
>Story boarding
>Outline Beginning, Middle, End
>Identify Purpose: To entertain - To teach a lesson -To narrate an event

Drafting
>Choose 1st or 3rd Person Point of View (POV)
>>Scholars should practice both writing in both POV's
>Complete a rough copy of narration: Beginning – Middle - End

Revising
>Include effective details make a stronger Beginning, Middle, and End of narrative
>Clarify purpose of narrative
>Clarify word choice
>Variety: Word Choice (diction) - Sentence Structure (syntax)
>Maintain consistent voice in narrative (may be different between narrative and dialogue)

Editing
>Use appropriate end punctuation effectively
>>Periods (.)
>>Question Marks (?)
>>Exclamation points (!)
>Spelling
>Subject-Verb agreement
>Quotation marks
>Paragraphs

Publishing
>Create a final draft
>>Neatly handwritten: Cursive - Print
>>Typed
>Present writing orally
>Record presentation

Expository (Informational) – Writing Outline

Informational writing is used to highlight details in an observation utilizing an Introduction with a Topic Statement, three supporting details about the observation, and a conclusion, written in 3rd person point of view that answers questions such as "How" and "What."

Pre-Writing

Free-writing
Planning
Outline Introduction, Body, Conclusion
Develop a Main Idea Statement
    Sharp, distinct, controlling point
    Placed at the end of the Introduction
Develop three supports for the Main Idea Statement

Drafting

Complete a rough copy

Introduction
    Topic
    Outline of "Essay"
    Main Idea about the Observation
Body
    Support 1
        Topic
        Information Supporting Main Idea
        Point about Support 1
    Support 2
        Transition to new Topic
        Information Supporting Main Idea
        Point about Support 2
    Support 3
        Transition to new Topic
        Information Supporting Main Idea
        Point about Support 3
Conclusion
    Restatement of Main Idea
    Anecdote, Real-World Connection, Historical Connection, Etc.
    Explanation of connection
    Final point

Revising

Ensure that Paragraphs end with points, and that transitions happen at the beginning of the next paragraph.
Clarify Main Idea Statement
Clarify word choice
Variety
    Word Choice (diction)
    Sentence Structure (syntax)
Maintain consistent voice

Editing

Use appropriate end punctuation effectively
    Periods (.)
    Question Marks (?)
    Exclamation points (!)
Spelling
Subject-Verb agreement
Quotation marks (only if using quotes from cited sources)
Paragraph structure

Publishing

Create a final draft
    Neatly handwritten
        Cursive
        Print
    Typed
Present writing orally
Record presentation

Persuasive Writing Outline

Persuasion is the art of defending, challenging, or clarifying an argument by making claims and counterclaims to prove the author's point through a well-organized essay written in 3rd person utilizing citations from credible sources.

Pre-Writing
Free-writing
Planning
Outline Introduction, Body, Conclusion
Develop a claim Statement
 Sharp, distinct, controlling point
 Placed at the end of the Introduction
Develop three supports for the claim

Drafting
Complete a rough copy of persuasive Writing
 Introduction
  Topic
  Outline of "Essay"
  claim
 Body
  Support 1
   Topic
   Information Supporting claim
   Point about Support 1
  Support 2
   Transition to new Topic
   Information Supporting claim
   Point about Support 2
  Support 3
   Transition to new Topic
   Information Supporting claim
   Point about Support 3
 Conclusion
  Restatement of claim
  Anecdote, Real-World Connection, Historical Connection, Etc.
  Explanation of connection
  Final point

Revising
Ensure that Paragraphs end with points, and that transitions happen at the beginning of the next paragraph.
Clarify claim Statement
Clarify word choice
Variety
 Word Choice (diction)
 Sentence Structure (syntax)
Maintain consistent voice

Editing
Use appropriate end punctuation effectively
 Periods (.)
 Question Marks (?)
 Exclamation points (!)
Spelling
Subject-Verb agreement
Quotation marks (only if using quotes from cited sources)
Paragraph structure

Publishing
Create a final draft
 Neatly handwritten
  Cursive
  Print
 Typed
Present writing orally
Record presentation

5 Paragraph Essay Outline

1.Introduction paragraph:

a.Get the readers attention by using a **"hook". Pull your audience in!**

A.Quote, Fact, something interesting to start essay

b.Give some **background information about topic.** Explain what the topic is and why it is controversial or important to you.

c.Thesis or focus statement (MUST BE STATED in the LAST sentence of your introduction paragraph).

A.This is a sentence stating your opinion about the topic and will be proven in the rest of your essay with 3 strong reasons and support.

1.Example: I am in favor of _____ because _____, ___, and ___.

2.Example: I am against _____because _____, _____, and ___.

2.Body Paragraphs:

a.(1st body paragraph)First argument or reason to support your position
A.Topic sentence explaining your first reason.
1.Example: My first reason for being against ___ is _____.
B.Provide support/evidence to prove your first reason.
1.Facts, data, examples, etc.
b.(2nd body paragraph) Second argument or reason to support your position.
A.Topic sentence explaining your second reason.
1.Example: Another reason I do not support _____is ___.
B.Provide support for your second reason
1.Facts, data, examples, etc.
c.(3rd body paragraph) Counter argument and third reason to support position.
A.State what the other side believes or may argue
1.Example: Some may argue _____
B.Challenge their argument with your third reason and provide support.
C. Example: but I disagree because _____.
D. Give support such as facts, data, examples, etc. explaining why your opinion is right and the other side is not right.

3. Conclusion Paragraph:

A. Sum up your main points and 3 reasons.
B. Restate your thesis. Example: I am strongly against
C. Final words: last comments or call to action.

Encourage the reader to agree with you and take your side on the issue

BEFORE SOCRATIC SEMINAR

Reading the Text
1. Read through the entire selection without stopping to think about any particular section. Pay attention to your first impression as to what the reading is about. Look for the main points and then go back and reread it.
2. The second time you read it, talk to the text.
   1. Underline major points or forceful statements.
   2. Put vertical lines at the margins to emphasize a statement already underlined or a passage too long to be underlined.
   3. Put an (*) to emphasize major points.
   4. Put numbers in margin to indicate sequence of points.
   5. Put numbers of other pages where point is also mentioned.
   6. Circle key words or phrases.
   7. Write in the margin questions that come to mi

Ground Rules of Socratic Seminar
1. Speak so that all can hear you.
2. Listen closely.
3. Speak without raising hands
4. Refer to and tie in the text
5. Talk to each other not just the teacher
6. Ask for clarification if you don't get it.
7. Invite and encourage others to speak
8. Be open to all ideas and viewpoints
9. You are responsible for the quality

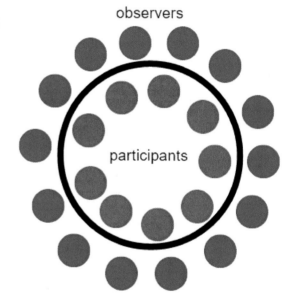

5 Responsibilities of the Leader
1. Preparing Students for dialogue
2. Selecting the text
3. Guiding the inner circle
4. Directing the outer circle
5. Providing assessment and feedback.

Socratic Seminar Participation Rubric

4	3	2	1
- Participate more than once, using <u>specific evidence</u>. - Encourage others to participate by asking questions	- Participate at least once using <u>specific evidence</u>.	- Participate in the discussion, but does not reference specific evidence.	- No participation. - Or, participation is off topic or does not add to the discussion (ex. "I agree." or "Yeah.")

Leading A Book Club

Starting the Discussion:

1. Did you enjoy the book? Why or why not?
2. What were your expectations before starting this book? Were they met?
3. How would you describe this book to a friend?
4. How did you experience the book? Were you immediately drawn into the story, or did it take a while?
5. What did you like best about this book? Like least?
6. Ending the Discussion:
7. Is there anything we haven't discussed yet that you'd like to talk about?
8. Did the ending of this book satisfy you? Why or why not?
9. What three words would you use to describe this book?
10. Out of a scale of 5, what would you rate this book? Why?
11. Would you recommend this book to other readers? To your close friends? Why or why not?

When No One Has Read the Book:

1. Why didn't you read the book? Expand on these themes as everyone shares?
2. Are there things in life people need help with? Can this become a bit of a therapy session?
3. Are these reasons specific to the book's length, genre, etc? Do we need to have a larger discussion about the types of books we select in the future?
4. Are there reasons related to the way your book club is run? If so, consider having a discussion to improve your current expectations, processes, and structure.
5. How can we take what we learned from no one reading this book and apply it to future meetings, so we don't run into this again?
6. Are there future books we have selected we should consider changing because the group isn't interested in reading this? Why or why not?
7. What about this book selection appealed to you when you found out we selected it? What turned you off?
8. Do you like the book blurb? What about this intrigues you and makes you want to read the book?
9. What do you think of the book cover? If there are multiple covers, look them up and compare. Which is the group's favorite?
10. Have you read other books by this author? What do you think of those books? Which books would you recommend and to whom?
11. If anyone did read the book, ask them to share their reflections, who they think in the group will enjoy it, and why. Discuss these speculations.
12. Did you read other books during this time instead? If so, what books? Would you recommend them?

Discussing Banned or Controversial Books

Challenged books are books where someone has formally questioned its appropriateness for a particular reason. Banned books are books that have been removed from a library shelf or school curriculum.

1. Do you think it's important to differentiate between these two? Why or why not?
2. Do you think the label we give these books, banned v. challenged, makes a difference in how important the book is? Does it make a difference in how you view the book?
3. Are there valid reasons to ban and challenge books?
4. What harm, if any is caused by having a book banned?
5. Why do you think the ALA hosts Banned Books Week? Does it matter?
6. Why is it important to talk about banned/challenged books?
7. What are your favorite banned and challenged books? Why are they banned/challenged? Do you agree with these concerns? What group(s) have banned/challenged this book?
8. What are the common elements of banned/challenged books today? Which are the most important to you? Why?
9. One of the most common reasons for banning/challenging a book is due to "age-appropriateness". What does this mean to you? Is it a valid reason?

What Makes A Book A Classic?

Discussing Classic Books:

What book did you read? Provide a brief synopsis.
1. Why did you select this particular book?
2. Did you enjoy the book? Why or why not?
3. Was this a re-read for you? If not, what insights did you glean from this book? If so, why did you choose to re-read this?
4. Why do you believe this book is considered a Classic? After reading it, do you agree this is a Classic?
5. Why does this book continue to appeal to modern-day readers? What are the timeless aspects of this story?
6. Did this book impact any modern works? How do you see this book reflected elsewhere?
7. What portions of the book could you personally relate to or connect with? Why?
8. What were your expectations before starting this book? Were they met?
9. Have you read other books by this author?
10. If so, how does this book compare?
11. If not, will you seek out this author in the future?
12. How did you experience the book? were you immediately drawn into the story, or did it take a while?
13. What did you like best about this book? Like the least?

201 Literary Themes to Start Conversation

Abandonment
Adolescence
Alcohol Abuse
Alienation
Ambition
Ambition and Self-Improvement
Anger
Appearances
Appearances are Deceptive
Beauty
Beauty (diversity/ simplicity)
Beauty (fading)
Betrayal
Bullying
Capitalism
Catastrophe
Change/Tradition
Chaos/Order
Character
Civilization vs. Savagery
Classics
Coming of Age
Communication
Community
Companionship
Compassion as Heroic
Conspiracy
Convention/Rebellion
Corruption (power)
Courage
Crime, Guilt, Innocence
Cruelty
Cyclical nature of life
Danger of Isolation
Dangerous Knowledge
Darkness
Death
Death and Rebirth
Deception
Decline of the American Dream
Desire
Destruction
Disillusionment
Displacement
Divorce
Dreams
Drug Abuse is Dangerous
Duty
Eating Disorders
Education
Empowerment
Emptiness
Equal Rights
Evil
Exclusion because of Racial or Religious Difference
Facing reality
Fairness and Loyalty
Faith/Doubt

Family
Family Struggles
Fate
Fate v. Free Will
Fear
Female Roles
Forgiveness
Freedom
Friendship
Fulfillment
Greed
Grief & Loss
Happiness
Heartbreak
Heroism
Home
Honor
Hope (loss)
Hopes, Dreams, and Plans
Household Governance
Human Nature
Humanity
Hysteria
Identity
Identity and Society
Ignorance
Immortality
Individual and Society
Individuality
Inhumanity towards other Humans
Inner/Outer Strength
Innocence (loss)
Interracial Love and Friendship
Intolerance
Isolation
Jealousy
Justice/Injustice
Knowledge/Ignorance
Literature and Writing
Loneliness
Loss of a Loved One
Loss of Innocence
Lost Dreams
Love
Love and Hate
Love's Difficulty
Loyalty
Malevolence/ Benevolence
Manipulation
Materialism
Memory and Vision
Money
Mortality
Motherhood
Nationalism
Nature
Nature (beauty/danger)
Necessity
Obsession

Oppression
Optimism
Overcoming (fear/weakness/vice)
Parenthood
Passing Judgment
Past Versus Present
People Hide their True Identity
People vs. Supernatural
Persecution
Pessimism
Poverty
Power
Prejudice
Pride
Progress
Quest
Race
Racism
Rebirth
Regret
Rejection
Relationships within Family
Religion
Reputation
Responsibility
Restricted Role of Women
Reunion
Rivalry
Roles (male/female)
Sacrifice
Secrecy
Self (awareness/ preservation)
Self vs. Alter Ego
Self-motivation and Self-reliance
Self-Sacrifice
Sexism/Misogyny
Sexuality
Silence
Social Class
Social mobility
Society's Treatment of the Powerless
Spirituality
Stages of Life
Struggle for Self-Definition
Struggle to Maintain Faith
Struggling with Depression
Success
Suffering
Suicide
Survival
Suspicion
Technology
Temptation
The American Dream
The Burden of Secrets
The Changing Idea of Family
The Chase
The Effects of Guilt on One's Conscience
Survival of the Fittest

The Importance of Establishing Identity
The Importance of Family
The Mystery of Death
The Nature of Evil
The Nature of Tragedy
The Need to Fight Racial Discrimination
The Pitfalls of Temptation
The Power of Language
The Power of Love
The Power of Skill over Strength
The Power of Storytelling
The Power of the Dead over the Living
The Problem of Immigrant Identity
The Quest
The Value and Purposes of Dreams
The Willingness to Ignore Truth
There are No Random Acts in Life
Totalitarianism
Tradition
Traditions and Customs
Trust is Betrayed
Truth
Upper Class vs. Lower Class
Vanity
Violence
Vulnerability
War (glory/necessity/ pain/tragedy)
Will
Wisdom
Work
Working class struggles
Youth

Literary Questions for Fun:

1. What is your favorite book of all time? Why?
2. Who are your insta-buy authors? If you don't have any, why?
3. What book did you read recently and absolutely hate?
4. What formats of books do you prefer to read? Why?
5. How do you organize your bookshelves at home?
6. What is your ideal book-themed vacation?
7. What is your favorite Classic? Your least favorite? Why?
8. Do you want to attend a bookish convention? Why or why not? Which ones?
9. Have you attended a bookish convention? Which one? Did you enjoy it? Why or why not?
10. Do you have any signed books? What books?
11. What book scares you the most now? As a child?
12. Name a TV or film adaptation that you think is better than the book. Now defend it.
13. Who is your favorite villain, and why?
14. What literary characters would you like to have a conversation with in real life? What would you discuss?
15. Which worlds within books do you want to visit? Why?
16. What book did you want to quit reading but you're glad you finished?
17. What is the most recent book you read?
18. What is the last book your purchased? For yourself or someone else?
19. Are there any books you enjoyed as a child but hate now? Which ones?
20. Are there any books you didn't like in school but love now? Which ones?

10 Key characteristics and criteria for historical fiction:

1. draws on two sources—fact and imagination (the author's information about the past and his/her power to speculate about how it was to live in that time
2. must tell a story that is interesting, and it must balance fact with fiction
3. does need to be accurate and authentic with details an essential part of the story
4. helps children understand the public events we label "history" and the private struggles that have characterized the human condition
5. offers youngsters the vicarious experience of participating in the life of the past
6. will bring students to a fuller understanding of human problems and human relationships
7. helps children to see that times change, nations rise and fall, but universal human needs have remained relatively unchanged
8. enables children to see human interdependence
9. is one-way children can develop a sense of history and begin to understand their place in the larger picture of human destiny assists children with seeing that today's way of life is a result of what people did in the past and that the present will influence the way people will live in the future.

Key characteristics of fantasy:

1. may reveal new insights into the world of reality
2. consistently asks the universal questions of good versus evil, the humanity of humankind, and the meaning of life and death
3. helps the child to develop imagination (to be able to imagine, to entertain new ideas, to create strange new worlds, to dream dreams)
4. has a well-constructed plot, convincing characterization, a worthwhile theme, and an appropriate style
5. must be believable (create belief in the unbelievable)
6. needs to be logical and consistent within the framework established by the author
7. is original and ingenious
8. has a universal truth underlying the metaphor of the fantasy ⮕ oftentimes introduces child to talking, animals, toys, and dolls

How To Use Our Lesson Cards

A Deeper Look On How Our Lesson Cards Fit Together

Thematic Units based on history are what makes Classical Education so effective. Using our color and date-coded lesson cards as a guide, we can help you teach your scholar a comprehensive Classical Education model.

This section explains the nuances of our lesson cards and how everything ties together.

What Is Classical Education?

6 Character Development Values and Virtue Education

Critical Thinking

Equip our Scholars with the Tools to decipher RIGHT from WRONG

CHALLENGE what is Presented with VERBAL and WRITING Proficiency

The Art of DEBATE Using Logical and Reason

Awareness of Others

Through the GREAT BOOKS, Scholars EXAMINE Character Through The Power of Story.

Awareness of Others - The Golden Rule The Golden Mean

Appreciation of the GOOD - TRUE - BEAUTIFUL

Life Long Learners

Instill WONDER and a JOY of learning by Making HISTORY come ALIVE.

Spark CURIOSITY Go DEEPER as opposed to WIDER into Subject Matter.

Hands on Learning in the Arts, Music, Science and Athletics

3 Three Stages of Learning The Trivium

Grammar Stage K-3

Heavier on Direct Instruction
Instill WONDER.
Math Facts
Grammar Rules
Recitations of Poetry
Beginning Socratic

Logic Stage 4-6

Scholars Start Asking 'Why?'
Connecting Facts with Ideas
Deeper Dive Into Concepts
Awareness of Others
The Good, True and Beautiful
Heavier Socratic Base

Rhetoric Stage 7-12

Socratic Discussions
Strong Verbal and Writing
Critical Thinking
Linking Past to Today
Capstone Projects
Personal Beliefs Explored

1 Pillars of Classical Ed

Teach Values and Virtues
Through great works of literature, art, music, math and scientific advancements from a historical view.

Natural Education Transitions
The Trivium - Education progression along the child's developmental stages. From Grammar to Logic To Rhetoric.

Interwoven Subjects
Subjects based on a year long, in depth study of a time period in history

Deeper Dives Into Learning
Explore in depth, the Society, Politics, Religions, Intellectual Advancements, Technology, Economics of societies from Ancient to Modern. Socratic Instruction and Source Document Analysis. Much More Than Dates and Facts.

Rigorous Academics
Heavy emphasis on writing, oratory and literature interpretation skills.

Pursuit of the Good, True and Beautiful

Classical Rome /Greece & America

What Is Classical Education?

4 **History Time Lines**
Year Long - Thematic Units

Ancient Times
1st - 5th - 9th Grades

Formation of Civilizations
Egypt - Mesopotamia
Ancient China - Confucius
Abraham - Moses
Babylon - Phoenicians

Medieval Times
2nd - 6th - 10th Grades

After The Fall of Rome
Magna Carta
The Rise of The Church
Knights and Samurais
Vikings Norsemen
Islam Begins
Ottoman Empire
Reformation - Martin Luther
Renaissance - The Masters

5 **Interwoven Disciplines**

rates
ne
s

Art - Music
Big Ideas
Great Literature
Values and Virtues
Great Men and Women

Rise & Fall of Civilizations
Inventions & Inventors
Astronomy
Science Advancements
Bio/Chem/Earth/Physics

Culture of the Day
Major Religions
Governments
Philosophers
Economies

America Founding
3rd - 7th - 11th Grades

Age of Exploration
America Colonized
American Revolution
Founding Fathers
Constitution - Bill of Rights
French Revolution
Industrial Revolution
Slavery Injustice
Civil War Divides The Nation

Modern Times
4th - 8th - 12th Grades

Reconstruction
Manifest Destiny
Roaring 20's
Great Depression
World War 1 and 2
Russian Revolution
Communist China
Cold War - Space Race
Vietnam to 9/11

Latin 1,2,3   **Logic 1,2**   **Recitations**   **Capstone**

Classical

Latin has been shown to increase student achievement and language mastery. Beginning in 3rd grade, scholars start their journey in learning Latin through exposure to the culture and history of ancient Rome. This cultural exposure combined with the basics of learning a new language is an effective way to engage students. **Logic** - Understanding arguments and fallacies are part of a Classical education and beginning in middle school, scholars are taught the theories that will improve their written and oral skills. **Recitations** are start in Kinder and continue up to Middle School. Scholars dissect and memorize the great works of poetry and learn the skill of presenting in front of their peers. Finally, the curriculum program includes **Capstone** modules that can be implemented in 5th to 12th grade. The capstones are typically year long projects that culminate in a summary of the scholars learning and personal reflections.

History The Arch In A Classical School

A Journey Through History's Great Ideas

Each card is a unit of instruction on a major topic in history. The graphical front of the card will have the major topics with big and overarching concepts.

Depending on your child's grade, age, and interest, these cards act as guides for their learning. In our model, the scholar will see a particular unit three times (e.g., Ancients are covered in 1st, 5th, and 9th grade), so it's not critical that students cover every item on every card every year.

Think of what you cover as foundations and building blocks for future years.
Remember, as your scholar is learning a particular unit and time period in history, they are also learning in different subjects such as English; expanded vocabulary, refined writing, oral presentation skills, and values and virtues. This thematic approach helps a scholar better understand and synthesize each unit at a deeper and deeper level.

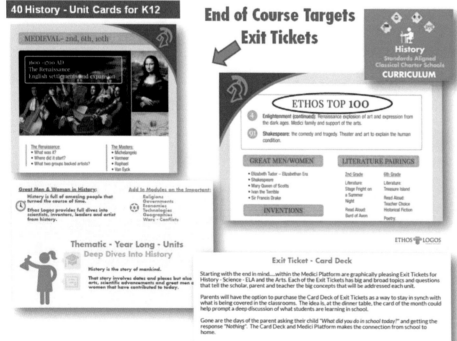

These oversized, laminated cards came about when we asked parents what was different at our schools. The feedback we received usually revolved around the dinner table. By that, what families found was that the history lessons that were explored in schools became the bonding conversations around the dinner table.

These graphical cards will be made into classroom posters to connect what your student is studying visually. Parents can purchase a complete deck of cards (oversized and laminated) to understand better what topic for which month the schools will be covering.

In many schools, history class takes on a minor role; in our Classical model, history is the arch from which all subjects are woven. We built out these cards for parents to use at the dinner table to prompt discussions and perhaps learn along with their children about a particular time in history.

Remember, Classical Education is all about going deeper into a time period or a story. We really want our scholars to experience what it was like to live in a particular time in history. Go deeply into the S.P.R.I.T.E. model of history and dissect the stories that accompany a time period.

The back of the history cards will include more specific events, people, inventions, and ideas that all align with the S.P.R.I.T.E. model of history instruction. The S.P.R.I.T.E. model is one of many that teachers use to triangulate a particular time in history. The acronym stands for the major topics explored when teaching a particular time period in history.

In Classical Education, it all starts with a THEME from a time in HISTORY.

Color Coded
By **SUBJECT**

For This Example –
The Unit/Month We Are Studying
The Civil War

MODERN- 4th, 8th, 12th

1861-1865 THE CIVIL WAR

The Leaders
Lincoln
Grant
Lee

The Battles
Ft Sumter

The Aftermath
The Assassination
Emancipation Proclamation
States Rights Argument

★ *Extra: Research the Strengths and Weakness*

MONTH 2 4 8 12   ETHOS L

History
- **Great Men & Women**
- **100 Top Events**

English
Historic
Novels
Recitations

Unit # & Grade
In this case: 4th, 8th, 12th
Grades 2nd month or
September

Arts
- **Top 50 Artists**
- **Top 25 Musical Moments**

ETHOS TOP 100

44 The American Civil War – The struggle of ideas of freedom, the role of the Federal government, and slavery lead to violence. With the north winning, America was kept intact for another 150 years.

GREAT MEN/WOMEN

- Jefferson Davis
- Robert E Lee
- Ulysses S Grant
- Stonewall Jackson
- William Sherman
- Clara Barton
- Jesse James
- Florence Nightingale

INVENTIONS

- The First Plastics
- Pasteur – Pasteurization of food
- Siemens Martin Steel process
- Mendel – Genetics
- Dynamite – Alfred Nobel
- Modern Sanitation
- Gatlin Gun

THE ARTS

- Verdi (1813-1901) • Renoir (1841-1919) (Featured Semester 1, 8th Grade)

- Tchaikovsky (1840-1893) • Degas (1834-1917) (Featured Semester 1, 4th Grade)

ECONOMICS

By 1860, 90 percent of the nation's manufacturing output came from northern states. The North produced 17 times more cotton and woolen textiles than the South, 30 x more leather goods, 20 x more pig iron, and 32 x more firearms.

The constitution was carefully crafted to protect the right to own slaves. 700,000 enslaved African Americans living in the United States were legally treated as property, not people. The Southern state used slave labor as the backbone of a plantation economy that produced tobacco, rice, sugar, and cotton.

LITERATURE PAIRINGS

4th	8th	12th
Lit. List: Mr. Lincoln's Drummer	Lit. List: Huckleberry Finn	Lit. List: Antigone
Read Aloud: Harriet the Spy	Read Aloud: Student Choice	Poetry: The Soldier
Poetry: O Captain, My Captain	Poetry: Gettysburg Address	

POLITICAL SYSTEM

Republicanism, the form of government — not to be conflated with the Republican political party specific to U.S. politics — refers to a system in which power is vested in the citizenry.

Federalism is a form of government that both combines and divides powers between a centralized federal authority and an array of regional and local authorities.

RELIGION/PHILOSOPHY –

Churches emphasized that the Union had to be preserved because of the special place that America occupied in world history. With its republican institutions, democratic ideals, and Christian values, the United States supposedly stood in the vanguard of civilization's forward march. Church ministers conceded that slavery was sanctioned by the scriptures, but the behavior of many slaveholders fell short of biblical standards. Reformers called for the legal recognition of slave marriages and laws prohibiting the breakup of families through a sale.

★ ETHOS LOGOS VALUE/VIRTUE OF THE MONTH: ★
Silence – Order

MCMLXIX5.2II

History
Politics
Religions
Economics

Each theme is one month of instruction. Themes of history start in ancient times all the way to modern era – Each scholar with cover each theme three times from Kinder to 12th grade. There are 40 themes with millions of combinations to explore.

Values & Virtues
- **2 Featured Per Month/Unit**

How To Use This Workbook

This workbook is broken into an overview of the connecting subjects to our HISTORY Lesson Cards. Your Classical Education journey starts with a time point in history. Each month-long history unit includes the English, Values/Virtues, Great Men and Women, Artists, Musicians, and Ethos 100 historic tie-ins. The entire course of instruction starts with a HISTORY Lesson Cards....

LESSON CARD:

This snapshot of the month covers the time period, lesson card, grade band, literature suggestions, artists and musicians, values, and virtues, great men and women from history, governance, and religion for a particular months worth of instruction.

Color and Icon denotes **HISTORY** Card

The Lesson Curriculum Cards
How To Connect History Cards

These oversized, laminated cards came about when we asked parents what was different at our schools. The feedback we received usually revolved around the conversations at the dinner table. Families found that the history lessons of the day in our schools became the bonding conversations around the dinner table.

In many schools, history class takes on a minor role; in our Classical model, history is the arch from which all subjects are woven. We built out these cards for parents to use at the dinner table to prompt discussions and perhaps learn along with their children about a particular time in history.

We built these Lesson Cards so that parents could better understand the topics our classroom teachers were covering. Aligning with our families is part of our school's mission. These cards put that mission into practice. From our history Lesson Cards, we know have over 800 Lesson Cards aligned to each grade and each subject that complete a K12 Classical Education.

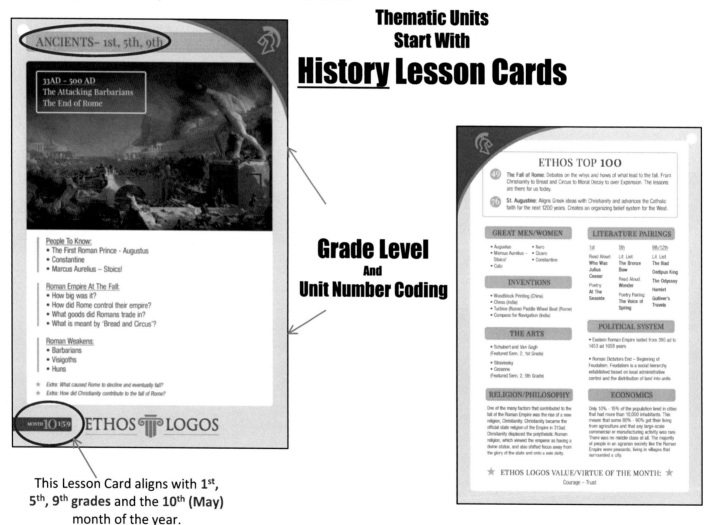

Thematic Units Start With

History Lesson Cards

Grade Level And Unit Number Coding

This Lesson Card aligns with 1st, 5th, 9th grades and the 10th (May) month of the year.

Remember, Classical Education is about going deeper into a time period or a story. We really want our scholars to experience what it was like to live in a particular time in history. Go deeply into the history and dissect the stories that accompany a time period.

The back of the history cards will include more specific events, people, inventions, and ideas that all align with history instruction.

Elements of a Unit Cards for K12

For Each Unit (1 month):
Unit Outline
The Big Areas To Cover
History Drives Everything

ETHOS TOP 100

Enlightenment: The ushering in of the age of Reason lead to the ideas of America, capitalism, Adam Smith, Milton Friedman and took the ideas of Greece/Rome and brought them forward 2000 years.

79 Isaac Newton: The birth of physics, scientific method.

80 Adam Smith: Wealth of Nations and the birth of Capitalism.

Top 100 Historical Events

The - *Ethos Logos 100* top events that appear in this unit **MUST** be covered. Everything else is a choice.

GREAT MEN/WOMEN

- Thomas More
- John Locke
- Adam Smith
- Rousseau
- Montesquieu
- Hobbes
- Voltaire
- Mary Wollstonecraft
- David Hume
- Immanuel Kant
- Isaac Newton

INVENTIONS

- Barometer
- Piston Engine (1680)

THE ARTS

- Bach and Vermeer
- Thomas Weelkes (1576-1623)
(Featured - Semester 2, 2nd Grade)

- Vivaldi, Thomas Morley (1557-1602)
- Durer (1471-1528)
(Featured Semester 2, 6th Grade)

RELIGION/PHILOSOPHY

The main religion of Renaissance Europe was Christianity and the main church was **the Catholic Church.** However, there were new ideas during this time including a new Christian church called Protestantism and a new philosophy called **Humanism.**

LITERATURE PAIRINGS

2nd Grade

Literature:
Stage Fright on a Summer Night

Read Aloud:
Gulliver's Stories

Poetry:
My Shadow

6th Grade

Literature:
Treasure Island

Read Aloud:
Teacher Choice
Historical Fiction

Poetry:
The Things That Haven't Been Done Before

POLITICAL SYSTEM

The Renaissance saw the rise of strong central **governments** and an increasingly urban economy, based on commerce rather than agriculture

ECONOMICS

Florence emerged as a prosperous city with rich merchants at its core. These merchants, and bankers, namely the Medici family, helped fund the arts and make the Renaissance possible. During this period, the joint stock company, the international banking system, a systematized foreign exchange market, insurance, and government debt developed.

★ **ETHOS LOGOS VALUE/VIRTUE OF THE MONTH:** ★

Integrity – Loyalty

Artist Musician

Gov. Religion

Explore The
Inventions
The Arts
Politics
Economics
Religion

Great Men/Women of History

Literature Pairing
Novel, Poetry, Read Aloud

Value/Virtue of the Month

GREAT MEN and WOMEN

For more impactful lessons and deeper learning, research has shown that the more you can connect your instruction with stories, the more impactful the learning. We have included listings and lesson cards on suggested **Great Men and Women** from history as a prompt for you to bring these stories to life in your instruction. We include suggested **Values and Virtues** that the historic figure exemplified as a way to feature character traits that your child may wish to emulate.

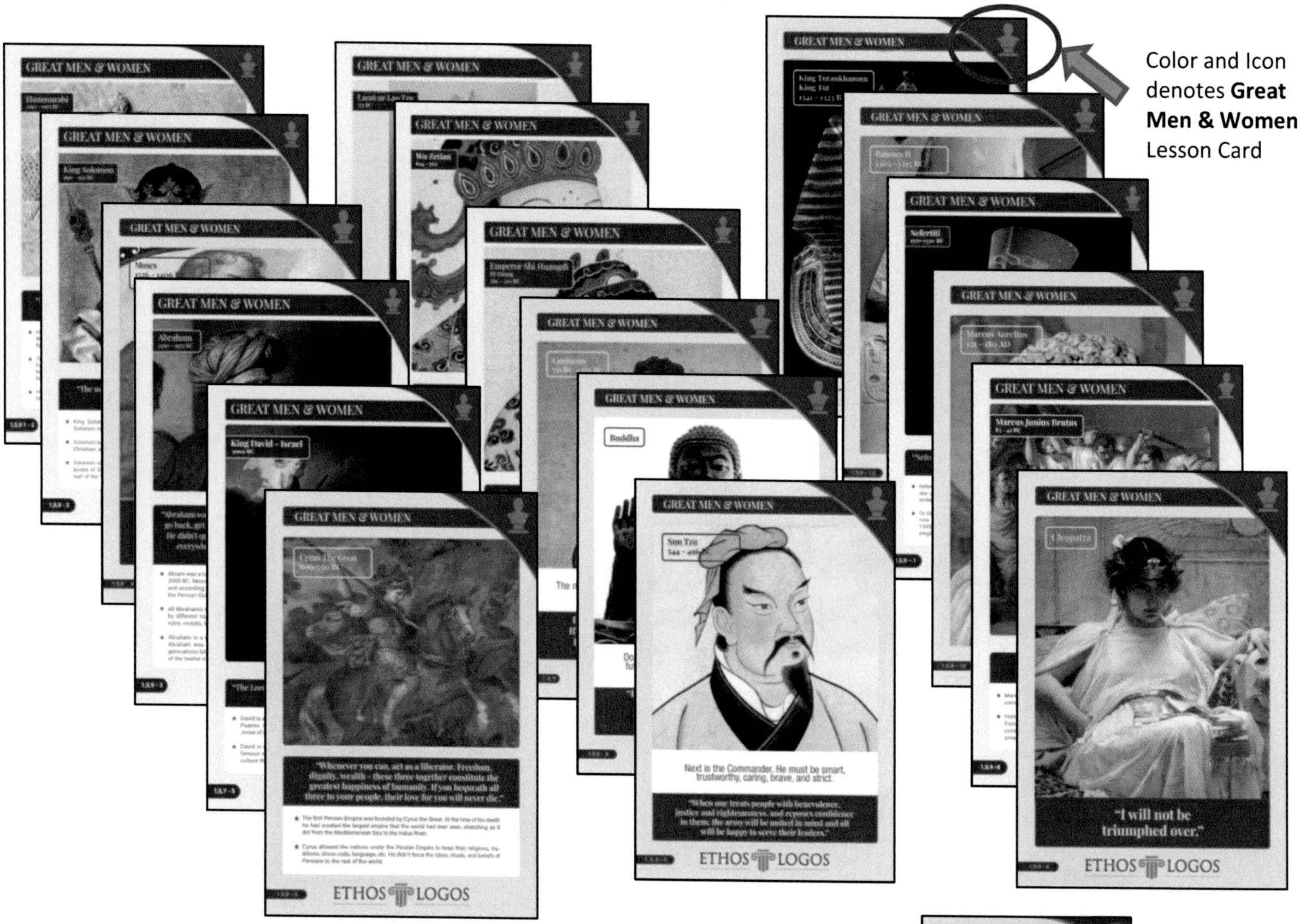
GREAT MEN & WOMEN
"I will not be triumphed over."
ETHOS LOGOS

Color and Icon denotes **Great Men & Women** Lesson Card

VALUES and VIRTUES

We specifically feature two **Values and Virtues** per month. The more ways you can connect your instruction to the featured values, the deeper the anchoring of the character traits you are working towards. Use these featured virtues as a guide.

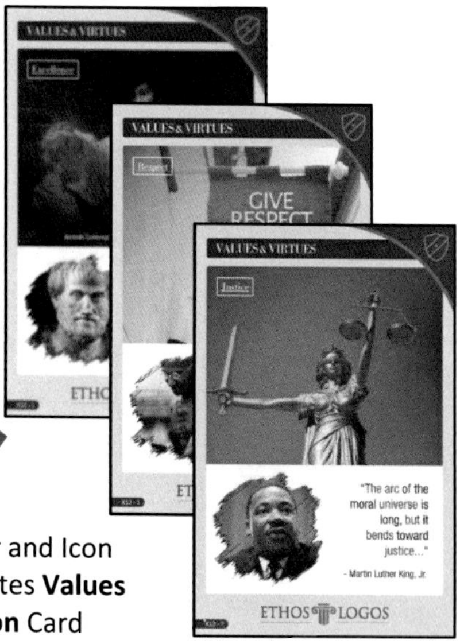
VALUES & VIRTUES
GIVE RESPECT
"The arc of the moral universe is long, but it bends toward justice..."
- Martin Luther King, Jr.
ETHOS LOGOS

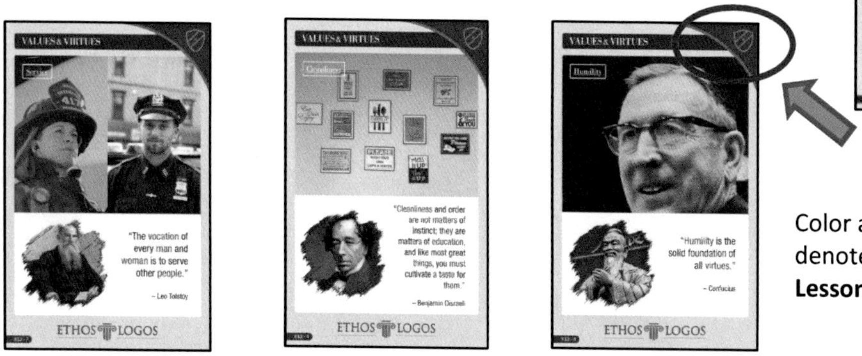
VALUES & VIRTUES
"The vocation of every man and woman is to serve other people."
- Leo Tolstoy
"Cleanliness and order are not matters of instinct; they are matters of education, and like most great things, you must cultivate a taste for them."
- Benjamin Disraeli
"Humility is the solid foundation of all virtues."
- Confucius
ETHOS LOGOS

Color and Icon denotes **Values Lesson** Card

ETHOS LOGOS All Rights Reserved ©

The Lesson Curriculum Cards
Sample Month

Because history is the arc with which we build all our curriculum around, the history card is your family's monthly starting point. From the history card, you'll be able to graphically see the areas you can cover (if you wish). We suggest the Ethos Logos 100 be integrated into each monthly unit, but from there, we encourage you and your child to explore what is interesting to you both.

We pair these history cards with more unit (monthly) cards including:

Great Men and Women
Science/Inventions
Literature (Historic novels, poetry)
Values and Virtues
Artists - Both visual and music

Along with the cards comes a workbook that is full of questions....no answers....just questions. We believe the fun and excitement of a Classical education is discovering new ideas. With easy access to the internet, this generation will forever have answers, the trick to pose the powerful questions.

One Unit/Month
Example 6th Grade May
Renaissance
Notice the color coding - corners

(1) History
(1) Novel (1) Poet
(3-5) Great Men/Women
(1) Science
(2) Artists (2)Musicians
(2) Values/Virtues
(1) World Religions
(1) World Governments
(1-2) US Civics
(1-3) Ethos Logos 100

English Novels

Poets

History

Artists

Musician

US Civics

Science

Ethos 100

Values/Virtues

Great Men Women

Order at:
EthosLogos.org

History and Classical Education

In the Classical Education model, history is the arch from which every other subject, assignment, and learning objective is tied. We form each grade around thematic units tied to a particular time period. The goal is to help our scholars get a deep sense of what it was like to live in a particular time period.

The deeper we delve into a time period, the deeper we understand motivations and outcomes of the people that shaped history. Our team of teachers, history professors, and researchers attempted to create an unbiased list that touches on the most influential events in world history.

These 100 events, people, and things are the historical events that shaped our world more than any other. As you review this list, you will find that some of the events cover just a few years, while others cover centuries. Some impacted only a single country or continent, while others spread out and touched every nation on earth. Some are violent conflicts like wars or revolutions, while others were scientific revolutions that ushered in entirely new ways of thinking and living.

What Do You Think Are History's 100 Milestone?

A deep understanding of history helps us to make sense of the times we live. History may not repeat, but it does rhyme. History rhymes because of human nature, market cycles, power, pride, envy, the power of human striving, and a burning desire for freedom. Every day, we are reminded of the power of the past to shape our lives. History and the narratives around events influence our family, nation, culture, religion, and future. A deep understanding of how history shapes the present and the future is paramount to engaging and understanding the world around us.

The Lesson Curriculum Cards
The Ethos Top 100

Do You Know The Top 100 Events In History?

After identifying the major historical occurrences, we organized, ranked, and debated each event's impact on the world. These top 100 events are included in each unit of our curriculum and are numbered on the actual time period that the event occurs.

We suggest that as you are covering a particular unit (month) of history, you focus on these top events to anchor the most important moments in the history of the west and east. The human odyssey is a fantastic adventure of good and bad, ups and downs. By focusing on these big events, you can ensure that your student is exposed to the religions, people, events, and cultures from all human recorded history.

These Top 100 Events were compiled and debated among history professors, K12 history teachers, history buffs and after combing through dozens and dozens of old and new textbooks, source documents, and novels. By no means are these the only events of impact on human history, and you and your family can debate for hours which events rank above others; we sure did! Once the events were outlined, organized, and then put into each monthly unit, you now have a platform to build projects, papers, and logical/rhetorical lessons.

Stand Alone Discussion Starter

These 100 Events can stand on their own and function as a dinner table conversation starter. Debate, explore and learn as a family. As you explore our history curriculum ask the big questions such as:

Should one event be higher on our list?

What didn't make our 100 list?

What did and may be controversial?

Color and Icon denotes **100 cards**

Integration In Our K12 Curriculum

As part of our K12 curriculum, we cover a time period in history in each grade and each month. You will notice on our Lesson Cards that there are many people, places, and things that occurred during the History Lesson Card's time frame. You will also notice that one or more of the **Ethos Logos 100 Events** will be found on the back of any one of the 60+ history Lesson Cards. We give our teachers tremendous flexibility on what they would like to teach and explore from our lesson cards in our classrooms.

The **Ethos 100 Logos Events** are the one subject area that we require our classroom teachers to cover each unit. How they explore these topics and tie the 100 Events into their lessons is up to each teacher's creativity.

We encourage our homeschool families to follow the same model. Enjoy exploring the 100 greatest events in history as part of your teaching experience.

You will find a listing of the 100 events aligned to one of four-time period historical bands. The first-time scholars see a time period (1st to 4th grades), we are introducing the basics of people, places, and events that define a particular unit. As scholars see a time period for the second (5th to 8th grades) or third time (9th to 12th grades), a deeper and deeper understanding of the events explored. Our curriculum platform helps a teacher along this journey with dozens of sample lessons and resources to use to make a unit come alive.

History Is The Arch In A Classical Education

A Journey Through History's Great Ideas

Each Lesson Card is a unit of instruction on a major topic in history. The graphical Lesson Cards give you an outline of major topics to explore for the unit. Each unit is designed to last one month.

In our model, the scholar will see a particular unit three times (e.g., Ancients are covered in 1st, 5th, and 9th grade), so it's not critical that students cover every item on every card every year. We do highly suggest you cover the **Top 100 Events** of history found in each history unit. Everything else is a guide based on the interest of the teacher or scholars.

Remember, as your scholar is learning a particular unit and time period in history, they are also learning different about the time period in their other subjects. This thematic approach helps a scholar better understand and synthesize each unit and time period at a deeper and deeper level.

The Lesson Curriculum Cards
Great Men and Women of History

The idea behind the Great Men and Women of History add-on units is that the teacher can further customize their history units by featuring the lives of heroes and legends that appeared during the particular time frame in history.

These Great Men and Women can be tailored to meet the students' interests or to better culturally represent a historical figure that a student may identify with. The goal is for teachers to weave these figures into their instructional lessons. We hope that students can see themselves in these Great Men and Women and one day goes on to change the world.

Learn Through Powerful Stories!

The front of the Great Men and Women unit cards have quotes or big questions to dig into on the particular character from history. The back has facts, dates, achievements, movies or books that may help to further explore the Great Men and Women of history.

The cards also include key Values and Virtues that made these people great. What an amazing way to make history come alive and set an example for your child of what greatness looks like.

The Lesson Curriculum Cards
Example of Values/Virtues Tie In

Character education develops knowledge, skills, and abilities that help scholars make informed and responsible choices. Character is derived from a Greek word meaning "to mark," as on an engraving. Character education enables students to come face-to-face with the realities of life and have the skill sets to deal with what is presented.

We have incorporated Values and Virtues into each of our month-long units. On the back/bottom of subject cards, we call out the featured Value and Virtue. Find the corresponding Values and Virtue Lesson Card and look for discussion or assignment prompts that tie the concepts together.

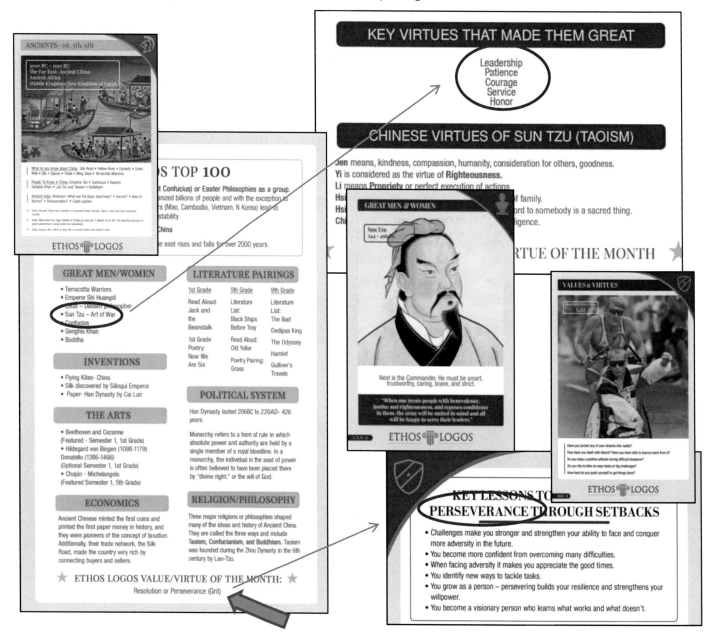

Putting It All Together

The above example explains how we connect history (in this case, Ancient China) with the Great Men and Women from history and a featured Value and Virtue that that character or time in history may have featured a particular virtue.

The Lesson Curriculum Cards
English Connections

From Grammar & Spelling to Literary Analysis and Writing

English courses in our model are critical and have several aspects both for English skills instruction and historical tie-ins. The Medici Classical English scope, sequence, and selection took years of classroom teachers back and forth to develop. We looked at top Classical schools around the country and interviewed teachers to find out which novels worked and which didn't. We added and subtracted and continue to do so. As you explore our selections, realize that you have complete flexibility in what to teach in English. If you follow our unit (monthly) sequence, the benefits of thematic units and cross-connections that make Classical education so impactful will be seamless.

We are firmly anchored in the classics, but we've incorporated abridged versions of classic novels for some of our lower grades and full versions for upper grades. The abridged versions introduce students to the famous English, American, European, and World literature. Our curriculum supports are built around novels, plays, poetry, short stories, speeches, and quotations from the great works of literary history.

Since many of these books have been in print for decades, many can be found online for no charge, used, or easily available from online booksellers.

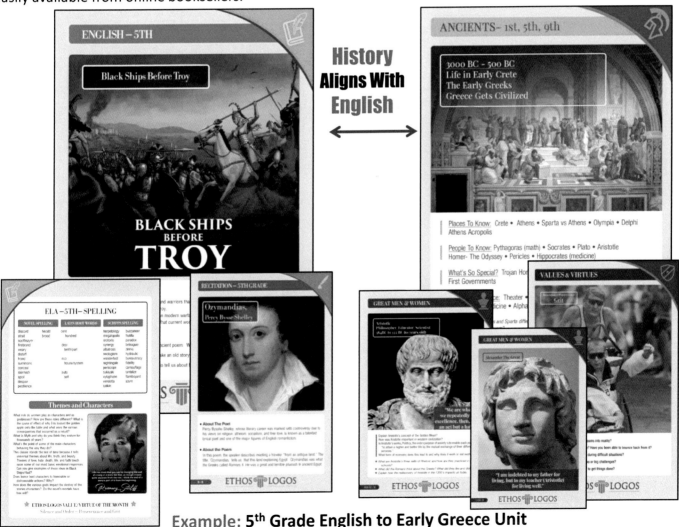

Example: 5th Grade English to Early Greece Unit
Novel: Black Ships Before Troy – **Poem:** Ozymandias, Shelley **Virtue:** Grit

The Lesson Curriculum Cards
Great Artists and Musicians

The arts help to identify the transition of time in both social, political, and economic stages. A historical perspective of the arts allows students to gather knowledge and inspiration that eventually contributes to how they speak and view the world around us as a people.

Artist – Musician Units Include:
50 Major Artists - 25 Major Composers

Ancient cave drawings to Egyptian mummification
Roman Architecture to Medieval Castles
Religious art to the Renaissance
DaVinci to Degas
Jackson Pollack to Picasso

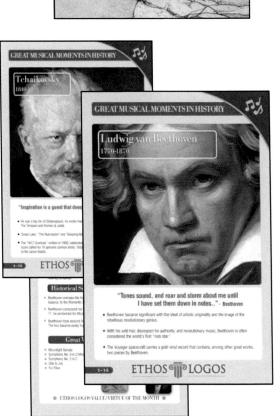

Color and Icon denotes
ART Card

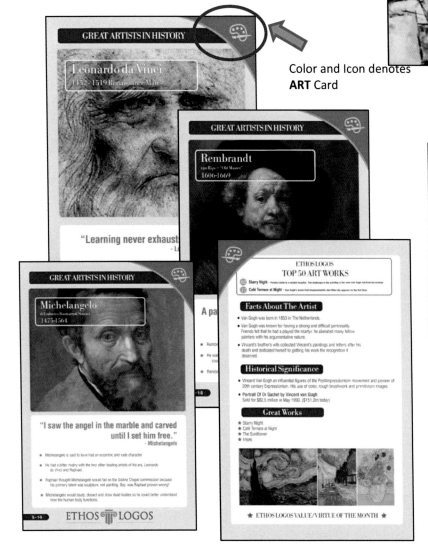

A Deeper Dive Into Our History Instruction Method
How S.P.R.I.T.E. Works

Behind each of the various S.P.R.I.T.E. topics are dozens of rich resources for the teacher to download from our Medici Learning Management System. These resources can be used as-is or customized in any way the teacher sees fit. To make history instruction come alive, we find that if the teacher is interested and if the scholar is interested, the learning and engagement are exponential. You know what your scholars' interests are better than any preplanned textbook. At Medici Classical, our role is to put a large selection of overarching topics together for you to pull from and customize.

The acronym stands for:

Society • Family • Gender Relations • Social Classes • Inequalities • Lifestyles

Politics • Leaders, Elites • State Structure • War • Diplomacy, Treaties • Courts, Laws

Religion • Holy Books • Beliefs, Teachings • Conversion • Sin/Salvation • Deities

Intellectual • Art, Music • Writing, Literature • Philosophy • Math & Science • Education

Technology • New Inventions • New Tools, Weapons • Ways to Improve Life • Technical Solutions

Economic • Type of System • Technology, Industry • Trade, Commerce • Capital/Money • Types of Businesses

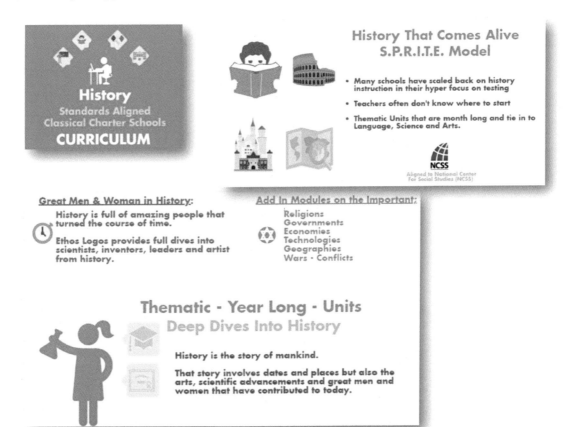

Themes For Quality Social Studies Curriculum

1. Culture

Culture

Learn the (S.P.R.I.T.E.) Society - Politics - Religion - Intellect (arts) - Technology - and Economics of ancient to modern cultures.

What is common among multiple cultures?
How did the S.P.R.I.T.E. subject areas affect the culture?
What do prior cultures tell us about our own?

2. Time, Continuity, Change

Change

This theme put history in perspective with scholars firm understanding of history, the questions of: Who Am I?
How Am I connected to the past?
How did the world change in the past?
How might the world change in the future?

3. People, Place, Environment

Geography

Helps scholars view the world beyond their own space and gives a geographical sense of the world: Where are things located?
Why did people settle where they did?
How did people manage their lives in different environments?

4. Individual Decisions and Development

Individuals

Individuals are shaped by culture, groups and institutions:
How do people learn?
Why do people behave in a good or bad way?
What role did ideas, religion and education have on history?
What spurred innovation or caused stagnation?

Each unit has a series of suggested questions to guide the teachers on grade-appropriate topics to explore these subjects deeper. You'll notice that we provide questions and not answers in our published workbooks. The power of a question is where all the magic in education resides. There are unlimited resources to find answers in our day and age of the internet, but the well-crafted questions guide the discovery of a particular topic. We list out questions based on complexity that we think would fit a specific grade level. By no means do you have to stay within the suggested grade band. If your scholar is in 1st grade but can decipher a 5th-grade level question, by all means, explore and research with them.

5. Power, Authority and Government

Government

Governments rise and fall. History is the understanding of leaders and society govern themselves:
What is power?
What forms does it take? From kings to despots to prime ministers, why do some rise?
How is power gained, used, abused and justified?
How is government created, maintained and changed?

6. Production, Distribution, Consumption

Economics

Resources are finite and history is riddled with scarcity and new technologies that create new resources:
What is grown, mined, manufactured?
How are goods and services distributed?
What economic systems worked until they didn't?

7. Science, Invention, Technology

Inventions

Science helps births technology and changes history:
Is new technology always better than the old?
How do we cope with the pace of change?
Can we maintain fundamental values with technology changes?
What are the major technology advancements by period of history?

8. Civic Engagement - Focused on US History

US Civics

History, especially with a US focus, covers the role of citizens stepping forward to set a new course to a better future:
What are a persons rights versus responsibilities?
How can one person make a difference?
What duties do I have as a citizen?
Why should I care about my society/country?

*NCSS Curriculum Standards - Executive Summary

The Medici Digital Curriculum Delivery system is built with all these themes in mind. Teachers have the leway and tools to deliver instruction that comes alive and answers these questions...and hopefully raises many many more.

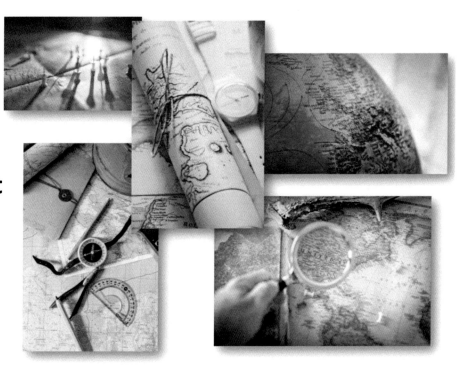

Geography
Location, Place, Human-Environment Interactions, Movement, Regions

Understand how to use maps, tools, and technologies to acquire, process, and report information from a spatial perspective.

1. Understand how to analyze the spatial organization of people, places, and environments on Earth's surface.
2. Understand the physical and human characteristics of places.
3. Understand how culture and experience influence people's perceptions of places and regions.
4. Understand the patterns and networks of economic interdependence on Earth's surface.
5. Understand the processes, patterns, and functions of human settlement.
6. Understand how the forces of cooperation and conflict among people influence Earth's surface division and control.
7. Understand how human actions modify the physical environment.
8. Understand how physical systems affect human systems.
9. Understand how to apply geography to interpret the past.
10. Understand how to apply geography to interpret the present and plan for the future.

A Deeper Dive Into Our History Instruction Method
Digital Instruction Option

Source Documents

What better way to learn history than from the actual artifacts written and preserved from a particular time period? The Magna Carta and The Mayflower Compact, compared to the US Constitution and Bill of Rights, are excellent ways to show our scholars how time, place, and context define historical narratives. We have done our best to source, organize and make available period-based source documents to our teachers so they can use these tools to create a more profound understanding.

The one who does not REMEMBER HISTORY is BOUND to live through it AGAIN.

George Santayana

Information Text - Close Reading

Along with Source Documents, we provide our teachers with digital documents that may include an old newspaper article, a current magazine piece, or other informational text on the particular topic being covered. A scholar's ability to read and understand informational text is an important skill and an academic standard that is often measured in state exams. Like any other skill, deciphering arguments, facts from opinion, and being able to dissect an article are valuable skills that will serve our scholars later in life.

History Standards – 3C Framework

Several states participated in a three-year effort to produce the C3 Framework for Social Studies State Standards. This effort aims to a) enhance the rigor of the social studies disciplines; b) build critical thinking, problem-solving, and participatory skills to become engaged citizens; and c) align academic programs to state standards for the English Language Arts and Literacy in History classes. Our curriculum team has worked within this framework to bolster our offerings and, in many cases, call out N.C.S.S. learning standards and or incorporate their overarching themes into our social studies print and digital resources.

The N.C.S.S. is organized into Curriculum Standards and not Content Standards. The N.C.S.S. curriculum standards provide a set of principles by which content can be selected and organized to build a viable, valid, and defensible social studies curriculum for grades from pre-K through 12. So our S.P.R.I.T.E. model and our selected topics (Ethos Logos 100 etc.) fit into a framework that all good instruction should follow.

As you plan your instruction and choose questions to tailor your lessons, keep in mind the 3C Framework. Our team has included many of these topics in our curriculum resources. The art and creativity tie these all together and make your history instruction come alive!

Themes For Quality Social Studies Curriculum

Culture

1. Culture

Learn the (S.P.R.I.T.E.) Society - Politics - Religion - Intellect (arts) - Technology - and Economics of ancient to modern cultures.
- What is common among multiple cultures?
- How did the S.P.R.I.T.E. subject areas affect the culture?
- What do prior cultures tell us about our own?

Change

2. Time, Continuity, Change

This theme put history in perspective with scholars firm understanding of history, the questions of:
- Who Am I?
- How Am I connected to the past?
- How did the world change in the past?
- How might the world change in the future?

Geography

3. People, Place, Environment

Helps scholars view the world beyond their own space and gives a geographical sense of the world:
- Where are things located?
- Why did people settle where they did?
- How did people manage their lives in different environments?

Individuals

4. Individual Decisions and Development

Individuals are shaped by culture, groups and institutions:
- How do people learn?
- Why do people behave in a good or bad way?
- What role did ideas, religion and education have on history?
- What spurred innovation or caused stagnation?

History Standards – 3C Framework

The NCSS framework looks at themes of how the content we provide is delivered. These themes include:

- **CULTURE** (in our model, (S)ociety and (I)ntellectual)
- **TIME, CONTINUITY, AND CHANGE** –
  (this would be higher-order thinking skills that show change over time, say using Geography changes or impacts)
- **PEOPLE, PLACES, AND ENVIRONMENTS**
- **INDIVIDUAL DEVELOPMENT AND IDENTITY**
  (Our English novel pairings and Great Men and Women add ons are excellent ways to tell this)
- **INDIVIDUALS, GROUPS, AND INSTITUTIONS**
- **POWER, AUTHORITY, AND GOVERNANCE** (in our model (P)olitics).
- **PRODUCTION, DISTRIBUTION AND CONSUMPTION** (in our model (E)conomics)
- **SCIENCE, TECHNOLOGY, AND SOCIETY** (in our model (T)echnology.
- **GLOBAL CONNECTIONS**
- **CIVIC IDEALS AND PRACTICES**

History Standards Aligned Classical Charter Schools **CURRICULUM**

Government

5. Power, Authority and Government

Governments rise and fall. History is the understanding of leaders and society govern themselves:
> What is power?
> What forms does it take? From kings to despots to prime ministers, why do some rise?
> How is power gained, used, abused and justified?
> How is government created, maintained and changed?

Economics

6. Production, Distribution, Consumption

Resources are finite and history is riddled with scarcity and new technologies that create new resources:
> What is grown, mined, manufactured?
> How are goods and services distributed?
> What economic systems worked until they didn't?

Inventions

7. Science, Invention, Technology

Science helps births technology and changes history:
> Is new technology always better than the old?
> How do we cope with the pace of change?
> Can we maintain fundamental values with technology changes?
> What are the major technology advancements by period of history?

US Civics

8. Civic Engagement - Focused on US History

History, especially with a US focus, covers the role of citizens stepping forward to set a new course to a better future:
> What are a persons rights versus responsibilities?
> How can one person make a difference?
> What duties do I have as a citizen?
> Why should I care about my society/country?

*NCSS Curriculum Standards - Executive Summary

The Medici Digital Curriculum Delivery system is built with all these themes in mind. Teachers have the leway and tools to deliver instruction that comes alive and answers these questions...and hopefully raises many many more.

US Citizenship – US Civics Unit Cards
Add One Unit Cards for 5th Grade and Up

Can you pass the US Citizenship Exam? A recent survey showed that only 19% of Americans under the age of 45 could pass the 120+ citizenship exam. Foreigners who are becoming US Citizens have a 95+% pass rate because they learn about what makes America great as part of their journey to becoming a part of the melting pot that is the United States of America.

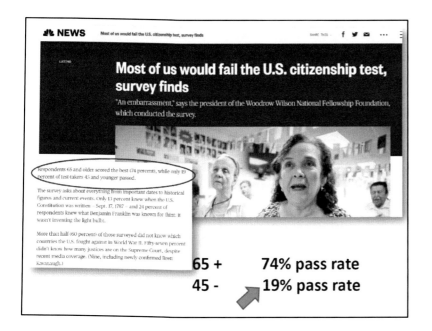

65 +   74% pass rate
45 -   19% pass rate

We have created a graphically appealing set of Unit Cards that help your scholar understand what it means to be an American.

This 38 Unit Card set and accompanying workbook features the actual questions and answers from the Citizenship Exam wrapped around background knowledge, the historical context of the answers, and graphically appealing images that help anchor the concepts.

We begin the US Citizenship Prep instruction in 5th grade and feature 20-25 of the questions each year. We aim for 100% proficiency by 8th grade. This series can be added to your instructional plan at any age.

Visit EthosLogos.org to add this series today.

English Done Classically
Add One Unit Cards for 1st to 12th Grade

- **Novel Historical Setting**
- **Author Intent and Voice**
- **Themes and Characters**
- **Spelling/Vocabulary**
  From the Novel
  Latin Root Words
  Scripps Spelling

Visit EthosLogos.org to add this series today.

K12 Science Instruction

- Next Generation Science Standards
- Includes Detailed Lessons and Enrichment
- Focus on Historical Impacts of Science
- Focus on Great Men and Women of Science
- Socratic Prompts Built Into Lessons
- Writing in Science Journals
- Ethics in Science Lesson Prompts

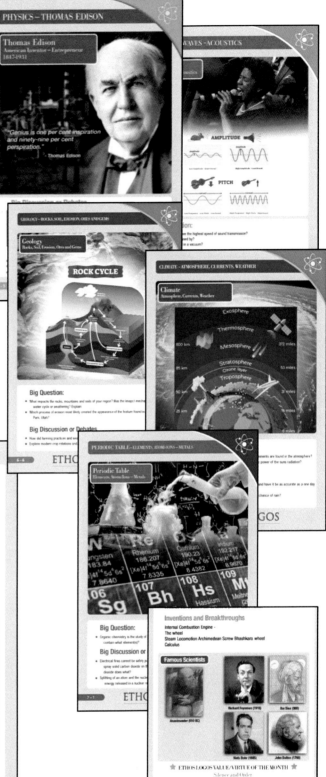

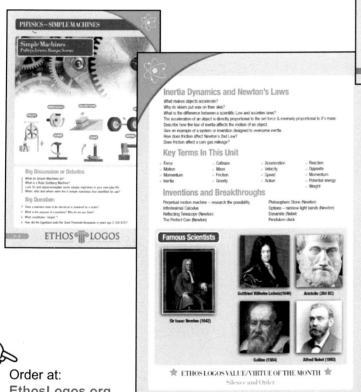

Order at:
EthosLogos.org

Each Unit Includes:
Key Terms
Historic Debates
Big Question
Unit Objectives
Inventions - Breakthroughs
Famous Scientists

NEXT GENERATION SCIENCE STANDARDS

Made in the USA
Las Vegas, NV
26 August 2024

94487986R00128